PENGUIN BOOKS

THE SHADOW OF THE S

'Suppose we were to launch a spacecraft with the intention of establishing literary contact with the residents of some remote part of the galaxy. If we had room for only one contemporary writer, whom would we send? I'd vote for Ryszard Kapuściński, because he has given the truest, least partial, most comprehensive and vivid account of what life is like on our planet' Geoff Dyer, *Guardian*

'[A] beautiful and extraordinary book. Like that other master of reportage, V. S. Naipaul, Kapuściński is a born storyteller and Africa provides him with some great tales to tell' Anthony Sattin, *Sunday Times*

'This book is a marvel of humane, sorrowful and lucid observation . . . Kapuściński has written a startling, sobering, mesmerizing account of a few isolated parts of a larger vastness, giving us sharper, clearer images and understandings than many more conventional and more comprehensive books have managed' Richard Bernstein, *The New York Times*

'This is the best book I have read about Africa in years . . . He gives quite the best account of the historical background to the prolonged crisis in Rwanda that I have read. He provides wonderful descriptions of the dictators Idi Amin and Samuel Doe . . . Kapuściński writes about a genuinely African Africa' Richard Gott, *Literary Review*

'Reading Kapuściński is a lot like reading Borges, with the fantastical imaginary continents replaced by an equally fantastical real one' Matt Steinglass, *Washington Post*

'Kapuściński has transformed journalism into literature in his writings about Africa . . . [and] got closer to African life than most Western reporters dream of doing' W. F. Deedes, *Daily Telegraph*

'A master reporter . . . for readers who have wanted to find a more African Africa, Ryszard Kapuściński has long been the most engaging guide . . . Kapuściński writes not about economic statistics or government policies, but about the lives of the poorest Africans struggling to survive . . . shows life through African eyes, and it begins to explain the nature of the resilience that provides the real hope for Africa' Anthony Sampson, *New Statesman*

'A loosely arranged, highly detailed, heartfelt but unsentimental introduction to Africa's afflictions and a quiet love song to its profound appeal' Roger Kaplan, *Wall Street Journal*

'He catches the heart of this vast continent by following his own intuitions, always going off the beaten track, away from the safe and air-conditioned . . . This book truly opens the doors to another world. A wonderful read' Malcolm Reid, *Time Out*

'Long-standing admirers of Kapuściński's writing will not be disappointed with *The Shadow of the Sun*; those who have yet to experience his uniquely brilliant blend of reportage and literature, and his passionate, compassionate tone, are urged to do so' Robert Macfarlane, *Tablet*

'Blessed with the acutest of antennae, this is a writer who feels with his eyes and thinks with his heart' Michela Wrong, *Financial Times*

'It bears the distinctive mark of all his work – raising reportage to the level of grand history and philosophy . . . Kapuściński is a masterful guide' Brett Martin, *Time Out New York*

'*The Shadow of the Sun* is a history of post-colonial Africa as seen through the eyes of a witness who is more poet than chronicler'
Blaine Harden, *The New York Times*

'Powerful, idiosyncratic, controversial, often deeply moving'
Dervla Murphy, *Irish Times*

'Sumptuous and meditative . . . a book that is both travelogue and history, a consummate, often hair-raising prose poem to the enduring strangeness and beauty of Africa. Landscapes require expert story telling to bring them to life, and time and again, Kapuściński rises to the challenge . . . an evocative and searching portrait of a continent wracked by constant change' John Freeman, *Star Tribune* (Minneapolis)

'A rare treat . . . Kapuściński doesn't just "cover" Africa - he knows it. By adhering steadfastly to the principle of "living where the Africans live", he sets himself apart from other Western correspondents . . . Kate Adie, Fergal Keane, Jeremy Bowen *et al*, could all learn by reading this' Keith Wilson, *Focus*

'A wise, engaging close-up filled with faces, landscapes, rutted roads and the daily perils of African life . . . There are many Africas, and Kapuściński is altogether enthralling as he guides us through them'
Patrick Smith, *Business Week*

'An excellent book, beautifully written by an accomplished storyteller . . . Revealed is a fauvist landscape of primary colours, bright calico dresses, painted buses, patchwork clothes and plastic water containers . . . an excellent book that will be of interest to all those concerned with Africa's post-colonial history' Nick Lodge, *West Africa*

Ryszard Kapuściński was born in Poland in 1932, and studied history and Polish language and literature at the University of Warsaw. As a foreign correspondent for PAP, the Polish news agency, until 1981, he was an eyewitness to revolutions and civil wars in Africa, Asia and Latin America, experiences that have made him one of the foremost writers on crises in the modern world. His texts have been published in *The New York Times*, *Time* magazine and *Frankfurter Allgemeine Zeitung* (among others), and have been translated into thirty languages. His books include *Another Day of Life* (1976; Penguin, 2001); *The Emperor: Downfall of an Autocrat* (1978), an account of the decline and fall of Haile Selassie of Ethiopia; *Shah of Shahs* (1982), on the last days of the Persian Shah; *The Soccer War* (1988), eyewitness accounts from Third World countries; *Imperium* (1992), memoirs and essays on the Soviet Union; and four volumes of *Lapidarium* (1990, 1995, 1997 and 2000), journalistic, political and poetic notes and essays. Kapuściński has been awarded several international literary prizes, such as the German Publishers' and Booksellers' Prize (1994), the Prix d'Astrolabe, France (1995), the Turzański Foundation Award, Canada (1996), the Joseph Conrad Literary Award, USA (1997), the Hansische-Goethe Preis, Germany (1998), the Göttingen–Toruń Partner Cities Literary Prize, Germany–Poland (1999) and the Premio Internazionale Viareggio, Italy (2000). He was recently made 'journalist of the century' in Poland.

Ryszard Kapuściński

The Shadow
of the Sun

My African Life

Translated from the Polish by

Klara Glowczewska

PENGUIN BOOKS

PENGUIN BOOKS

Published by the Penguin Group
Penguin Books Ltd, 80 Strand, London WC2R 0RL, England
Penguin Putnam Inc., 375 Hudson Street, New York, New York 10014, USA
Penguin Books Australia Ltd, 250 Camberwell Road, Camberwell, Victoria 3124, Australia
Penguin Books Canada Ltd, 10 Alcorn Avenue, Toronto, Ontario, Canada M4V 3B2
Penguin Books India (P) Ltd, 11 Community Centre, Panchsheel Park, New Delhi – 110 017, India
Penguin Books (NZ) Ltd, Cnr Rosedale and Airborne Roads, Albany, Auckland, New Zealand
Penguin Books (South Africa) (Pty) Ltd, 24 Sturdee Avenue, Rosebank 2196, South Africa

Penguin Books Ltd, Registered Offices: 80 Strand, London WC2R 0RL, England

www.penguin.com

First published in Poland under the title *Heban* by Czytelnik, Warsaw 1998
First published in the USA by Alfred A. Knopf 2001
First published in Great Britain by Allen Lane The Penguin Press 2001
Published in Penguin Books 2002

032

Original text copyright © Ryszard Kapuściński, 1998
Translation copyright © Klara Glowczewska, 2001

ISBN-13: 978–0–140–29262–6

www.greenpenguin.co.uk

I lived in Africa for several years. I first went there in 1957. Then, over the next forty years, I returned whenever the opportunity arose. I traveled extensively, avoiding official routes, palaces, important personages, and high-level politics. Instead, I opted to hitch rides on passing trucks, wander with nomads through the desert, be the guest of peasants of the tropical savannah. Their life is endless toil, a torment they endure with astonishing patience and good humor.

This is therefore not a book about Africa, but rather about some people from there—about encounters with them, and time spent together. The continent is too large to describe. It is a veritable ocean, a separate planet, a varied, immensely rich cosmos. Only with the greatest simplification, for the sake of convenience, can we say "Africa." In reality, except as a geographical appellation, Africa does not exist.

R.K.

The Shadow of the Sun

The Beginning:
Collision, Ghana, 1958

M ore than anything, one is struck by the light. Light everywhere. Brightness everywhere. Everywhere, the sun. Just yesterday, an autumnal London was drenched in rain. The airplane drenched in rain. A cold wind, darkness. But here, from the morning's earliest moments, the airport is ablaze with sunlight, all of us in sunlight.

In times past, when people wandered the world on foot, rode on horseback, or sailed in ships, the journey itself accustomed them to the change. Images of the earth passed ever so slowly before their eyes, the stage revolved in a barely perceptible way. The voyage lasted weeks, months. The traveler had time to grow used to another environment, a different landscape. The climate, too, changed gradually. Before the traveler arrived from a cool Europe to the burning Equator, he already had left behind the pleasant warmth of Las Palmas, the heat of Al-Mahara, and the hell of the Cape Verde Islands.

Today, nothing remains of these gradations. Air travel tears us violently out of snow and cold and hurls us that very same day into the blaze of the tropics. Suddenly, still rubbing our eyes, we find ourselves in a humid inferno. We immediately start to sweat. If we've come from Europe in the wintertime, we discard overcoats, peel off sweaters. It's the first gesture of initiation we, the people of the North, perform upon arrival in Africa.

People of the North. Have we sufficiently considered the fact that northerners constitute a distinct minority on our planet? Canadians and Poles, Lithuanians and Scandinavians, some Americans and Germans, Russians and Scots, Laplanders and Eskimos, Evenkis and Yakuts—the list is not very long. It may amount to no more than 500 million people: less than 10 percent of the earth's population. The overwhelming majority live in hot climates, their days spent in the warmth of the sun. Mankind first came into being in the sun; the oldest traces of his existence have been found in warm climes. What was the weather like in the biblical paradise? It was eternally warm, hot even, so that Adam and Eve could go about naked and not feel chilled even in the shade of a tree.

Something else strikes the new arrival even as he descends the steps of the airplane: the smell of the tropics. Perhaps he's had intimations of it. It is the scent that permeated Mr. Kanzman's little shop, Colonial and Other Goods, on Perec Street in my hometown of Pińsk. Almonds, cloves, dates, and cocoa. Vanilla and laurel leaves, oranges and bananas, cardamom and saffron. And Drohobych. The interiors of Bruno Schulz's cinammon shops? Didn't their "dimly lit, dark, and solemn interiors" smell intensely of paints, lacquer, incense, the aroma of faraway countries and rare substances? Yet the actual smell of the tropics is somewhat different. We instantly recognize its weight, its sticky materiality. The smell makes us at once aware that we are at that point on earth where an exuberant and indefatigable nature labors, incessantly reproducing itself, spreading and blooming, even as it sickens, disintegrates, festers, and decays.

It is the smell of a sweating body and drying fish, of spoiling meat and roasting cassava, of fresh flowers and putrid algae—in short, of everything that is at once pleasant and irritating, that attracts and repels, seduces and disgusts. This odor will reach us from nearby palm groves, will escape from the hot soil, will waft above stagnant city sewers. It will not leave us; it is integral to the tropics.

And finally, the most important discovery—the people. The locals. How they fit this landscape, this light, these smells. How they are as one with them. How man and environment are bound in an indissoluble, complementary, and harmonious whole. I am struck by how firmly each race is grounded in the terrain in which it lives, in its climate. We shape our landscape, and it, in turn, molds our physiognomy. Among these palm trees and vines, in this bush and jungle, the white man is a sort of outlandish and unseemly intruder. Pale, weak, his shirt drenched with sweat, his hair pasted down on his head, he is continually tormented by thirst, and feels impotent, melancholic. He is ever afraid: of mosquitoes, amoebas, scorpions, snakes—everything that moves fills him with fear, terror, panic.

With their strength, grace, and endurance, the indigenous move about naturally, freely, at a tempo determined by climate and tradition, somewhat languid, unhurried, knowing one can never achieve everything in life anyway, and besides, if one did, what would be left over for others?

I've been here for a week. I am trying to get to know Accra. It is like an overgrown small town that has reproduced itself many times over, crawled out of the bush, out of the jungle, and come to a halt at the shores of the Gulf of Guinea. Accra is flat, single-storied, humble, though there are some buildings with two or more floors. No sophisticated architecture, no excess or pomp. Ordinary plaster, pastel-colored walls—pale yellow, pale green. The walls have numerous water stains. Fresh ones. After the rainy season, entire constellations of stains appear, collages, mosaics, fantastical maps, flowery flourishes. The downtown is densely built up. Traffic, crowds, bustle—life takes place out in the street. The street is a roadway delineated on both sides by an open sewer. There are no sidewalks. Cars mingle with the crowds. Everything moves in concert—pedestrians, automobiles, bicycles, carts, cows, and goats. On the sides, beyond the sewer, along the entire length of the street, domestic scenes unfold. Women are pounding manioc, baking taro bulbs over the coals, cooking dishes of one sort or another, hawking chewing gum, crackers, and aspirin, washing and drying laundry. Right out in the open, as if a decree had been issued commanding everyone to leave his home at 8 a.m. and remain in the street. In reality, there is another reason: apartments are small, cramped, stuffy. There is no ventilation, the atmosphere inside is heavy, the smells stale, there is no air to breathe. Besides, spending the day in the street enables one to participate in social life. The women talk nonstop, yell, gesticulate, laugh. Standing over a pot or a washbasin, they have an excellent vantage point. They can see their neighbors, passersby, the entire street; they can listen in on quarrels and gossip, observe accidents. All day long they are among others, in motion, and in the fresh air.

A red Ford with a speaker mounted on its roof passes through the streets. A hoarse, penetrating voice invites people to attend a meeting. The main attraction will be Kwame Nkrumah— Osagyefo, the prime minister, the leader of Ghana, of Africa, of all downtrodden peoples. There are photographs of Nkrumah everywhere—in the newspapers (every day), on posters, on flags, on ankle-length percale skirts. The energetic face of a middle-aged man, either smiling or serious, at an angle meant to suggest that he is contemplating the future.

"Nkrumah is a savior!" a young teacher named Joe Yambo tells me with rapture in his voice. "Have you heard him speak? He sounds like a prophet!"

Yes, in fact, I had heard him. He arrived at the stadium with an entourage of his ministers—young, animated, they created the impression of people who were having a good time, who were full of joy. The ceremony began with priests pouring bottles of gin over the podium—it was an offering to the gods, a way of making contact with them, a plea for their favor, their goodwill. Among the adults in the audience there were also children, from infants strapped to their mothers' backs, to babies beginning to crawl, to toddlers and school-age children. The older ones take care of the younger ones, and those older ones are taken care of by ones older still. This hierarchy of age is strictly observed, and obedience is absolute. A four-year-old has full authority over a two-year-old, a six-year-old over a four-year-old. Children take care of children, so that the adults can devote themselves to their affairs—for instance, to listening carefully to Nkrumah.

Osagyefo spoke briefly. He said that the most important thing was to gain independence—everything else would follow naturally, all that is good would emerge from the very fact of independence.

A portly fellow, given to decisive gestures, he had shapely, expressive features and large, lively eyes, which moved over the sea of dark heads with an attention so concentrated as to suggest he wanted to count each and every one of them.

After the rally, those on the podium mingled with the audience. It was loud, chaotic, and there was no visible police protection or escort. Joe, who had brought me, elbowed his way toward a young man (whom he identified as a minister) and asked him if I could come see him tomorrow. The other one, not really able to hear over the buzz and commotion what the issue was, replied, at least partially to get rid of us, "Fine! Fine!"

The next day, I found my way to the Ministry of Education and Information, a new building set amid a growth of royal palms. It was Friday. On Saturday, sitting in my small hotel, I wrote a description of the preceding day:

The way is open: neither policeman, nor secretary, nor doors.

I draw aside a patterned curtain and enter. The minister's office is warm. In semidarkness, he is standing at his desk organizing his papers: crumpling those he will throw into the wastepaper basket, smoothing out others to place in his briefcase. A thin, slight figure, in a sports shirt, short trousers, sandals, with a flowery kente cloth draped over his left shoulder; nervous gestures.

This is Kofi Baako, minister of education and information.

At thirty-two, he is the youngest minister in Ghana, in the entire British Commonwealth, and he has already had his portfolio for three years now. His office is on the third floor of the ministry building. The hierarchy of positions is reflected in the ladder of floors. The higher the personage, the higher the floor. Fittingly, since on top there is a breeze, while toward the bottom the air is heavy as stone, motionless. Petty bureaucrats suffocate on the ground floor; above them, the departmental directors enjoy a slight draft; and at the very top, the delicious breeze caresses the ministers.

Anyone who wants to can come and see a minister whenever he wants to. If someone has a problem, he travels to Accra, finds out where, for instance, the minister of agriculture can be found. He goes to his office, parts the curtain, sits down, and sets forth in detail what's bothering him. If he doesn't find the official at the agency, he will find him at home—even better, because there he'll get a meal and something to drink. People felt a remoteness from the white administration. But now these are their own people, they don't have to feel inhibited. It's my government, so it must help me. If it's to help me, it has to know the situation. For it to know, I have to come and explain. It's best that I do this on my own, in person and direct.

There is no end of these supplicants.

"Good morning!" said Kofi Baako. "And where are you from?"

"From Warsaw."

"You know, I almost went there. I was traveling all over

Europe: France, Belgium, England, Yugoslavia. I was in Czechoslovakia, about to go to Poland, when Kwame sent me a telegram calling me back for the party congress, our ruling Convention People's Party."

We were sitting at a table, in his doorless office. Instead of window panes there were shutters with widely spaced slats, through which a gentle breeze passed. The small room was piled high with papers, files, brochures. A large safe stood in a corner, several portraits of Nkrumah hung on the walls, a speaker wired to a central system stood on a shelf. Tomtoms pounded from it, until finally Baako turned it off.

I wanted him to tell me about himself, about his life. Baako enjoys great prestige among the young. They like him for being a good athlete. He plays soccer, cricket, and is Ghana's Ping-Pong champion.

"Just a minute," he interrupted, "I just have to place a call to Kumasi, because I'm going there tomorrow for a game."

He called the post office for them to connect him. They told him to wait.

"I saw two films yesterday," he told me, as he waited, holding the receiver to his ear. "I wanted to see what they're showing. They're playing films schoolchildren shouldn't go to. I must issue a decree that forbids young people to see such things. And this morning I spent visiting book stalls throughout the city. The government has established low prices for schoolbooks, but the word is that retailers are marking them up. I went to check for myself. Indeed, they are selling them for more than they're supposed to."

He dialed the post office again.

"Listen, what are you so busy with over there? How long am I supposed to wait? Do you know who this is?"

A woman's voice answered, "No."

"And who are you?" Baako asked.

"I'm the telephone operator."

"And I am the minister of education and information, Kofi Baako."

"Good morning, Kofi! I'll connect you right away."

And he was talking to Kumasi.

I looked at his books, stacked on a small cabinet: Hemingway, Lincoln, Koestler, Orwell, *The Popular History of Music, The American Dictionary,* as well as various paperbacks and crime novels.

"Reading is my passion. In England I bought myself the *Encyclopaedia Britannica,* and now I'm reading it little by little. I cannot eat without reading, I have to have a book lying open in front of me."

A moment later:

"I've got another, even greater hobby: photography. I take pictures all the time and everywhere. I have more than ten cameras. When I go to a store and see a new camera, I immediately have to buy it. I bought a film projector for the children, and show them films in the evening."

He has four children, ranging in age from three to nine. All of them attend school, even the youngest. It is not unusual here for a three-year-old to be enrolled in school. The mother will send him off, especially if he's a handful, just to have some peace.

Kofi Baako himself first went to school at three. His father was a teacher and liked being able to keep his eye on his children. When he finished elementary school, he was sent for high school to Cape Coast. He became a teacher, and then a civil servant. At the end of 1947, Nkrumah had returned to Ghana having finished university studies in America and England. Baako listened to his speeches, which spoke of independence. Then Baako wrote an article, "My Hatred of Imperialism." He was fired from his job. He was blacklisted, and no one would employ him. He hung around the city, eventually meeting Nkrumah, who entrusted him with the position of editor in chief of the *Cape Coast Daily Mail.* Kofi was twenty years old.

He wrote another article entitled "We Call for Freedom," and was jailed. Arrested with him were Nkrumah and several other activists. They spent thirteen months behind bars, before finally being released. Today, this group constitutes Ghana's government.

Now Baako speaks about broad issues. "Only thirty percent of the people in Ghana can read and write. We want to abolish illiteracy within fifteen years. There are difficulties: a shortage of teachers, books, schools. There are two kinds of schools: missionary-run and state-run. But they are all subject to the state and there is a single educational policy. In addition, five thousand students are being educated abroad. What frequently happens is that they return and no longer share a common language with the people. Look at the opposition. Its leaders are Oxford- and Cambridge-educated."

"What does the opposition want?"

"Who knows? We believe that an opposition is necessary. The leader of the opposition in parliament receives a salary from the government. We allowed all these little opposition parties and groups to unite, so they would be stronger. Our position is that in Ghana, anyone who wants to has the right to form a political party—on the condition that it not be based on criteria of race, religion, or tribe. Each party here can employ all constitutional means to gain political power. But, you understand, despite all this, one doesn't know what the opposition wants. They call a meeting and shout: 'We've come through Oxford, and people like Kofi Baako didn't even finish high school. Today Baako is a minister, and I am nothing. But when I become minister, then Baako will be too stupid for me to make him even a messenger.' But you know, people don't listen to this kind of talk, because there are more Kofi Baakos here than all those in the opposition put together."

I said that I should get going, as it was dinnertime. He asked me what I was doing that evening. I was supposed to go to Togo.

"What for?" He waved his hand. "Come to a party. The radio station is having one tonight."

I didn't have an invitation. He looked around for a piece of paper and wrote: "Admit Ryszard Kapuściński, a journalist from

Poland, to your party. Kofi Baako, Minister of Education and Information."

"There. I'll be there too, we'll take some photographs."

The guard at the gates of the radio building saluted me smartly and I was promptly seated at a special table. The party was already in full swing when a gray Peugeot drove up to the dance floor out in the garden, and Kofi Baako emerged from inside. He was dressed just as he had been in his office, only he held a red sweat suit under his arm, because he was going to Kumasi tonight and it might get cold. He was well known here. Baako was the minister of schools, of all the universities, the press, the radio, the publishing houses, the museums—of everything that constitutes culture, art, and propaganda in this country.

We soon found ourselves in a crowd. He sat down to drink a Coca-Cola, then quickly stood up.

"Come, I will show you my cameras."

He pulled a suitcase out of the trunk of his car, set it on the ground, knelt down, and began taking out the cameras, laying them out on the grass. There were fifteen of them.

Just then two boys walked up to us, slightly drunk.

"Kofi," one of them began in a plaintive tone, "we bought a ticket and they're not letting us stay here because we don't have jackets. So what did they sell us a ticket for?"

Baako rose.

"Listen," he answered, "I am too important a man for such matters. There are lots of little guys here, let them take care of it. I have issues of government on my mind."

The twosome sailed off unsteadily, and we went to take pictures. Baako had only to approach, cameras hanging around his neck, for people to start calling to him, asking for a photograph.

"Kofi, take one of us."

"Of us!"

"And us too!"

He circulated, picking tables with the prettiest girls, arranging them, and telling them to smile. He knew them by name: Abena, Ekua, Esi. They greeted him by extending their hands, without getting up, and shrugging their shoulders, which is an expression of seductive flirtatiousness here. Baako walked on; we took many photographs. He looked at his watch.

"I have to go."

He wanted to get to the game on time.

"Come tomorrow, and we'll develop the photographs."

The Peugeot flashed its lights and vanished in the darkness, while the party swayed and surged till dawn.

The Road to Kumasi

What does the bus station in Accra most resemble? The caravan of a huge circus that has come to a brief stop. It is colorful, and there is music. The buses are more like circus wagons than the luxurious vehicles that roll along the highways of Europe and North America.

A bus in Accra has a wooden body, its roof resting on four posts. Because there are open walls, a pleasant breeze cools the ride. In this climate, the value of a breeze is never to be taken for granted.

In the Sahara, the palaces of rulers have the most ingenious constructions—full of chinks, crannies, winding passageways, and corridors so conceived and constructed as to maximize cross-ventilation. In the afternoon heat, the ruler reclines on a mat optimally positioned to catch this refreshing current, which he breathes with delight. A breeze is a financially measurable commodity: the most expensive houses are built where the breeze is best. Still air has no value; it has only to move, however, and then immediately acquires a price.

The buses are brightly ornamented, colorfully painted. On the cabs and along the sides, crocodiles bare their sharp teeth, snakes stretch ready to attack, and flocks of peacocks frolic in trees, while antelope race through the savannah pursued by a lion.

Birds are everywhere, as well as garlands, bouquets of flowers. It's kitsch, but full of imagination and life.

The inscriptions are most important of all. The words, adorned with flowers, are large and legible from afar, meant to offer important encouragements or warnings. They have to do with God, mankind, guilt, taboos.

The spiritual world of the "African" (if one may use the term despite its gross simplification) is rich and complex, and his inner life is permeated by a profound religiosity. He believes in the coexistence of three differerent yet related worlds.

The first is the one that surrounds us, the palpable and visible reality composed of living people, animals, and plants, as well as inanimate objects: stones, water, air. The second is the world of the ancestors, those who died before us, but who died, as it were, not completely, not finally, not absolutely. Indeed, in a metaphysical sense they continue to exist, and are even capable of participating in our life, of influencing it, shaping it. That is why maintaining good relations with one's ancestors is a precondition of a successful life, and sometimes even of life itself. The third world is the rich kingdom of the spirits—spirits that exist independently, yet at the same time are present in every being, in every object, in everything and everywhere.

At the head of these three worlds stands the Supreme Being, God. Many of the bus inscriptions speak of omnipresence and his unknown omnipotence: "God is everywhere," "God knows what he does," "God is mystery." There are also some more down-to-earth, human injunctions: "Smile," "Tell me that I'm beautiful," "Those who bicker like each other," etc.

We have only to show up in the square, which teems with dozens of buses, before a group of shouting children surrounds us—where are we going? to Kumasi? to Takoradi? or to Tamale?

"To Kumasi."

Those who are hunting for passengers to Kumasi shake our hands and, bouncing with glee, lead us to the appropriate bus. They are happy, because, having found him a passenger, the bus driver will reward them with a banana or an orange.

We climb into the bus and sit down. At this point there is a risk of culture clash, of collision and conflict. It will undoubtedly occur if the passenger is a foreigner who doesn't know Africa. Someone like that will start looking around, squirming, inquiring, "When will the bus leave?"

"What do you mean, when?" the astonished driver will reply. "It will leave when we find enough people to fill it up."

The European and the African have an entirely different concept of time. In the European worldview, time exists outside man, exists objectively, and has measurable and linear characteristics. According to Newton, time is absolute: "Absolute, true, mathematical time of itself and from its own nature, it flows equably and without relation to anything external." The European feels himself to be time's slave, dependent on it, subject to it. To exist and function, he must observe its ironclad, inviolate laws, its inflexible principles and rules. He must heed deadlines, dates, days, and hours. He moves within the rigors of time and cannot exist outside them. They impose upon him their requirements and quotas. An unresolvable conflict exists between man and time, one that always ends with man's defeat—time annihilates him.

Africans apprehend time differently. For them, it is a much looser concept, more open, elastic, subjective. It is man who influences time, its shape, course, and rhythm (man acting, of course, with the consent of gods and ancestors). Time is even something that man can create outright, for time is made manifest through events, and whether an event takes place or not depends, after all, on man alone. If two armies do not engage in a battle, then that battle will not occur (in other words, time will not have revealed its presence, will not have come into being).

Time appears as a result of our actions, and vanishes when we neglect or ignore it. It is something that springs to life under our influence, but falls into a state of hibernation, even nonexistence, if we do not direct our energy toward it. It is a subservient, passive essence, and, most importantly, one dependent on man.

The absolute opposite of time as it is understood in the European worldview.

In practical terms, this means that if you go to a village where a meeting is scheduled for the afternoon but find no one at the appointed spot, asking, "When will the meeting take place?" makes no sense. You know the answer: "It will take place when people come."

Therefore the African who boards a bus sits down in a vacant seat, and immediately falls into a state in which he spends a great portion of his life: a benumbed waiting.

"These people have a fantastic talent for waiting!" an Englishman who has lived here for years tells me. "Talent, stamina, some peculiar kind of instinct."

Africans believe that a mysterious energy circulates through the world, ebbing and flowing, and if it draws near and fills us up, it will give us the strength to set time into motion—something will start to happen. Until this occurs, however, one must wait; any other behavior is delusional and quixotic.

What does this dull waiting consist of? People know what to expect; therefore, they try to settle themselves in as comfortably as possible, in the best possible place. Sometimes they lie down, sometimes they sit on the ground, or on a stone, or squat. They stop talking. A waiting group is mute. It emits no sound. The body goes limp, droops, shrinks. The muscles relax. The neck stiffens, the head ceases to move. The person does not look around, does not observe anything, is not curious. Sometimes his eyes are closed—but not always. More frequently, they are open but appear unseeing, with no spark of life in them. I have observed for hours on end crowds of people in this state of inanimate waiting, a kind of profound physiological sleep: They do not eat, they do not drink, they do not urinate; they react neither to the mercilessly scorching sun, nor to the aggressive, voracious flies that cover their eyelids and lips.

What, in the meantime, is going on inside their heads?

I do not know. Are they thinking? Dreaming? Reminiscing? Making plans? Meditating? Traveling in the world beyond? It is difficult to say.

Finally, after two hours of waiting, the bus, now packed full, leaves the station. On the rough potholed road, shaken this way and that, the passengers come to life. Someone reaches for a biscuit, someone else peels a banana. People look around, wipe sweaty faces, neatly fold wet handkerchiefs. The driver is talking nonstop, holding the steering wheel with one hand, gesticulating with the other. Everyone keeps bursting out in laughter, the driver the loudest, the others more softly; perhaps they're just doing it out of politeness, because they feel they should.

We're on our way. My fellow passengers are only the second, perhaps even the first generation of Africans fortunate enough to be conveyed to their destinations. For thousands and thousands of years, Africa walked. People here did not have a concept of the wheel, and were unable to adopt it. They walked, they wandered, and whatever had to be transported they carried—on their backs, on their shoulders, and, most often, on their heads.

How is it that during the nineteenth century there were ships on lakes deep in the interior of the continent? They were first disassembled at oceanic ports, then carried piecemeal on people's heads and put back together again on the shores of the lakes. Cities, factories, mining equipment, electrical plants, hospitals, all were carried in sections deep into Africa. All the products of nineteenth-century technology were transported into Africa's interior on the heads of its inhabitants.

The people of northern Africa, even of the Sahara, were more fortunate in this respect: they could use a beast of burden, the camel. But neither the camel nor the horse was able to adapt to regions south of the Sahara—they perished, decimated by the encephalitis borne by the tsetse fly, as well as by other fatal diseases of the tropics.

The problem of Africa is the dissonance between the environment and the human being, between the immensity of African space (more than thirty million square kilometers!) and the defenseless, barefoot, wretched man who inhabits it. Whichever direction he turns, there is distance, emptiness, wilderness, boundlessness. Often one had to walk for hundreds, thousands of miles to encounter other people (to say "another human being" would be inappropriate, for a lone individual could not survive in these conditions). For the most part information, knowledge, technological innovation, goods, commodities, and the experiences of others did not penetrate here, could not find a way in. Exchange as a means of participating in world culture did not exist. If it appeared, it did so only accidentally, as a rare event, an exception. And without exchange there is no progress.

Most frequently, people lived in small groups, clans, tribes isolated and scattered over vast, hostile territories, in mortal peril from malaria, drought, heat, hunger.

Living and moving about in small groups allowed them to flee danger more easily and thereby survive. These peoples applied the same tactic once practiced by light cavalry on the European field of battle: the keys were mobility, the avoidance of head-on confrontation, the skirting and outsmarting of peril. As a consequence, the African was a man on the move. Even if he led a sedentary life in a village, he was also on the move, for periodically the entire village would set off: either the water had run out, or the soil had ceased to bear crops, or an epidemic had broken out, and off they would go, in search of succor, in the hope of finding something better. Only city life brought them a measure of stability.

The population of Africa was a gigantic, matted, crisscrossing web, spanning the entire continent and in constant motion, endlessly undulating, bunching up in one place and spreading out in another, a rich fabric, a colorful arras.

This compulsory mobility of the population resulted in Africa's interior having no old cities, at least none comparable in age to those that still exist in Europe, the Middle East, or Asia. Similarly—again in contrast to those other regions—many African societies (some claim all of them) today occupy terrain that they did not previously inhabit.

All are arrivals from elsewhere, all are immigrants. Africa is their common world, but within its boundaries they wandered and shifted about for centuries, a process that continues in certain parts of the continent to this day. Hence the striking physical characteristic of civilization is its temporariness, its provisional character, its material discontinuity. A hut put up only yesterday has already vanished. A field still cultivated three months ago is today lying fallow.

The continuity that lives and breathes here, and that creates the threads of the social fabric, is the continuity of family tradition and ritual, and the pervasive and far-reaching cult of the ancestor. Rather than a material or territorial community, it is a spiritual community that binds the African to those closest to him.

The bus is going deeper and deeper into the thick, tall, tropical forest. Biology in the temperate zones exhibits discipline and order: there is a little stand of pines here, some oaks over there, and birch trees somewhere else. Even in mixed forests a certain clarity and propriety prevail. In the tropics, however, the flora exists in a state of frenzy, in an ecstasy of the most untrammeled procreation. One is struck immediately by a cocky, pushy abundance, an endless eruption of an exuberant, panting mass of vegetation, all the elements of which—tree, bush, liana, vine, growing, pressing, stimulating, inciting one another—have already become so interlocked, knotted, and clenched that only sharpened steel, wielded with a horrendous amount of physical force, can cut through it a passage, path, or tunnel.

Because in the past there was no wheeled transport on this enormous continent; there were also no roads. When the first cars were brought here, early in the twentieth century, they didn't really have anywhere to go. A paved road is something new in Africa, at most several decades old. And in certain areas it still remains a rarity. Instead of roads, there were trails, usually shared by people and cattle alike. This age-old system of paths explains why people here are still in the habit of walking single file, even if they're traveling along one of today's wide roads. It explains, too, why a walking group is silent—it is difficult to conduct a conversation single file.

One can't afford to be less than a great expert on the geography of these paths. Whoever knows them less than well will lose his way, and if forced to wander too long without water and food will of course perish. Various clans, tribes, and villages have their own paths, which cross one another, and someone unfamiliar with their points of intersection can walk along one assuming it is taking him in the right direction, while in fact it may be leading him astray, even toward death. The most perplexing and dangerous are jungle paths. You are constantly caught on thorns and branches, reaching a destination all scratched and swollen. It is a good idea to carry a stick, for if a snake is lying across the path (as happens often), you must scare it off, and this is best accomplished with a stick. Talismans present further dilemmas. Inhabitants of the tropical forest, living in an impenetrable wilderness, are by nature wary and superstitious. To scare off evil spirits, they hang all kinds of talismans along the pathways. What should you do when you come upon a lizard's skin left hanging, a bird's head, a bunch of grass, or a crocodile's tooth? Should you risk continuing, or, rather, turn back, knowing that beyond this warning sign something truly evil might be lurking?

Every now and then our bus stops along the side of the road. Someone wants to get off. If it's a young woman with a child or two (a young woman without a child is a rare sight), there unfolds a scene of extraordinary agility and grace. First, the woman will secure the child to her body with a calico scarf (her small charge sleeping the entire time, not reacting). Next, she will squat down and place the bowl from which she is never separated, full of food and goods of all kinds, on her head. Then, straightening up, she will execute that maneuver of a tightrope walker taking his first step above the abyss: carefully, she finds her equilibrium. With her left hand she now clutches a woven sleeping mat, and with her right the hand of a second child. And this way—stepping at once with a very smooth, even gait—they enter a forest path leading to a world I do not know and perhaps will never understand.

My neighbor on the bus. A young man. An accountant from a firm in Kumasi whose name I don't catch.

"Ghana is independent!" he says ecstatically. "Tomorrow, Africa will be independent!" he assures me. "We are free!"

And he shakes my hand in a way meant to signify that now a black man can offer a white man his hand without self-consciousness.

"Did you see Nkrumah?" he asks, interested. "Yes? Then you

are a lucky man! Do you know what we'll do with the enemies of Africa?"

He laughs, ha-ha, but doesn't say exactly what will be done.

"Now the most important thing is education. Education, schooling, the acquiring of knowledge. We are so backward, so backward! I think that the whole world will come to our aid. We must be the equals of the developed countries. Not only free— but also equal. But for now, we are breathing freedom. And this is paradise. This is wonderful!"

This enthusiasm of his is universal here. Enthusiasm, and pride that Ghana stands at the head of the independence movement, sets an example, leads all of Africa.

My other neighbor, sitting to my left (the bus has three seats in a row), is different: withdrawn, taciturn, unengaged. He immediately draws attention to himself, for people here are generally open, eager to converse, quick to tell stories and deliver various opinions. Thus far he has told me only that he is working and that he is having some troubles at work. What sorts of troubles, he's not saying.

Finally, however, as the great forest starts to shrink and grow thinner, signaling that we are slowly approaching Kumasi, he decides to confess something to me. So—he has problems. He is sick. He is not sick always, not continuously, but intermittently, periodically. He has already been to see various native specialists, but none of them has been able to help him. The thing is that he has animals in his head, under his skull. It's not that he sees these animals, that he thinks about them or is afraid of them. No. It's nothing like that. The animals are literally in his head; they live there, run around, graze, hunt, or just sleep. If they happen to be gentle animals, like antelopes, zebras, or giraffes, he tolerates them well; it is even quite pleasant then. But sometimes a hungry lion arrives. He is hungry, he is furious—so he roars. And then this roar makes his head explode.

The Structure of the Clan

I arrived in Kumasi with no particular goal. Having one is generally deemed a good thing, the benefit of something to strive toward. This can also blind you, however: you see only your goal, and nothing else, while this something else—wider, deeper—may be considerably more interesting and important.

Kumasi lies amid greenery and flowers, on gentle hillsides. It is like a giant botanical garden in which people were allowed to settle. Everything here seems kindly disposed to man—the climate, the vegetation, other people. The dawns are dazzlingly beautiful, although they last but a few minutes. It is night, and out of this night the sun suddenly emerges. Emerges? This verb suggests a certain slowness, a leisurely process. In reality, the sun comes out as if it were a ball catapulted into the air. We suddenly see a fiery sphere, so near to us that we can't help experiencing a frisson of fear. Moreover, this sphere is gliding toward us, closer and closer.

The sight of the sun acts like a starter's pistol: the town instantly springs into motion. It's as if all night long everyone was crouching on his starter blocks and now, at the signal, at that shot of sunlight, they all take off full speed ahead. No intermediate stages, no preparations. All at once, the streets are full of people, the shops are open, the fires and kitchens are smoking.

Yet the bustle of Kumasi differs from Accra's. It is local, regional, as if self-enclosed. The town is the capital of the kingdom of Ashanti (which is part of Ghana), and it vigilantly guards its otherness, its colorful and robust traditions. Here you can see tribal chiefs strolling along the streets, or the performance of a rite that dates back to ancient times. And in this culture, the world of magic, of spells and enchantments, thrives and prospers.

The road from Accra to Kumasi is not just the five hundred kilometers from the Atlantic coast to the interior; it is also a voyage into those areas of the African continent where there are fewer vestiges of colonialism than along the coastlines. For Africa's immensity, its dearth of navigable rivers and its lack of roads, as well as its difficult, murderous climate, while presenting an impediment to its development, also furnished a natural defense against invasion: colonialists were unable to penetrate very deeply. They kept to the shores, to their ships and fortifications, their supplies of food and quinine. In the nineteenth century, if someone—like Stanley—dared to traverse the continent from east to west, the feat was widely celebrated for years to come. And it was largely due to these obstacles to communication that many African cultures and traditions have been able to survive intact to this day.

Officially, but only officially, colonialism reigned in Africa from the time of the Berlin West Africa Conference (1884–85), during which several European states (mainly England and France, but also Belgium, Germany, and Portugal) divided the whole continent among themselves, a status that persisted until Africa won independence in the second half of the twentieth century. In reality, however, colonial penetration began much earlier, as long ago as the fifteenth century, and flourished over the next five hundred years. The most shameful and brutal phase of this conquest was the trade in African slaves, which went on for more than three hundred years. Three hundred years of raids, roundups, pursuits, and ambushes, organized, often with the help of African and Arab partners, by white men. Millions of young Africans were deported across the Atlantic in horrific conditions, stuffed down the hatches of ships; those lucky to emerge alive would with their sweat build the riches and might of the New World.

Africa—persecuted and defenseless—was depopulated, destroyed, and ruined. Whole stretches of the continent were deserted; barren bush supplanted what had been sunny flowering lands. But the most painful and lasting imprints of this epoch were left upon the memory and consciousness of the Africans: centuries of disdain, humiliation, and suffering gave them an inferiority complex, and a conviction, deep in their hearts, of having been wronged.

When World War II erupted, colonialism was at its apogee. The course of the war, however, its symbolic undertones, would sow the seeds of the system's defeat and demise.

How and why did this happen? First, a short detour into the foul realm of racial thinking. The central subject, the essence, the core of relations between Europeans and Africans during the colonial era, was the difference of race, of skin color. Everything—each exchange, connection, conflict—was translated into the language of black and white. And, of course, white was better, higher, more powerful than black. Whites were sir, master, sahib, bwana kubwa, unchallenged lords and rulers, sent by God to hold sway over the blacks. Into the African was inculcated the notion that the white man was untouchable, unconquerable, that whites constituted a homogeneous, cohesive force. Such was the ideology that ably supported the system of colonial domination, by teaching that to question or contest the system was absolutely pointless.

Then, suddenly, Africans recruited into the British and French armies in Europe observed that the white men were fighting one another, shooting one another, destroying one another's cities. It was a revelation, a surprise, a shock. African soldiers in the French army witnessed their colonial sovereign, France, defeated and conquered. African soldiers in the British army saw the imperial capital, London, bombed; they saw whites seized with panic, fleeing, pleading, sobbing. They saw ragged, hungry whites, crying for bread. As they moved east, fighting white Germans alongside white Englishmen, they encountered columns of white people dressed in stripes, people-skeletons, people-rags.

The shock the African experienced as scenes from the white man's war passed before his eyes was all the more powerful because earlier the inhabitants of Africa (with few exceptions, and in the case of the Congo, for example, none) were not permitted to travel to Europe, or anywhere else beyond their continent. And so their views of the lives of white men was based only on the luxurious circumstances whites enjoyed in the colonies.

And another thing: the inhabitant of Africa in the middle of the twentieth century had no sources of information other than what a neighbor, his village chief, or a colonial administrator told him. Therefore he knew of the world only as much as he was able to glean from his immediate surroundings, or what he heard from others during an evening's chat by the fire.

The veterans of World War II who returned from Europe to Africa shortly reappear in the ranks of various movements and parties fighting for national independence. The number of these organizations swells rapidly; they spring up like mushrooms after a rain. They have various points of view, and various goals.

Those from the French colonies initially make limited demands. They do not speak yet of freedom. They ask only that all the inhabitants of the colony be made French citizens. Paris rejects this. Yes, someone who has been educated in French culture, who raises himself to its level—the so-called *évolué*—can become a French citizen. But such individuals will turn out to be exceptions.

The organizations in the British colonies are more radical.

Their inspiration and program are the bold visions of the future as formulated by the descendants of slaves, Afro-American intellectuals of the second half of the nineteenth century and first half of the twentieth. They called their doctrine pan-Africanism. Its principal creators: the activist Alexander Crumwell, the writer W. E. B. Du Bois, and the journalist Marcus Garvey (this last one from Jamaica). They differed among themselves, but agreed on two points: (1) that all blacks in the world—be they in South America or in Africa—constitute a single race, a single culture, and they should be proud of the color of their skin; (2) that all of Africa should be independent and united. Their slogan was "Africa for Africans!" On other matters they differed, W. E. B. Du Bois for example proclaimed that blacks should remain in the countries in which they now live, while Garvey held that all blacks, wherever they may be, should return to Africa. For a time he even sold photographs of Haile Selassie, proclaiming each was a valid return visa. He died in 1940 never having seen Africa himself.

A young activist and theoretician from Ghana, Kwame Nkrumah, became an enthusiast of pan-Africanism while studying in America. He returned home in 1947 and founded a political party into which he recruited former World War II combatants as well as the young. At a rally in Accra he issued a war cry: "Independence now!" In those days, in colonial Africa, this resounded like a bomb exploding. Ten years later, Ghana became the first independent African country south of the Sahara, and Accra immediately became the provisional, informal center of all movements, ideas, and activities for the entire continent.

The town burned with liberation fever, and people flocked here from all over Africa. Journalists from around the world also arrived. They came out of curiosity, uncertainty, and even the fear growing in Europe's capitals—what if Africa explodes, what if the blood of white men flows here, and, even, what if armies are formed, and then, supplied with weapons by the Soviets, attempt—in a gesture of hateful vengeance—to strike at Europe?

. . .

In the morning I bought the local newspaper, *Ashanti Pioneer,* and set out in search of its editorial offices. Experience teaches that one can learn more passing an hour in such an office than in a week of walking around to see various institutions and notables. And so it was this time.

In a small, shabby room, with a strange mix of odors, overly ripe mango and printer's ink, I was greeted effusively by a cheerful, corpulent man, Kwesi Amu. "I am also a reporter!" he exclaimed by means of introduction, and as though he had been waiting for this visit for who knows how long.

The course and temperature of the first greeting are of utmost significance to the ultimate fate of a relationship, which is why people here set much store by the way they salute each other. It is essential to exhibit from the very beginning, from the very first second, enormous, primal joy and geniality. So, for starters, one extends one's hand. But not in a formal manner, reticently, limply: just the opposite—a large, vigorous gesture, as if one's intention were not so much to offer one's hand as to tear the other's off. If, however, the other manages to keep his hand, whole and in its proper place, it is because, understanding the ritual rules of the greeting, he has likewise executed the same broad, forceful gesture. Both of these extremities, bursting with tremendous energy, now meet halfway and, with a terrifying impact of collision, cancel out the two opposing forces. Simultaneously, as the hands are rushing toward each other, the two individuals share a prolonged cascade of loud laughter. It is meant to signify that each is happy to be meeting and warmly disposed to the other.

There ensues a long list of questions and answers, such as "How are you? Are you feeling well? How is your family? Are they all healthy? And your grandfather? And your grandmother? And your aunt? And your uncle?"—and so forth and so on, for families here are large with many branches. Custom dictates that each positive answer be offered with yet another torrent of loud and vibrant laughter, which in turn should elicit a similar or perhaps an even more homeric cascade from the one posing the questions.

You often see two (or more) people standing in the street and dissolving with laughter. It does not mean that they are telling each other jokes. They are simply saying hello. And if the laughter dies down, then either the act of greeting has come to an end and they will now move on to the substance of the conversation, or, simply, the newly met have fallen silent to allow their tired vocal cords a moment's respite.

After completing the raucous and cheerful ritual, Kwesi and I started to talk about the Ashanti kingdom. The Ashanti resisted the British until the end of the nineteenth century, and really never fully capitulated to them. Even now, after independence, they hold themselves at a distance from Nkrumah and his supporters from the coast, whose culture they don't value highly. They are closely attached to their extremely rich history, their traditions, beliefs, and laws.

In all of Africa, each larger social group has its own distinct culture, an original system of beliefs and customs, its own language and taboos, and all of this is immensely complicated, intricate, and mysterious. That is why anthropologists never spoke of "African culture," or "African religion," knowing that no such thing exists, and that the essence of Africa is its endless variety. They saw the culture of each people as a discrete world, unique, unrepeated. And they wrote accordingly: E. E. Evans-Pritchard published a monograph on the Nuer, M. Gluckman on the Zulu, G. T. Basden on the Ibo, and so on. Meantime, the unschooled European mind, inclined to rational reduction, to pigeonholing and simplification, readily pushes everything African into a single bag and is content with facile stereotypes.

"We believe," Kwesi told me, "that man is composed of two elements. Blood, which he inherits from his mother, and spirit, donated by his father. The stronger of these components is blood, which is why the child belongs to the mother and her clan—not to the father. If the wife's clan orders her to leave her husband and return to her native village, she takes all the children with her, for although the wife lives in her husband's village and house, she is there really only as a guest. This possibility of returning to her clan gives the woman a place to go should her husband abandon her. She can also move out herself, should he prove to be a despot. But these are extreme situations; usually, the family is a strong and vibrant unit in which everyone has a traditionally assigned role and everyone understands his or her duties.

"The family is always large—several dozen people. The husband, the wife (or wives), the children, the cousins. The family gathers as frequently as possible and spends time together. Time spent communally is highly valued and accorded much respect. It is important to live together, or near one another: there are many tasks which can be accomplished only collectively—otherwise, there is no chance of surviving.

"The child is raised familialy, but as he grows, he sees that the borders of his social world extend further, that other families live nearby, and that these families together constitute the clan. A clan comprises all those who believe that they have a common ancestor. If I believe that you and I have an ancestor in common, then we belong to the same clan. Such a belief carries enormous consequences. For example, a man and a woman from the same clan are forbidden to have sexual relations. This is subject to the strongest possible taboo. In the past, parties violating it were both condemned to death. But even today it is a serious transgression, one that can anger the spirits of the ancestors and bring great misfortune down upon the clan.

"At the head of the clan stands the chief. He is chosen by a clan assembly, which is led by a council of elders. The elders are village chiefs, heads of individual clans, functionaries of all kinds. There can be several candidates and many rounds of voting, for the choice matters deeply: the position of chief is hugely important. From the moment of his selection, the chief becomes a holy person. Henceforth, he is not permitted to walk barefoot. Or to sit directly on the ground. One is not allowed to touch him or speak a bad word about him. One can tell from afar that a chief is coming—because of the open umbrella. A great chief has an enormous, decorative umbrella, held by a special servant; a lesser chief walks about with an ordinary umbrella purchased from an Arab in the marketplace.

"The clan chief has a function of the utmost significance. The central element of the Ashanti faith is the cult of ancestors. The clan comprises a great number of individuals, but we can see and meet only a small percentage of them—those that live on earth. The others—the majority—are ancestors who have partially departed, though in reality they still participate in our lives. They look at us, observe our behavior. They are everywhere, they see everything. They can help us, but they can also punish us. Bestow happiness upon us, or bring about our ruination. They decide everything. That is why maintaining good relations with the ancestors is a precondition for the welfare of the whole clan and of each and every one of us. And it is the chief who is responsible for the quality and closeness of these relations. He is the mediator and link between two integral parts of the clan: the world of the ancestors and the world of the living. It is he who communicates to the living the ancestors' will and decision regarding any given matter, and it is he who pleads with them for forgiveness if the living have violated custom or law.

"One can obtain this forgiveness by making offerings to the ancestors: sprinkling the earth with water or palm wine, laying food aside for them, slaughtering a sheep. But it all might not suffice—the ancestors might continue to be angry, which for the living means endless misfortunes and illnesses. The greatest anger is caused by incest, murder, suicide, assault, insulting the chief, witchcraft."

"Suicide?" I was surprised. "How can you punish someone who has committed suicide?"

"Our law commanded us to cut off his head. Suicide was the violation of a taboo, and the principle tenet of the clan legal code is that each offense must be punished. If an offense goes unpunished, the clan will meet with catastrophe, will face ruin."

We were sitting on the porch of one of the numerous local bars, drinking Fanta, which clearly holds a monopoly here. A young barmaid was napping behind the counter, leaning her head on her hands. It was hot and sleepy.

"The chief," Kwesi continued, "has many other duties. He decides disputes and resolves conflicts, and is therefore also a judge. An important fact, especially important in the villages, is that the chief allocates land to families. He cannot give them this land, or sell it, for land belongs to the ancestors. They dwell in it, inside it. The chief can only allot it for cultivation. If a field grows barren, he will assign the family another piece of ground, and the former one will lie fallow, gaining strength for the future. The land is sacred. The land gives people life, and that which gives life is sacred.

"While the chief enjoys the greatest respect, he is surrounded by a council of elders and cannot decide anything without seeking their opinion and gaining their consent. That is how we understand democracy. In the morning, each member of the council visits the chief's house, to greet him. That is how the chief knows that he is governing well and enjoying support. Should these morning visits cease, it means that he has lost the council's confidence and must go. This will happen if he commits any one of five offenses: drunkenness, gluttony, collusion with sorcerers, bad rapport with people, and governing without seeking the opinion of the council of elders. He must also step down if he is blinded, infected with leprosy, or becomes mentally unsound.

"Several clans together form what Europeans call a tribe. The Ashanti is a union of eight clans. At their head stands a king, the Ashantehene, also surrounded by a council of elders.

The Shadow of the Sun

Such a union is cemented not only by shared ancestors. It is also a territorial, cultural, and political community. It can be very powerful at times, numbering many millions, larger than many a European nation."

I hesitated a long time, then finally asked him: "Tell me something about witchcraft." I hesitated, because it is a subject about which one speaks reluctantly here, and often simply passes over in silence.

"Not everyone believes in it anymore," Kwesi answered. "But a lot of people still do. Many are simply afraid of not believing. My grandmother thinks that witches exist and meet at night on tall solitary trees standing in fields. 'But has Grandma ever seen a witch?' I once asked her. 'That would be impossible,' she answered with conviction. 'At night, witches envelop the whole world with a spider's web. They hold one end in their hands, and the other is fastened to every door in the world. If someone tries to open a door and go outside, he moves the spider's web. The witches feel this and, alarmed, vanish into the darkness. In the mornings one can only see shreds of spiders' webs hanging down from tree branches and doorknobs.' "

I, a White Man

I n Dar es Salaam I bought an old Land Rover from an Englishman who was returning to Europe. It was 1962, several months after Tanganyika had gained independence, and many Englishmen from the colonial administration had lost their jobs, positions, even houses. In their increasingly deserted clubs, someone was always recounting how he had walked into his office at the ministry, and there, smiling at him from behind his desk, was one of the locals. "Excuse me. I'm very sorry!"

This changing of the guard is called Africanization. There are those who applaud it as a symbol of liberation, while others are outraged by the process. It is clear who is for and who is against. London and Paris, in order to induce their civil servants to go work in the colonies, created for those amenable to the idea a grand quality of life. A minor clerk from the post office in Manchester received upon arrival in Tanganyika a villa with a garden and swimming pool, cars, servants, holidays in Europe, etc. Members of the colonial bureaucracy lived truly magnificently. And now, between one day and the next, the inhabitants of the colony receive their independence. They take over the colonial state in an unaltered form. They even take great care not to alter anything, because such a state offers fantastic privileges, which its new administrators naturally do not wish to renounce. The colonial origins of the African state—a state wherein the civil servant received renumeration beyond all measure and reason—ensured that in independent Africa, the struggle for power instantly assumed an extremely fierce and ruthless character. All at once, in the blink of an eye, a new ruling class arises—a bureaucratic bourgeoisie that creates nothing, produces nothing, but merely governs the society and reaps the benefits. The twentieth-century principle of vertiginous speed applied in this instance as well—once, decades, even centuries, were needed for a new social class to emerge, and here all it took was several days. The French, who were observing the struggle for positions with some wry amusement, called the phenomenon *la politique du ventre* (politics of the belly), so closely was a political appointment connected with huge material gains.

But this is Africa, and the fortunate nouveau riche cannot forget the old clan tradition, one of whose supreme canons is share everything you have with your kinsmen, with another member of your clan, or, as they say here, with your cousin. (In Europe, the bond with a cousin is by now rather weak and distant, whereas in Africa a cousin on your mother's side is more important than a husband.) So—if you have two shirts, give him one; if you have a bowl of rice, give him half. Whoever breaks this rule condemns himself to ostracism, to expulsion from the clan, to the horrifying status of outcast. Individualism is highly prized in Europe, and perhaps nowhere more so than in America; in Africa, it is synonymous with unhappiness, with being accursed. African tradition is collectivist, for only in a harmonious group could one face the obstacles continually thrown up by nature. And one of the conditions of collective survival is the sharing of the smallest thing. One day a group of children surrounded me. I had a single piece of candy, which I placed in my open palm. The children stood motionless, staring. Finally, the oldest girl took the candy, bit it into pieces, and equitably distributed the bits.

If someone has become a government minister, replacing a

white man, and has received his villa, garden, salary, and car, word of this quickly reaches this fortunate one's place of origin. It spreads like wildfire to neighboring villages. Joy and hope well up in the hearts of his cousins. Soon they begin their pilgrimage to the capital. Once here, they easily locate their distinguished distant relative. They appear at the gate of his house, greet him, ritualistically sprinkle the ground with gin to thank the ancestors for such a felicitous turn of events, and then make themselves at home in the villa, in the yard, in the garden. Before long, we can observe how the quiet residence where an elderly Englishman lived with his taciturn wife is now noisily teeming with the new official's kinsmen. From the earliest morning, a fire is going in front of the house, women are mashing cassava in wooden mortars, a gaggle of children are romping among the flower beds and borders. In the evenings, the entire extended family sits down to dinner on the lawn—for although a new life has begun, an old custom from the days of unremitting poverty remains: one eats only once a day, in the evening.

Whoever has a more mobile occupation, and less respect for tradition, tries to cover his tracks. In Dodoma, I once ran into a street vendor hawking oranges who used to bring these fruits to my house in Dar es Salaam. I was happy to see him, and asked him what he was doing here, five hundred kilometers from the capital. He had had to flee from his cousins, he explained. He had shared his meager profits with them for a long time, but finally had had enough, and ran. "I will have a few cents for a while," he said happily. "Until they find me again!"

Social advancements of this type are still relatively infrequent in Dar es Salaam in the years immediately following independence. In the white neighborhoods, whites still dominate. For Dar es Salaam, like other cities in this part of the continent, consists of three distinct quarters, separated from one another either by water or by a stretch of bare ground.

The best neighborhood, close to the sea, belongs of course to the whites. It is called Oyster Bay: magnificent villas, gardens exploding with flowers, thick lawns, smooth, gravel-strewn avenues. Yes, you can live truly luxuriously here, especially since you don't have to do anything yourself: everything is taken care of by quiet, vigilant, discreetly moving servants. Here, a man ambles along as he probably would do in paradise: slowly, loosely, content that he is here, enchanted by the beauty of the world.

Beyond the bridge, on the other side of the lagoon, significantly farther from the sea, lies a paved-over, crowded, busy, mercantile neighborhood. Its inhabitants are Indians, Pakistanis, natives of Goa, arrivals from Bangladesh and Sri Lanka, all of them collectively called Asians here. Although there are several men of great wealth among them, the majority are middle class, living without any excess. They are traders. They buy, sell, act as middlemen, speculate. They are always counting something, counting endlessly, shaking their heads, quarreling. Dozens, hundreds of shops, wide open, their goods spilling out onto the sidewalks, onto the streets. Fabrics, furniture, lamps, pots and pans, mirrors, knickknacks, toys, rice, syrups, spices—everything. In front of a shop sits a Hindu, one foot resting on the seat of his chair, his fingers digging at his toes.

Every Saturday afternoon, the inhabitants of this airless, swarming neighborhood go to the seashore. They dress in their finest clothes—the women in golden saris, the men in neat shirts. They travel by car. The whole family piles in, perched on one another's laps, shoulders, heads—ten, fifteen people. They stop the car on the steep slope above the ocean. At this time of day, the incoming tide pounds the beach with powerful, deafening waves. They open the windows. They breathe in the salty smell. They air themselves. On the other side of the immense body of water before them lies their country, which some don't even know anymore: India. They spend fifteen minutes here, maybe a half hour. Then the convoy drives off and the shore is empty again.

The farther from the sea, the greater the heat, the aridity, and the dust. It is there, on the dry sand, on the bare, barren earth, that stand the clay huts of the African quarter. Its individual neighborhoods bear the names of the old slave villages of the sultan of Zanzibar: Kariakoo, Hala, Magomeni, Kinondoni. The names may vary, but the quality of their clay houses is uniformly low, and their standard of living wretched, with no prospect of improvement.

For the people of those neighborhoods, independence means being free to walk at will the main streets of this city of more than a hundred thousand, and even to venture into the white areas. It was never really forbidden, because the African could always turn up there, but he had to have a clear, concrete goal: he either had to be going to work, or going home from work. The policeman's eye easily distinguished between the gait of someone hurrying to some task and purposeless, suspicious loafing. Everyone, depending on the color of his skin, had his assigned role and prescribed place.

Those who wrote about apartheid emphasized that this was a system invented and enforced in South Africa, a state governed by white racists. But apartheid is a much more universal, common phenomenon. Its critics maintained that it is a system instituted by rabid Boers so that they could rule indivisibly and keep the blacks in the ghettos, which were called bantustans. The ideologists of apartheid defended themselves: We believe that all people are entitled to better their circumstances and to develop, but, depending on the color of their skin and their ethnicity, to develop separately. This was a piece of fraudulence, for whoever knew the reality understood that behind this support for equal development lay a deeply inequitable and unjust state of affairs: the whites possessed the best plots of land and the cities' richest neighborhoods, and they controlled industry, while the blacks were consigned to crowded, wretched scraps of semi-arid land.

The concept of apartheid was so perverse that with time its principal victims began to discover certain advantages in it, a chance for a kind of self-reliance, the comfort of being in one's

39

own backyard. The African could say: "It is not only I, the black man, who cannot enter your area, but you, too, the white man, if you want to stay in one piece and not place yourself in danger, you had better not come into my neighborhood!"

It was in such a city that I arrived as the correspondent of the Polish Press Agency, and in which I was to spend several years. Going about its streets, I quickly realized I was in the net of apartheid. First of all, the issue of skin color suddenly loomed large. In Poland, in Europe, I never thought about it. Here, in Africa, it was becoming the most important determinant of my identity, and for simple people, the sole one. The white man. White, therefore a colonialist, a pillager, an occupier. I subjugated Africa, conquered Tanganyika, put to the sword the entire tribe of the man just now standing before me, the tribe of his ancestors. I made him an orphan. Moreover, a humiliated and powerless orphan. Eternally hungry and sick. Yes, when he looks at me, this is exactly what he must be thinking: the white man, the one who took everything from me, who beat my grandfather on his back, who raped my mother. Here he is before me, let me take a good look at him!

I could not adequately resolve the question of guilt. In their eyes, I was guilty. Slavery, colonialism, five hundred years of injustice—after all, it's the white men's doing. The white men's. Therefore mine. Mine? I was not able to conjure within myself that cleansing, liberating emotion—guilt; to show contrition; to apologize. On the contrary! From the start, I tried to counterattack: "You were colonized? We, Poles, were also! For one hundred and thirty years we were the colony of three foreign powers. White ones, too." They laughed, tapped their foreheads, walked away. I angered them, because they thought I wanted to deceive them. I knew that despite my inner certainty about my own innocence, to them I was guilty. These barefoot, hungry, and illiterate boys had a moral advantage over me, the sole advantange an accursed history bestows upon its victims. With rare exceptions, they, the black men, had never conquered anybody, hadn't occupied, hadn't enslaved. They could regard me from a position of superiority. They were of a black race, but a pure one. I stood among them weak, with nothing more to say.

I didn't feel comfortable anywhere. The color of my skin, albeit privileged, also confined me to the cage of apartheid. A gilded cage—Oyster Bay—but a cage nonetheless. Oyster Bay is a beautiful neighborhood. Beautiful, blooming with flowers—and boring. Granted, one could stroll here amid tall palm trees, admire the billowing bougainvillea and the elegant, delicate tuberose, the cliffs covered with thick seaweed. But what else? Besides this, what? The residents of the neighborhood were colonial bureaucrats, who thought only of getting to the end of their contract, buying a crocodile skin or a rhinoceros horn as a souvenir, and leaving. Their wives discussed either the children's health or a past or upcoming party. And I had a daily story to file! About what? Where would I get the material? There was one small local newspaper, the *Tanganyika Standard*. I visited its editorial offices, but the staff consisted of these very same Englishmen from Oyster Bay. And they too were already packing.

I went to the Indian quarter. But what was I to do here? Where was I to go? Who was there for me to talk to? The heat was dreadful, and it was impossible to walk for any length of time: there is no air to breathe, your legs grow weak, your shirt drips with sweat. After an hour of wandering around, you are fed up with everything. You have but one desire left: to sit down somewhere in the shade. Better yet, beneath a fan. And then a thought strikes you: do the inhabitants of the North appreciate what a treasure they possess in that gray, drab, perpetually cloudy sky, with its one great, miraculous advantage—that there is no sun in it?

My main goal, of course, was the African suburbs. I had their names written down. I had the address for the office of the ruling party, TANU (Tanganyika African National Union). But I couldn't find it. Identical streets, sand up to your ankles, children who won't let you pass, crowding around you, amused, aggressively curious—a white man in these inaccessible back alleys is a sensation and a spectacle. With each step I lose my confidence. I feel the attentive gaze of men sitting idly in front of houses, following me with their eyes. The women don't look, turning their heads away: they are Muslims, dressed in black, loosely draped gowns called bui-bui, which completely conceal their bodies as well as part of their faces. The irony of the situation is that even if I were to strike up a conversation with one of the Africans and wished to talk further to him, we would have nowhere to go. The good restaurant is for Europeans, the bad one for Africans. They never frequent each other's establishments; it isn't the custom. Each one would feel ill at ease if he found himself in a place inconsistent with the dictates of apartheid.

Now that I had a powerful, four-wheel-drive vehicle, I could set off. And there was reason to: in early October, a neighbor of Tanganyika's, Uganda, was gaining its independence. The wave of liberation was sweeping the entire continent: in one year alone, 1960, seventeen African countries ceased being colonies. And this process was continuing, though at a diminished pace.

From Dar es Salaam to Uganda's capital, Kampala, where the ceremony was to take place, is three days' solid driving, going from dawn to dusk at maximum speed. Half the route is asphalt, the other half consists of reddish laterite roads, called African graters because they have a crenellated surface over which you can only drive fast, so as to skim over the tops of the crenellations.

A Greek went along with me, Leo—a part-time broker, part-time correspondent for various Athenian newspapers. We took four spare tires, two barrels of gasoline, a barrel of water, food. We set out at dawn, heading north, to the right of us the Indian Ocean, invisible from the road, to the left first the massif of Nguro, and then, for the rest of the way, the plain of the Masai.

Both sides of the road are dense with greenery. Tall grasses, thick, fleecy shrubs, spreading umbrella trees. It's this way all the way to Kilimanjaro and the two little towns nearby, Moshi and Arusha. In Arusha we turned west, toward Lake Victoria. Two hundred kilometers on, the problems started. We drove onto the enormous plain of the Serengeti, the largest concentration of wild animals on earth. Everywhere you look, huge herds of zebras, antelopes, buffalo, giraffes. And all of them are grazing, frisking, frolicking, galloping. Right by the side of the road, motionless lions; a bit farther, a group of elephants; and farther still, on the horizon, a leopard running in huge bounds. It's all improbable, incredible. As if one were witnessing the birth of the world, that precise moment when the earth and sky already exist, as do water, plants, and wild animals, but not yet Adam and Eve. It is this world barely born, the world without mankind and hence also without sin, that one can imagine one is seeing here.

The Cobra's Heart

This mood of elation quickly dissipated in the fact of the realities and riddles of the journey. The first, most important question was, which way should we go? For when we emerged onto the great plain, what was heretofore a single broad trail suddenly forked into several identical-looking dirt paths, all leading in entirely different directions. And no guidepost, sign, or arrow in sight. The plain smooth as a tabletop, overgrown with tall grasses, no mountains or rivers, no natural orientation points of any kind, only this unending, increasingly unreadable, tangled net of trails.

There weren't even any intersections, but every few kilometers, sometimes every few hundred meters, more and more radiating tentacles, coils, and knots, from which secondary offshoots of the same kind branched out chaotically this way and that.

I asked Leo what he thought we should do, but he just looked about uncertainly and answered my question with an identical one. We drove on randomly, choosing roads that seemed to head west (and therefore toward Lake Victoria), but whichever the road, suddenly, after several kilometers and for no apparent reason, it would begin to turn in some unknown direction. Utterly confused, I would stop the car, wondering, now where? It was an especially urgent question, since we had neither a detailed map nor even a compass.

Soon, a new difficulty developed, for noontime arrived, and with it the hours of the greatest heat, when the world sinks into insensibility and silence. Animals seek shelter in the shade of trees. But the herds of buffalo have nowhere to hide. They are too large, too numerous. Each might be a thousand strong. Such a herd, in the hour of the greatest heat, simply grows motionless, dead still. It so happens that one has frozen this way precisely on the road along which we want to drive. We approach. Before us stand a thousand dark, granitelike statues, firmly set on the ground, as if petrified.

A mighty force slumbers in the herd, mighty and—should it explode anywhere near us—deadly. It is the force of a mountain avalanche, only inflamed, frenzied, driven by foaming blood. The zoologist Bernhard Grzimek tells of flying a small plane over the Serengeti and observing for months on end the behavior of buffalo. A lone buffalo didn't react at all to the whir of the descending plane: it calmly continued grazing. When Grzimek flew over a large herd, however, it was different. It sufficed for there to be among them a single overly sensitive one, a hysteric, a hothouse flower, who at the sound of the engine would start to thrash around waiting to flee. The entire herd would immediately panic and, in terror, begin to move.

And here is just such a herd. What should we do? Stop and stand? For how long? Turn around? It's too late for that; I am afraid to turn around, for they might rush us. They are fantastically swift, stubborn, and persistent animals. I make a sign of the cross and slowly, slowly, in first gear, the clutch only half engaged, drive into the herd. It is enormous, stretching almost to the horizon. I observe the bulls, who are at the head. Those who are standing in the path of the car begin drowsily, sluggishly to step aside so that the car can pass. They do not move even a centimeter farther than is absolutely necessary, and still the Land Rover is constantly scraping against their sides. I am drenched in sweat as we drive through this minefield. Out of the corner of my eye I look at Leo. His eyes are shut. One meter after another, meter by meter. The herd is silent. Immobile. Hundreds of pairs of dark, bulging eyes in massive heads, filmy, dull, expressionless. The passage lasts a long time, a crossing seemingly without end, but at last we emerge on the other shore—the herd is now behind us, its deep, dark stain against the green surface of the Serengeti growing smaller and smaller.

The more time passed, the farther we drove, circling and straying, the more anxious I became. We had not encountered any people since morning. We had also not come upon either a larger road or any kind of signpost. The heat was terrifying, and it intensified with every minute, as if the road we were on, and all others as well, led directly toward the sun, and as we drove we were inexorably approaching the moment we would be consumed by fire, like offerings laid at its altar. The burning air started to quiver and undulate. Everything was becoming fluid, each view blurred and washed out as in a film left running out-of-focus. The horizon receded and smudged, as if subject to the oceanic law of ebb and flow. The dusty gray parasols of the acacias swayed rhythmically and moved about—as if some confused madmen were tossing them here and there, at a loss for anything better to do.

But the worst by far was that the tangled net of roads that had held us in its treacherous and suffocating grip for several hours now itself twitched and began to move. I could see that the web, the entire intricate geometry, which admittedly I had not been able to decipher but which nonetheless was a kind of constant, a fixed element upon the surface of the savannah, was now thrashing about and drifting. Where was it drifting to? Where was it pulling us, entwined in its coils? We were all being swept somewhere, Leo, the car and I, the roads, the savannah, the buffalo, and the sun, toward some unknown, shining, white-hot space.

Suddenly, the engine stopped and the car came to an abrupt halt. Leo, seeing that something was wrong with me, had turned off the ignition. "Give it to me," he said. "I'll drive." We continued this way until the heat diminished, and it was then that we spotted two African huts in the far distance. We drove up. They were empty, with no doors or windows. There were some wooden bunks inside. The houses clearly did not belong to anyone, and were simply intended for travelers who happened by.

I don't know how I found myself on one of the bunks. I was half dead. My head was pounding from the sun. To overcome drowsiness, I lit a cigarette. It didn't taste good. I wanted to put it out, and when I looked at my hand, which was reaching instinctively for the ground, I saw that I was about to extinguish the cigarette on the head of a snake lying under the bed.

I froze. Froze to such a degree that instead of quickly pulling back my hand, I left it suspended, cigarette burning, over the snake's head. Slowly, the reality of my position dawned on me: I was the prisoner of a deadly reptile. I knew one thing for certain: I could not move a muscle, because then the snake would attack. It was an Egyptian cobra, yellowish gray, neatly coiled on the floor. Its venom brings death quickly, and in our situtation—with no medicines, and the nearest hospital probably a day's driving away—death would be inevitable. It was possible that at that very moment the cobra was in a state of light catalepsy (a condition of numbness and lethargy apparently typical of these reptiles), because it did not stir. My God, what should I do? I thought feverishly, by now completely wide awake.

"Leo," I whispered loudly. "Leo, a snake!"

Leo had been in the car, getting our luggage out. We stared at each other silently, not knowing how to proceed. Yet time was running out: Were the cobra to awaken, it would probably attack instantly. Because we had no weapons of any kind, not even a machete, we decided that Leo would get a metal canister from the car and with it we would try to crush the cobra. It was a risky plan, but it was all we could come up with. We had to do something. Our inaction was giving the snake an advantage.

The canisters, from old British army supplies, were large, with sharp, protruding edges. Leo, who was a powerful man, grabbed one and started to creep toward the hut. The cobra was still just lying there, motionless. Leo, grasping the canister by its handles, lifted it up and waited. He was calculating, positioning himself, aiming. I lay still as stone on the bunk, tense, ready. And then suddenly, in a split second, Leo, holding the canister before him, threw his entire weight upon the snake. At which moment I too fell with my whole body on top of him. In these seconds, our lives hung in the balance—we knew this. Actually, we only thought of it later, for the instant the canister, Leo, and I came down on top of the snake, the interior of the hut exploded.

I never suspected there could be so much power within a single creature. Such terrifying, monstrous, cosmic power. I had assumed that the canister's edge would easily cut through the snake—nothing of the kind! I now saw we had beneath us not a snake, but a throbbing, vibrating steel spring, impossible to either break or crush. The cobra was thrashing and pounding the ground with such demented fury that the hut's interior grew dark from the dust. Under the powerful blows of its tail, the clay floor was crumbling and scattering, blinding us with clouds of debris. At one point it suddenly occurred to me with horror that we wouldn't manage, that the reptile would slip out from under us and, in pain, wounded, enraged, would start to bite us. I pressed down even harder on my friend. He was groaning, his chest crushed against the canister, unable to breathe.

Finally, but this took a long time, an eternity, the cobra's blows started to lose their impetus, vigor, frequency. "Look," Leo said. "Blood." Indeed, into a crevice along the floor, which now resembled a shattered clay dish, a narrow trickle of blood was slowly seeping. The cobra was weakening, and the vibrations of the canister, which we felt the whole time and by means of which the snake signaled us about her pain and her hatred, vibrations that terrified and panicked us, were also diminishing. But now, when it was all over, when Leo and I rose and the dust began to settle and thin out and I gazed down again at the narrow ribbon of blood being quickly absorbed, instead of satisfaction and joy I felt an emptiness inside, and something else as well: I felt sad that that heart, which inhabited the very pit of hell we had all shared through a bizarre coincidence only a moment ago, that that heart had stopped beating.

The next day we stumbled upon a wide, rust-colored track that, in a wide arc, circumscribed Lake Victoria. Driving several hundred kilometers through a green, luxuriant, fertile Africa, we reached the Ugandan border. It wasn't really a border. A simple shed stood by the side of the road, with the sign "Uganda" burned out on a wooden board above the door. The shed was empty and shuttered. The kinds of borders for which blood is spilled were still to come into being.

We drove on. Night had already fallen. Everything that in Europe is called dusk and evening here lasts only a few minutes, if it exists at all. It is daytime, and then night, as if someone has turned off the sun's generator with one flip of the switch. All at once, all is black. In one instant we are inside the night's darkest core. If this change surprises you as you are walking through the bush, you must stop immediately: you can see nothing, as if somebody has unexpectedly pulled a sack over your head. You become disoriented, you don't know where you are. In such darkness people converse without seeing one another. They might call out to one another, not realizing they are standing side by side. The darkness separates people, and thereby intensifies all the more their desire to be together, in a group, in a community.

The first hours of the night are the most social time in Africa. No one wants to be alone then. Being alone? That's misfortune, perdition! Children don't go to sleep early here. We enter the land of dreams together—as a family, a clan, a village.

We drove through an already sleeping Uganda, invisible behind the curtain of night. Somewhere nearby must have been Lake Victoria, somewhere the kingdoms of Ankole and Toro, the pastures of Mubende, Murchison Falls. All this surrounded by a night black as soot. A night full of silence. The car's headlights pierced the darkness, and in their glow whirled a frenzied swarm of little flies, beetles, and mosquitoes, which appeared as if out of nowhere, for a fraction of a second played out before our eyes their role of a lifetime—the insect's demonic dance—before perishing, splattered mercilessly upon the windshield of the speeding car.

Every now and then an oasis of light appeared in the undifferentiated blackness—a roadside shack lit up colorfully as though at a fair, glittering from afar: an Indian shop, a *duka*. Above the mounds of biscuits, tea bags, cigarettes, and matches, over the cans of sardines and the sticks of butter, we could make out, illuminated by a fluorescent lamp, the head of the proprietor, who sat motionless, waiting with patience and hope for late clients. The glow of these shops, which seemed to appear and disappear as if at our command, lit for us, like solitary lampposts on an empty street, the whole road to Kampala.

Kampala was readying for celebration. In several days, on October 9, Uganda was to receive its independence. The complicated deals and maneuvers continued up to the very last minute. Everything about the internal politics of Africa's states is intricate and entangled. This stems directly from the fact that European colonialists, dividing Africa among themselves under Bismarck's leadership during the Berlin conference, crammed the approximately ten thousand kingdoms, federations, and stateless but independent tribal associations that existed on this continent in the middle of the nineteenth century within the borders of barely forty colonies. Meantime, many of these kingdoms and tribal groups shared a long history of conflict and wars. And here, without being asked their opinion on the matter, they suddenly found themselves within one and the same colony, subject to the same (and foreign) authority, the same laws.

Now, with decolonization, the old interethnic relationships, which European rule only froze or simply ignored, suddenly sprang back to life and were becoming relevant again. The chance for liberty appeared, yes, but liberty with a proviso: that yesterday's opponents and enemies form one nation and become its joint managers, patriots, and defenders. The former European colonial capitals and the leaders of Africa's independence movements adopted the principle that if bloody internal conflicts erupted within a given colony, that territory would not become free.

The process of decolonization was to occur through what were stipulated as constitutional methods, at a round table, without great political dramas, ensuring the preservation of that which was most important: the uninterrupted flow of goods and riches between Africa and Europe.

The circumstances under which the leap to the kingdom of liberty was to be accomplished presented many Africans with a difficult choice. Colliding within them were two sets of considerations, two loyalties, in painful, almost insoluble conflict. On the one hand lay the deeply encoded remembrance of the history of one's clan and people, of the allies one could turn to in times of need and of the enemies one had to despise, and on the other hand was the awareness that one was supposed to be entering the community of independent, modern societies, a precondition of which was the renunciation of all ethnic egoism and blindness.

It is this very problem that existed in Uganda. As defined by its current borders, it was a young country, barely several decades old. But its territory encompassed parts of four ancient kingdoms: Ankole, Buganda, Bunyoro, and Toro. The history of their mutual animosities and conflicts was as colorful and rich as anything between the Celts and the Saxons, or the Montagues and the Capulets.

Preeminent among them was the kingdom of Buganda, whose capital, Mengo, made up one of Kampala's neighborhoods. Mengo is also the name of the hill upon which the royal palace stands. For Kampala, a city of extraordinary beauty, full of flowers, palm trees, mango trees, and poinsettia, is laid out across seven gentle green hills, several of which descend directly to the lake.

Once, royal palaces kept springing up on these hills, one by one: when a king died, his residence was abandoned and a new one was built on the next hilltop. The object was to not disturb that ongoing rule of the deceased, which continued, albeit from the other world. Thus the entire dynasty held power at once, with the actual living king as its guardian, its temporary representative.

In 1960, two years prior to liberation, people who did not consider themselves subject to the king of Buganda formed the UPC party (Uganda People's Congress), which won the first elections. At its head stood a young civil servant, Milton Obote; I met him while he was still in Dar es Salaam.

The journalists who were expected in Kampala were to live in the barracks of an old hospital, situated slightly outside of town (the new one, a gift from Queen Elizabeth, was awaiting its dedication). We were the first to arrive; the barracks, white and clean, were still empty. In the main building, I was handed the room key. Leo was driving north to see Murchison Falls. I envied him, but had to stay behind to gather some material for my story. I found my building, which stood at some remove, on a slope amid luxuriant cinnamon and tamarind trees. The entrance to the room was at the end of a long corridor. I walked in, set down my bag and suitcase, closed the door. And at that moment I noticed that the bed, table, and chest of drawers were rising, and high up, beneath the ceiling, starting to whirl faster and faster.

I lost consciousness.

Inside the Mountain of Ice

When I opened my eyes, I saw a large white screen, and against its brightness the face of a black girl. Her eyes observed me for a moment, then vanished together with the rest of her face. A moment later the head of an Indian appeared on the screen. He must have leaned over me, for suddenly I saw him in close-up, as if magnified many times over.

"Thank God, you're alive," I heard. "But you're sick. You have malaria. Cerebral malaria."

I came to instantly. I wanted to sit up, but felt that I didn't have the strength to, that I was paralyzed. Cerebral malaria is the terror of tropical Africa. Once, it was inevitably fatal. Even now it is dangerous, and frequently still deadly. Driving here, we passed near Arusha a cemetery of its victims, a vestige of the epidemic that had passed that way several years ago.

I tried to look around. The white screen above me was the ceiling of the room in which I was lying. I was in the just-opened Mulago Hospital, one of its first patients. The girl was a nurse called Dora, and the Indian was a doctor, Patel. They told me that an ambulance called by Leo had brought me here the day before. Leo had gone to the north, seen Murchison Falls, and three days later returned to Kampala. He walked into my room and saw me lying there unconscious. He ran to the reception desk for help,

but it was Uganda's independence day, the entire town was dancing, singing, swimming in beer and palm wine, and poor Leo
didn't know what to do. Finally he drove to the hospital himself
and arranged for an ambulance. And that is how I found myself
here, in a private room, in which everything still smelled of fresh-
ness, peace, and order.

The first signal of an imminent malaria attack is a feeling of anxiety, which comes on suddenly and for no clear reason. Something
has happened to you, something bad. If you believe in spirits, you
know what it is: someone has pronounced a curse, and an evil
spirit has entered you, disabling you and rooting you to the
ground. Hence the dullness, the weakness, the heaviness that
comes over you. Everything is irritating. First and foremost, the
light; you hate the light. And others are irritating—their loud
voices, their revolting smell, their rough touch.

But you don't have a lot of time for these repugnances and
loathings. For the attack arrives quickly, sometimes quite abruptly,
with few preliminaries. It is a sudden, violent onset of cold. A
polar, arctic cold. Someone has taken you, naked, toasted in the
hellish heat of the Sahel and the Sahara, and thrown you straight
into the icy highlands of Greenland or Spitsbergen, amid the
snows, winds, and blizzards. What a shock! You feel the cold in a
split second, a terrifying, piercing, ghastly cold. You begin to
tremble, to quake, to thrash about. You immediately recognize,
however, that this is not a trembling you are familiar with from
earlier experiences—say, when you caught cold one winter in a
frost; these tremors and convulsions tossing you around are of a
kind that at any moment now will tear you to shreds. Trying to
save yourself, you begin to beg for help.

What can bring relief? The only thing that really helps is if
someone covers you. But not simply throws a blanket or quilt
over you. This thing you are being covered with must crush you
with its weight, squeeze you, flatten you. You dream of being

pulverized. You desperately long for a steamroller to pass over you.

I once had a powerful malaria attack in a poor village, where there weren't any heavy coverings. The villagers placed the lid from some kind of wooden chest on top of me and then patiently sat on it, waiting for the worst tremors to pass. The most wretched are those who have a malaria attack and there is nothing to wrap them in. You can see them by the roadsides, in the bush, or in the clay huts, lying semicomatose on the ground, drenched in sweat, confused, their bodies rent by rhythmic waves of malarial convulsions. But even snuggled under a dozen blankets, jackets, and coats, your teeth chatter and you moan with pain, because you sense that this cold does not come from without— it's forty degrees Celsius out there!—but that it's within, inside you, that these Greenlands and Spitsbergens are in you, that all those floes, sheets, and mountains of ice are advancing through your veins, muscles, and bones. Perhaps this thought would fill you with fear—were you able to summon the strength to feel anything at all. But the thought occurs just as the peak of the attack, after several hours, is gradually subsiding, and you start a helpless descent into a state of extreme exhaustion and weakness.

The malaria attack is not merely painful, but like every pain also a mystical experience. We enter a realm about which a moment ago we knew nothing, though it now turns out that it had existed alongside us all the while, finally capturing and incorporating us: we discover within ourselves icy crevasses, chasms, and abysses, whose presence fills us with suffering and fear. But this moment of discovery, too, passes, the spirits desert us, depart, and disappear, and that which remains, under the mountain of the most bizarre coverings, is truly pitiful.

A man right after a strong attack of malaria is a human rag. He lies in a puddle of sweat, he is still feverish, and he can move neither hand nor foot. Everything hurts; he is dizzy and nauseous.

He is exhausted, weak, limp. Carried by someone else, he gives the impression of having no bones or muscles. And many days must pass before he can get up on his feet again.

Each year in Africa malaria afflicts tens of millions of people, and in those areas where it is most prevalent—in wet, low-lying, marshy regions—it kills one child out of three. There are many types of malaria; some, the gentle ones, you should be able to recover from as you would from the flu. But here, even those can lay waste whoever succumbs to them. First, because in this murderous climate one endures with difficulty even the slightest indisposition; second, because Africans are often malnourished, attenuated, hungry. Time and again you encounter here drowsy, apathetic, benumbed people. They sit or lie for hours on end on the streets, by the roadsides, doing nothing. You speak to them and they do not hear you; you look at them and have the impression that they do not see you. It is unclear if they are ignoring you, if these are just idle lazybones and do-nothings, or if they are being ravaged by a malaria that is slowly and inexorably killing them. You do not know how to behave toward them, or what to think.

I lay for two weeks in the Mulago Hospital. The attacks recurred, but each one less intense and exhausting than the preceding. I got countless injections. Dr. Patel came every day, examined me, told me that when I was better he would introduce me to his family. He has a wealthy family, owners of large stores in Kampala and in the provinces. They were able to educate him in England, and he received his medical degree in London. How did his ancestors come to find themselves in Uganda? At the end of the nineteenth century, his grandfather and thousands of other young Indians were brought by the English to eastern Africa to build the railway line from Mombasa to Kampala. It was a new phase of colonial expansion: the conquest and subjugation of the continent's interior. If you look closely at old maps of Africa, you will notice a peculiarity: inscribed along the coastlines are dozens, hundreds of names of ports, cities, and settlements, whereas the rest, a vast 99 percent of Africa's surface, is a blank, essentially virgin area, only sparsely marked here and there.

The Europeans clung to the coasts, to their ports, eating houses, and ships, reluctantly and only sporadically making incursions into the interior. They were hampered by the lack of roads, fearful of hostile tribes and tropical diseases—malaria, sleeping sickness, yellow fever, leprosy. And although they inhabited the coasts for more than four centuries, they did so in a spirit of impermanence, with a narrow-minded goal of quick profits and easy spoils. Their ports were really only leeches on the body of Africa, points of export for slaves, gold, and ivory. Their goal: to carry away everything, and at the lowest possible price. Consequently, many of these European beachheads resembled the poorest sections of old Liverpool or Lisbon. In the course of four hundred years in Luanda, the Portuguese did not dig a single well for potable water, or illuminate the streets with lanterns.

The construction of the railway line to Kampala was the symbol of a new, more paternalistic approach to Africa on the part of the colonial powers, especially London and Paris. With the division of Africa among the European states already securely accomplished, they could turn their attentions to investing in those parts of their colonies whose rich and fertile soils held the promise of huge profits from coffee, tea, cotton, and pineapple plantations, or, in other places, from diamond, gold, or copper mines. But there were no means of transport. The old way—porters carrying everything on their heads—no longer sufficed. Roads, railway lines, and bridges had to be built. Yes, but who would do this? They could not bring in white workers: the white man was master here, he could not do physical labor. Initially, the local African worker was also out of the question: he simply did not exist. It was impossible to induce the local population to work for wages, because they didn't yet understand the concept of money (for centuries, trade here was based on barter, and one paid for slaves, for example, with firearms, lumps of salt, calico fabrics).

With time, the British introduced a system of forced labor: the tribal chief had to supply a given number of people to work for free. They were placed in camps. Large concentrations of these gulags indicated places where colonialism had settled for good. Before this occurred, however, other quick alternatives had to be found. One of them was to import to eastern Africa cheap labor from another British colony: India. In this way Dr. Patel's grandfather found himself first in Kenya, and then in Uganda, where he later settled permanently.

During one of his visits, the doctor told me how in the course of the railroad's construction, when the tracks began to draw away from the shores of the Indian Ocean and enter the vast territories covered with dense bush, terror began spreading among the Hindu workers: lions had started to attack them.

A lion in his prime does not like to hunt humans. He has his own predatory customs, his favorite tastes and gustatory preferences. He loves the meat of antelope and zebra. He also likes giraffe, although they are difficult to hunt, being so tall and large. And he doesn't turn his nose up at beef, which is why at night shepherds gather their herds within enclosures built in the bush out of thorny branches. But even such a fence is not always an effective barrier, for the lion is a superb jumper and can soar over the goma, as they call it, or just as adroitly crawl under it.

Lions hunt at night, usually in a pride, organizing approaches and ambushes. Immediately before a hunt, a division of roles takes place. There are those who are in charge of driving the prey, directing it toward the jaws of the executioners. The lionesses are the most active, and it is they who attack most frequently. The males are the first to feast: they slurp the freshest blood, swallow the most tender morsels, lick up the fatty marrow.

The daytime hours are spent digesting and sleeping. The lions lie drowsily in the shade of the acacias. If one doesn't irritate them, they will not attack. Even if one approaches them, they will get up and walk farther away. This is a risky maneuver, however, for a predator like this can execute a leap in a split second. Once, on the drive across the Serengeti, we got a flat tire. Instinctively I jumped out of the car to change it, and suddenly realized that around us in the tall grass, next to the bloody shreds of an antelope, lay several lionesses. They watched us but didn't move. Leo and I sat shut in the car, waiting, wondering what they would do. After a quarter of an hour they rose and, tawny, shapely, beautiful, calmly ambled off into the bush.

Lions going forth to hunt announce this with a mighty roar that carries over the entire savannah. The sound frightens, panics the other animals. Only elephants are oblivious to these battle horns: elephants are not afraid of anyone. The others scatter wherever they can, or else stand, paralyzed with terror, waiting until the predator emerges from the darkness and delivers the mortal blow.

The lion is an efficient and formidable hunter for about twenty years. After that he begins to show his age. His muscles weaken, his speed diminishes, his leaps grow shorter. It is difficult for him to chase down a skittish antelope, a swift and vigilant zebra. He walks around hungry, a burden to the pride. It is a dangerous moment for him—the pride does not tolerate the weak and the ill, and he can fall prey to it himself. More and more frequently, he fears that the younger ones will bite him to death. He gradually detaches himself from the pride, lags behind, and finally is alone. He is tormented by hunger, but can no longer chase game. He has only one recourse: to hunt humans. Such a lion is commonly referred to here as a man-eater, and he terrorizes the local population. He lurks near streams where women go to do the wash, near paths along which children walk to school (being hungry, he now hunts by day as well). People are afraid to walk out of their huts, but he attacks them there, too. He is fearless, merciless, and still relatively strong.

It was lions like these, Dr. Patel continued, that started to attack the Indians building the railway line to Kampala. The men slept in cotton tents, which the predators easily slashed to pieces as they pulled out a steady supply of victims. No one protected these people, and they didn't have their own guns. In any event, to battle a lion in the African darkness is a losing proposition. The doctor's grandfather and his companions heard at night the screams of men being torn apart, for the lions feasted fearlessly, in close proximity to the tents, and then, sated, vanished into the gloom.

The doctor always found time for me and conversed willingly, for which I was grateful since even several days after an attack I would still be unable to read, the print blurring, the letters swimming about, as if lifted up and rocked on invisible waves.

"Have you seen a lot of elephants already?" he asked me once.

"Oh, hundreds," I answered.

"And do you know," he said, "that long ago, when the Portuguese first arrived here and started buying up ivory, they were struck by the fact that Africans didn't have a great deal of it. Why, they wondered? After all, the tusks are very rugged and long-lasting, and if it is difficult for them to hunt down a live elephant for its ivory—they usually did this by chasing the animal into a hole they had dug earlier—then why don't they collect the tusks from elephants that have already died, and whose corpses are doubtless lying somewhere? They suggested this idea to their African middlemen, but heard something astonishing by way of reply: there are no dead elephants, there are no elephant cemeteries. The Portuguese were intrigued. How do elephants die? Where are their remains? At issue were the tusks, the ivory, and the large sums of money they commanded.

"The manner in which elephants die was a secret Africans long guarded from the white man. The elephant is sacred, and so is his death. Everything sacred is surrounded by an impenetrable mystery. What caused the elephant to be so admired was that he had no enemies in the animal world. No other beast could conquer him. He could die (in the past) only a natural death. It occurred usually at dusk, when the elephants came to the water. They would stand at the edge of a lake or river, reach out far with their trunks, and drink. But the day would come when a tired old elephant could no longer raise his trunk, and to drink clear water he would have to walk farther and farther out into the lake. His legs would sink into the muck, deeper and deeper. The lake pulled him into its cavernous interior. He fought for a time, thrashed about, attempted to extricate himself from the bog and get back to the shore, but his own weight was so great, and the pull of the lake's bottom so paralyzing, that finally the animal would lose its balance, fall, and vanish under the water forever.

"There," Dr. Patel finished, "on the bottoms of our lakes, are the age-old elephant cemeteries."

Dr. Doyle

My apartment in Dar es Salaam consists of two rooms, a kitchen, and a bathroom, on the first floor of a house that stands amid coconut palms and luxuriant, feathery banana trees not far from Ocean Road. In one room I have a table and chairs, in the other a bed draped with mosquito netting; its festive presence—it resembles a white, trailing wedding train—is meant more to reassure the tenant than to deter mosquitoes: a mosquito will always manage to slip through. It almost seems that these small but insistent aggressors establish each evening a battle plan meant to exhaust their victims, because if there are ten of them, say, they do not attack all together—which would allow you to deal with them all at once and have peace for the rest of the night—but one by one. The first to take off is, as it were, the scout, whose reconnaissance mission the rest closely observe. Well rested after a good day's sleep, he torments you with his demonic buzzing, until finally, sleepy and furious, you organize a hunt, kill him; you are just lying down again, confident of returning to sleep, just turning off the light, when the next one begins his loops, spirals, and corkscrews.

After years (or, rather, years of nights) spent observing mosquitos, I reached the conclusion that this creature is possessed of a deeply seated suicidal instinct, some uncontrollable need for self-destruction. Witnessing the demise of the predecessors does not discourage them, instead they hurl themselves one after the other, clearly excited and desperately determined, toward an inevitable and quick death.

Whenever I return to my apartment from some longer trip, I bring great confusion and discomfort into the lives of those I find there. For the place doesn't stay empty during my absence. Barely have I shut the door behind me than a teeming, bustling, and meddlesome world of insects takes possession. From cracks in the floor and walls, from behind window frames and out of corners, from under moldings and parapets emerge into the light of day armies of ants and centipedes, of spiders and beetles; out fly swarms of flies and moths: the rooms fill up with the countless and varied little nothings, which I am unable to either describe or name; and all this moves its wings, grinds its chops, and minces its limbs. I most admire a certain variety of red ants, who appear suddenly out of nowhere, marching in a superbly even formation and in a perfectly synchronized rhythm, briefly enter one cabinet or another, consume whatever is sweet there, then leave their feeding ground and, walking again as before in an equally ideal order, disappear without a trace whence they came.

It was this way now, too, when I returned from Kampala. At the sight of me, part of the assembled company departed without any deliberation or delay, the others reluctantly, pouting. I drank some juice, looked through the letters and newspapers, and went to sleep. In the morning I got up with difficulty—I had no strength. Making matters worse, it was already the dry season, a time of terrible, withering heat waves that begin from the earliest morning hours. Rallying what strength I had, I wrote several dispatches about the situation in Uganda during the first weeks of independence and drove them to the post office. The clerk who took them from me wrote the date and time into my notebook. They were transmitted via teleprinter to our office in London, and from there to Warsaw: it was the cheapest way. I was astonished by the skill of the local teletypists: they transcribed the Polish text onto the telex without making a single error. I asked them once how this was possible. Because, they answered, they had been taught to copy not words or sentences, but letter after letter. "That is why it makes no difference to us in which language the telegram is written," one of them explained to me. "So far as we're concerned, we are not sending meanings, but marks."

Despite the fact that quite some time had already elapsed since I'd left Kampala, instead of feeling better, I was feeling increasingly worse. It's the remains of the malaria, I told myself, and on top of that the unbearable temperatures of the dry season. Despite the fact that I now began to feel an unfamiliar, intense warmth within, I thought it was the external heat somehow settling down inside me and radiating from there. I was dripping with sweat, but others, too, were drenched—sweat prevented you from being incinerated on the summer's blazing pyre.

After a month of this diminished and wretched existence, I awoke one night feeling that my pillow was wet. I turned on the light and froze: my pillow was covered with blood. I rushed into the bathroom and looked in the mirror: my whole face was smeared with it. In my mouth I felt something sticky, with a salty taste. I washed, but was unable to get back to sleep until morning.

I remembered seeing a sign on one of the houses near the main street, Independence Avenue, with the name of a doctor on it. I went there. John Laird, a tall, slim Englishman, was bustling about his office, which was stacked high with crates and packages. He was returning to Europe in two days, but gave me the name and address of a colleague whom I should see. Close by, near the railway station, there's an outpatient clinic; I would find him there. His name is Ian Doyle. "And," he added, "he's an Irishman" (as if in medicine, at least in this country, what mattered was not so much one's specialty as one's nationality).

The clinic occupied an old military building, which had

served as the army barracks during the days when Tanganyika was a German colony. A listless crowd of Africans was camped out in front, suffering no doubt from all manner of illness. Inside I was greeted by a tired, drawn-looking middle-aged man, whose warmth and kindness struck me momentarily. His very presence, his smile and friendliness, acted like a balm on me. He told me to come to the Ocean Road Hospital that afternoon, because that was the only place with an X-ray machine.

I knew things weren't right with me, but blamed everything on the malaria, and very much wanted the doctor to confirm my diagnosis. As we left the X-ray ward—Doyle had X-rayed me himself—he placed his hand on my shoulder, and we started to stroll over the gently rolling grounds covered with tall palm trees. It was pleasant here, for the palm trees gave shade and a light breeze blew from the ocean.

"Yes," Doyle said finally, and lightly squeezed my arm, "it's definitely tuberculosis."

And he fell silent.

My legs buckled under me and grew so heavy I could raise neither one. We came to a stop.

"We will take you to the hospital," he said.

"I can't go to the hospital," I said. "I don't have enough money."

A month's stay in the hospital cost more than my quarterly salary.

"Then you have to return home," he said.

"I can't go home," I replied. I felt the fever consuming me, I was thirsty and weak.

Then and there I decided to tell him everything. I had trusted this man from the start, and believed he would understand. I explained to him that this stay in Africa was the chance of a life-time for me. That an appointment like mine was the first of its kind in my country: Poland had never before had a permanent correspondent in sub-Saharan Africa. That it came to pass thanks only to an enormous effort on the part of the editorial department, which is poor, for ours is a country where every dollar is precious. That if I inform Warsaw of my illness, they will be unable to pay for my hospitalization and will simply order me to return, and that I will most likely never come here again. And that the thing that had been a lifelong dream of mine—to work in Africa—will vanish forever.

The doctor listened to all this in silence. We were walking again among the palm trees, shrubs, and flowers, amid all that tropical beauty, poisoned for the moment by my defeat and despair.

Silence. Doyle was weighing something, deliberating.

"There is really only one solution," he said at last. "You were at the local clinic this morning. Poor Africans go there for medical attention, because it's free. Unfortunately, conditions are dismal. I don't go there often myself, because I am the only pulmonologist in this whole large country, where tuberculosis is common. Your case is fairly typical: a strong malaria so weakens the system that you then easily succumb to another illness, frequently tuberculosis. Starting tomorrow, I will put your name down on the list of the clinic's patients. I am authorized to do so. I will introduce you to the staff. You'll come every day for an injection. We'll try, we'll see."

Dr. Doyle's staff consisted of two people, who did everything: they cleaned, gave injections, and for the next part directed the flow of traffic, admitting some of the sick, and for reasons unclear to me, chasing others away before they so much as got to the door (suspicions of corruption did not apply here—none of the prospective patients had any money).

The older and heavier one was called Edu, the younger, shorter, and muscular one Abdullahi. In many African societies, children are named for an event that occurred on the day of their birth. Edu is an abbreviation of "education," for on the day he came into the world, the first school was opened in his village.

In places where Christianity and Islam had not yet become deeply rooted, there was an infinite richness to given names. They were expressions of the poetry of adults, who called a child Brisk Morning (if he was born at dawn), or Shadow of the Acacia (if he came into the world beneath an acacia tree). In societies without a tradition of written history, names were used to affix in memory the more important events, long past or recent. If a child was born as Tanganyika was obtaining its independence, it was called Independence (Uhuru in Swahili). If the parents were supporters of President Nyerere, they might name their child Nyerere.

Thus a historical record, albeit a spoken one, was created over centuries, and being highly personal, one with a particularly strong claim on the individual: I am at one with my community because my name celebrates a deed inscribed in the collective memory of the people to whom I belong.

The introduction of Christianity and Islam reduced this exuberant world of poetry and history to several dozen names from the Bible and the Koran. From then on there were only Jameses and Patricks, or Ahmeds and Ibrahims.

Edu and Abdullahi had hearts of gold. We quickly became friends. I tried to create the impression that my life was in their hands (and it was, actually), and they were tremendously impressed by this fact. When I needed help, they dropped everything. I arrived every day after four, when the afternoon heat was waning, the clinic was already closed, and the two of them were sweeping the old wooden floors, raising unimaginably large clouds of dust. Everything proceeded just as Dr. Doyle had ordered. In a glass cabinet in his office stood an enormous metal can (a gift from the Danish Red Cross) full of large gray pills, a drug called PAS. I took twenty-four of those a day. As I was counting them out into a bag, Edu would remove a massive metal syringe from boiling water, snap on the needle, and draw two centimeters of streptomycin from a bottle. Drawing his hand far back, as if to hurl a spear, he would then drive the needle into me. I would leap—with time this became part of the ritual—and emit a sharp hiss, at which Edu and Abdullahi (who was observing everything) would explode with homeric laughter.

Nothing creates a bond between people in Africa more quickly than shared laughter—for example, at a white man jumping up because of a little thing like an injection. So I began to play the game with them, and despite the pain from the needle that Edu plunged into me with such dreadful force, I laughed with them.

In the disturbed, paranoid world of racial inequality, in which everything is determined by the color of one's skin (calibrated by shades of difference), my illness, while physically incapacitating, had an unexpected benefit. Rendering me weak and defective, it diminished my prestigious white status—that of someone formidable, untouchable—and put me on a more even footing with the black men. Now a diminished, disowned, flawed white man I could be treated with familiarity, although I was still a white man. A warmth entered my relations with Edu and Abdullahi. It would have been unthinkable had they met me as a strong, healthy, imperious European.

First of all, they started to invite me to their homes. I gradually became a habitué of the African districts of the city and came to know their life as never before. In African tradition, the guest is treated with the utmost consideration. The saying "Guest in the house, God in the house" has a nearly literal meaning here. The hosts prepare a long time for the occasion. They clean, they cook the best possible meal. I am referring to the home of someone like Edu—an attendant at a city clinic. When I met him, his position was relatively good. Good, because Edu had a steady job, and there are few of those. The majority of the city's inhabitants work sporadically and rarely, or not at all for long periods of time. Perhaps the greatest riddle of Africa's cities is how these masses of people earn a living. How, and from what? They are here not because there was a demand for them, but because poverty expelled them from the villages—poverty, hunger, and helplessness. They are fugitives seeking rescue, refugees cursed by fate. When a group of such people finally reaches the outskirts of town, driven from areas affected by drought or famine, you will notice the fear in their eyes. They must now search among these slums and mud houses for their El Dorado. What will they do now? How will they proceed?

So it was with Edu and several cousins from his clan. They belong to the Sango-speaking people from the interior. They had been farmers, but their land grew barren, so several years ago they came to Dar es Salaam. Their first step: to find other Sango-speaking people. Or people from communities who are affiliated with the Sango through ties of friendship. The African is well versed in this geography of intertribal friendships and hatreds, no less critical than those existing today in the Balkans.

Following a ball of yarn, they will finally arrive at the house of a countryman. The neighborhood is called Kariakoo, and its layout is more or less planned—straight, perpendicularly aligned sandy streets. The construction is monotonous and schematic. The so-called swahili houses predominate, a type of Soviet-style housing—a single one-storied building with eight to twelve rooms, one family in each. The kitchen is communal, as are the toilet and the washing machine. Each dwelling is unbelievably cramped, because families here have many children, each home being in effect a kindergarten. The whole family sleeps together on the clay floor covered with thin raffia matting.

Arriving within earshot of such a house, Edu and his kinsmen stop and call out: *"Hodi!"* It means, in effect: "May I come in?" In these neighborhoods the doors are always open, if they exist at all, but one cannot just walk in without asking, so this

"*Hodi!*" can be heard from quite a distance. If someone is inside, he answers, "*Karibu!*" This means: "Please come in. Greetings." And Edu walks in.

Now begins the interminable litany of greetings. It is simultaneously a period of reconnaissance: both sides are trying to establish their precise degree of kinship. Concentrated and serious, they enter the primevally thick and tangled forest of genealogical trees that is each clan and tribal community. It is impossible for an outsider to make heads or tails of it, but for Edu and his companions, this is a critical moment of the meeting. A close cousin can be a great help, whereas a distant one—significantly less so. But even in this second instance, they will not go away empty-handed. Without a doubt, they will find a corner under the roof here. There will always be a little room for them on the floor—an important consideration, since despite the warm climate it is difficult to sleep outside, in the yard, where one is tormented by mosquitoes, by spiders, earwigs, and various other tropical insects.

The next day will be Edu's first in the city. And despite the fact that this is a new environment for him, a new world, he doesn't create a sensation walking down the streets of Kariakoo. It is different with me. If I venture far from downtown, deep into the remote back alleys of this neighborhood, small children run away at the sight of me as fast as their legs can carry them, and hide in the corners. And with reason: whenever they get into some mischief, their mothers tell them: "You had better be good, or else the *mzungu* will eat you!" (*Mzungu* is Swahili for the white man, the European.)

Once, I was telling some children in Warsaw about Africa. A small boy stood up and asked, "And did you see many cannibals?" He did not know that when an African returns to Kariakoo from Europe and describes London, Paris, and other cities inhabited by *mzungu,* his African contemporary might also get up and ask: "And did you see many cannibals there?"

Zanzibar

I was driving west—from Nairobi to Kampala. It was early Sunday morning, and the road, running over creased, hilly land, was empty. On the asphalt ahead of me, the rays of the sun created lakes of light, glistening, vibrating. As I approached, the light would vanish, the asphalt would be gray for a moment, then turn to black, but soon the next lake would flame up, and the next. The journey was being transformed into a cruise through a realm of radiant waters, abruptly igniting and dying out, like strobe lights in a crazed discotheque. Both sides of the road were lushly green—forests of eucalyptus, large plantations of the Tea and Bond Co. Here and there among the cypress and cedars one caught a glimpse of an Englishman's white farmhouse. Suddenly, far, far away, at the farthest visible point on the highway, I spotted a glowing sphere, which grew rapidly and drew closer. I barely managed to move to the shoulder of the road when a column of cars and motorcycles sped past, at its center a black Mercedes carrying Jomo Kenyatta. Kenyatta was seldom in his prime minister's office in Nairobi, preferring to spend most of his time in Gatundu, a private residence 160 kilometers from the capital. His favorite pastime was watching dance troupes from various Kenyan tribes, who arrived there to sweeten their leader's days. Despite the noise of the drums, the pipes, and the shouts of the dancers, Kenyatta would fall asleep in his armchair, reviving only when the dancers tiptoed out after their performance and silence descended.

But Kenyatta here, now? On a Sunday morning? His motorcade rushing at such breakneck speed? Something extraordinary must have happened.

Without hesitating, I turned around and followed the convoy. A quarter of an hour later we were in the capital. The cars pulled up to the prime minister's office—a modern, twelve-story structure on City Square in downtown Nairobi—but the police barred my way and I had to stop. I was left alone on the empty street, with no one in sight from whom to get information. In any event, it didn't look as if anything was happening in Nairobi itself: the city was slumbering, in a Sunday torpor, deserted.

It occurred to me that it might be a good idea to drop by Felix's place—he might know something. Felix Naggar was the bureau chief of Agence France Presse in East Africa. He lived in a villa in Ridgeways, an exclusive, hyperelegant Nairobi neighborhood. Felix was an institution. He knew everything, and his net of informers stretched from Mozambique to the Sudan, from the Congo to Madagascar. He himself rarely stepped outside his house. He was either supervising his cooks—he had the best kitchen in all of Africa—or sitting in front of the fireplace reading crime novels. In his mouth he held a cigar. He never removed it—unless it was just for a moment, in order to swallow a bite of baked lobster or taste a spoonful of pistachio sorbet. Every now and then the phone would ring. Naggar would pick up the receiver, scribble something down on a bit of paper, and walk to the other end of the house, where his aides sat at teleprinters (they were the most handsome young Indians he could find in Africa). He would dictate to them the text of the telegram, fluently, with no hesitations or corrections, then return either to the kitchen, where he would stir something in the pots, or before the fireplace, to continue reading.

I found him now sitting in the armchair, as usual, with a cigar and a crime novel.

"Felix!" I shouted from the threshhold. "Something is happening, because Kenyatta just returned to Nairobi!" And I told him about the government motorcade I had encountered on my way to Uganda. Naggar ran to the phone and started dialing everywhere. I turned on his radio. It was a Zenith, a shortwave receiver, phenomenal—I had been dreaming about one for years. It picked up several hundred stations, even shipboard transmissions. At first all I could hear were broadcasts of masses, Sunday sermons, and organ music. Commercials, programs in unintelligible languages, the calls of muezzins. Then, suddenly, through the noise and static, a barely audible voice came through: ". . . the tyranny of the sultan of Zanzibar has ended once and for all . . . the governments of bloodsuckers, which . . . signed, general headquarters of the revolution, the field marshal . . ."

More noise and static, then the loose, flowing words and rhythms of the fashionable band, Mount Kenya. That was it, but we now knew the most important thing: a coup in Zanzibar! It must have happened last night. That's why Kenyatta had returned in such haste to Nairobi. The revolt could spread to Kenya, to all of East Africa. It could transform it into another Algeria, another Congo. But at this moment, for us—for Felix and for me—there was but one issue: to get to Zanzibar.

We began by calling East African Airways. The first flight to Zanzibar, they informed us, is on Monday. We booked places. An hour later, however, they called us back to say that the airport in Zanzibar had been closed and all flights canceled. What now? How do we get there? There was an evening flight to Dar es Salaam. From there, it's not far to the island: forty kilometers across the water. We had no choice; we decided to fly to Dar and set out from there for Zanzibar. As we were figuring all this out, the rest of Nairobi's foreign correspondents arrived at Felix's house. There were forty of us. Americans, Englishmen, Germans, Russians, Italians. We all decided to take the same plane.

In Dar es Salaam we took over the Imperial Hotel, an old building with a spectacular veranda, from which the bay is visible. Rocking on its waters was the white yacht of the sultan of Zanzibar. The young sultan—Seyyid Jamshid bin Abdulla bin Harub bin Thwain bin Said—had escaped on this yacht, leaving behind the palace, the treasury, and his red Rolls-Royce. The crew of the yacht tell us about the great carnage overtaking the island. Blood is flowing in the streets. The rabble are looting, raping, setting fire to houses. No one is safe.

For the time being, Zanzibar is cut off from the world. Their radio announces every hour that any airplane attempting to land on the island will be shot down. And any approaching boat or ship will be sunk. They are sending out these warnings, we reason, because they must be afraid of intervention. We sit around listening to the communiqués, condemned to idleness and interminable waiting. In the morning, we receive news that British warships are sailing toward Zanzibar. Tom, from Reuters, is rubbing his hands in anticipation, convinced that he will be transported aboard ship by helicopter and will land on the island with the first division of the marines. All of us can think of one thing only: how can we get to Zanzibar? I have the fewest options, because I have no money. In cases of revolutions, coups, and wars, the large agencies don't worry about expenditures. They pay whatever is necessary to obtain firsthand information. The correspondent from AP, AFP, or the BBC charters a plane or a ship, or purchases a car that he will need for only several hours—anything to get to where the action is. I stood no chance on such a playing field; I could only hope for some opportunity, for a stroke of luck.

At noon, a fisherman's boat pulled up near our hotel. Aboard were several American journalists, their faces burned lobster red by the sun. They had tried to reach Zanzibar that morning, their boat was already close, when those onshore started shooting at them, bullets flying so thick and fast that they had to give up and turn around. The sea route was closed.

After lunch I drove to the airport to see what was happening there. The terminal was full of journalists, piles of cameras and suitcases everywhere. Many of the reporters were dozing in armchairs, others were drinking beer at the bar, sweaty, exhausted by the heat, tropically disheveled. The plane for Cairo departed, and it grew quiet all around. A herd of cows walked slowly across the runway. Other than that, there was no sign of life in this hot, dead space, this desolate emptiness at the end of the world.

I was thinking of returning to town when suddenly Naggar appeared, stopped me, and took me aside. Although we were alone in this place, he looked around to make sure no one could hear him, and, speaking in a whisper, mysteriously, he said that he and Arnold (a cameraman from NBC) had hired a small plane and paid a pilot to fly them to Zanzibar. They couldn't get going, however, because the airport there was still closed. They had just come from the air traffic control tower, and had spoken to the one at the airport on Zanzibar, asking if they would be allowed to land. No, they were told; they would be fired upon if they tried.

Relating all this, Naggar was nervous. I noticed that he threw away a barely lit cigar and quickly pulled out another one.

"What do you think?" he said. "What can we do?"

"What sort of plane is it?" I asked.

"A Cessna," he answered. "A four-seater."

"Felix," I said, "if I manage to secure permission to land, will you take me for free?"

"Of course!" He agreed instantly.

"Good. I need one hour."

As I was saying all this, I was aware I was bluffing (though it turned out later not to have been a complete bluff). I jumped in the car and raced back to town.

In the very center of Dar es Salaam, halfway along Independence Avenue, stands a four-story, poured-concrete building encircled with balconies: the New Africa Hotel. There is a large terrace on the roof, with a long bar and several tables. All of Africa conspires here these days. Here gather the fugitives, refugees, and emigrants from various parts of the continent. One can spot sitting at one table Mondlane from Mozambique, Kaunda from Zambia, Mugabe from Rhodesia. At another—Karume from Zanzibar, Chisiza from Malawi, Nujoma from Namibia, etc. Tanganyika is the first independent country in these parts, so people from all the colonies flock here. In the evening, when it grows cooler and a refreshing breeze blows in from the sea, the terrace fills with people discussing, planning courses of action, calculating their strengths and assessing their chances. It becomes a command center, a temporary captain's bridge. We, the correspondents, come by here frequently, to pick up something. We already know all the leaders, we know who is worth sidling up to. We know that the cheerful, open Mondlane talks willingly, and that the mysterious, closed Chisiza won't even part his lips.

On the terrace one could always hear music coming from below. Two floors down, Henryk Subotnik, from Lodz, Poland, ran the Paradise nightclub. When World War II broke out, Subotnik found himself in the Soviet Union, and then, by way of Iran, reached Mombasa by ship. Here he fell ill with malaria, and instead of joining the Second Polish Army Corps in Italy, under the command of General Wladyslaw Anders, he stayed in Tanganyika.

His club is always jammed, crowded, and noisy. Customers are drawn here by the charms of the chocolate-colored Miriam, a beautiful stripper from the distant Seychelles. For a show-stopper she has a special way of peeling and eating a banana.

"Did you know, Mr. Henryk," I asked Subotnik, whom I just happened to find at the bar, "that there is turmoil on Zanzibar?"

"Do I know!?" he exclaimed with surprise. "I know everything!"

"Mr. Henryk," I asked again, "do you think that Karume is over there?"

Abeid Karume was the leader of Zanzibar's Afro-Shirazi Party. Although this party, representing the island's black African population, won a majority in the last elections, the government was formed by an Arab minority party supported by London— the Zanzibar Nationalist Party. The Africans, outraged by this fact, organized a revolt and abolished Arab rule. That is what had just transpired two days ago.

"Is Karume there?!" Subotnik laughed in such a way that I knew one thing for certain: he was there.

And that is all I needed.

I returned to the airport. Dodging about with Felix so that no one could make out where we were headed, we reached the control tower. Felix asked one of those on duty to connect us by telephone with the tower at the airport in Zanzibar. When a voice answered on the other end, I took the receiver and asked to speak to Karume. He wasn't there, but was expected at any minute. I put down the receiver and we decided to wait. A quarter of an hour later, the telephone rang. I recognized Karume's thundering, hoarse voice. For twenty years he had sailed the world as an ordinary sailor, and now, even if he was speaking into someone's ear, he thundered as loudly as if he were trying to outshout the roar of a stormy ocean.

"Abeid," I said, "we have a small plane here, and there are three of us: an American, a Frenchman, and myself. We wanted to fly to you. Is it possible? We won't write any dirt, I promise you that. I swear—no lies. Could you arrange for them not to shoot us down as we land?"

A long silence ensued, and then I heard his voice again. We had permission, he said, and we would be met at the airport. We ran to the plane, and moments later were airborne, over the sea. I was sitting next to the pilot, Felix and Arnold in the back. The cabin was silent. Yes, we were happy that we had succeeded in getting through the blockade, and that we would be the first ones on the island, but at the same time we didn't know what, actually, awaited us.

On the one hand, experience had taught me that situations of crisis appear more dire and dangerous from a distance than they do up close. Our imaginations hungrily and greedily absorb every tiny bit of sensational news, the slightest portent of peril, the faintest whiff of gunpowder, and instantly inflate these signs to monstrous, paralyzing proportions. On the other hand, however, I also knew something about those moments when calm, deep waters begin to churn and bubble into general chaos, confusion, frantic anarchy. During social explosions, it is easy to perish by accident, because someone didn't hear something fully or didn't notice something in time. On such days, the accidental is king; it becomes history's true determinant and master.

Less than an hour's flying time, and we are approaching the airport. Zanzibar: the old Arab town, like a brooch skillfully sculpted out of white stone, and further on forests of coconut palms, enormous, branching clove trees, and fields of corn and cassava, all of it framed by the brilliant sandy beach punctuated by aquamarine inlets in which bob flotillas of fishermen's boats.

When we are already close to the ground, we see armed men positioned on both sides of the runway. A feeling of relief, because they are not taking aim at us, are not shooting. There are several dozen of them, and one notices immediately that they are poorly, carelessly dressed—half-naked, in fact. The pilot taxis the plane to the main building. Karume is not there, but there are some people who introduce themselves as his aides. They will take us to the hotel, they say, and request that the plane take off again at once.

We drive to town in two police vans. The road is empty, there are hardly any people visible. We pass some ruined houses, a destroyed, disemboweled shop. One enters the city through a magnificent, massive gate, beyond which immediately begin narrow streets, so narrow that a car can barely fit through. If someone were walking toward us, he would have to duck into a doorway and wait until we passed.

But at this time the city is silent; doors are either shut or torn out of their frames, windows tightly shuttered. A torn-off signboard on which is written "Maganlal Yejchand Shah"; a broken window in the shop Noorbhai Aladin and Sons; a similarly gaping and empty store next door, M. M. Bhagat and Sons, Agents for Favre Leuba, Geneva.

Several barefoot boys are walking by, one of them holding a gun.

"This is our problem," says one of our guides. His name is Ali. He worked on a clove plantation. "We had only several dozen old guns, confiscated from the police. Very few automatic weapons. The principal arms are machetes, knives, clubs, sticks, axes, hammers. But you'll see for yourselves."

We got rooms in the deserted Arab neighborhood, in the Zanzibar Hotel. The building was constructed in such a way that it always provided coolness and shade. We sat down at the bar, to catch our breath. Every now and then some people we didn't know would come up to see and greet us. At one point, a slight, energetic old woman came in. She began questioning us: What are we doing here? what for? where from? When she got to me and I told her where I was from, she seized me by the hand, paused, and began reciting in flawless Polish:

Pogodą rana lśni polana,
Cisza opieszcza smukłość drzew,
Dygotem liści rozszeptana,
Źdźbla trawy kłoni lekki wiew.

Naggar, Arnold, our escort, all those barefoot warriors now congregating in the hotel's reception area, were frozen in astonishment.

Tak cicho jest i slodko wszędy,
I tak przedziwny wkoło świat,
Jakbyś przed chwilą przeszła tędy,
Musnąwszy trawy skrajem szat.

"Staff?" I asked, hesitatingly.

"Of course it's Staff. Leopold Staff!" she said triumphantly. "My name is Helena Trębecka. From Podole. I have a hotel right next door. It's called Pigalle. Please come. You will find Karume there and all his people, because I am serving them free beer!"

What happened on Zanzibar? Why are we here, in a hotel guarded by a troop of barefoot zealots with machetes? (If truth be told, their leader has a rifle, but there's no telling whether it's loaded.)

If someone looks carefully at a detailed map of Africa, he will notice that the continent is surrounded by numerous islands. Some are so small they are registered only on highly specialized navigational maps, but others are large enough to appear on ordinary atlases. On the northern side of the continent lie Dzalita and Kerkenna, Lampione and Lampedusa; on the western side of the Canary and Cape Verde Islands, Gorée and Fernando Po, Príncipe and São Tomé, Tristan da Cunha and Annobón; and on the eastern side Shaduan and Gifatun, Suakin and Dahlak, Socotra, Pemba, and Zanzibar, Mafia Island and the Amirante Islands, the Comoros, Madagascar, and the Mascarene Islands. In reality, there are many, many more; one can count dozens, if not hundreds of them, for some branch out into whole archipelagos, while others are encircled by mysterious worlds of coral beds and sandy shoals, which emerge only at low tide to display their dazzle of colors and shapes. The abundance of these islands and promontories suggests the act of creation being as it were interrupted, never completed, so that the continent which is visible and palpable today is merely that part of geologic Africa that has managed to emerge from the oceans, while the rest remains at the bottom, and these islands are just those of its peaks that have broken the surface.

One can imagine this geological phenomenon had historical consequences. Africa had long been at once a place of terror and of temptation. On the one hand, it struck fear into foreigners, and remained unexplored and unconquered. For centuries, its interior was successfully defended by a difficult tropical climate, long incurable diseases (malaria, smallpox, sleeping illness, leprosy, and the like), the lack of roads and means of transport, and, also, the frequently fierce resistance of its inhabitants. This inaccessibility of Africa gave birth to the myth of its mystery: Conrad's "Heart of Darkness" began at the continent's sunny coasts, as one disembarked from the ship onto solid ground.

But at the same time Africa seduced, beckoning with its dream of rich spoils, lavish booty.

Whoever set out for its shores embraced a most risky undertaking, an endgame of life and death. As late as the first half of the nineteenth century, more than half the Europeans who made it here died of malaria—but many of those who survived returned with sudden and great fortunes: loads of gold, ivory, and, first and foremost, black slaves.

And it is in this connection that the dozens of islands scattered along the continent's shores come into the picture, aided by a multinational band of sailors, merchants, and robbers. The islands become for them toeholds, mainstays, havens, and factories. They are, first of all, safe: too far from the mainland for

Africans to reach in their unstable boats carved from tree trunks, yet close enough for the Europeans to establish and maintain contact.

The role of these islands increases especially during the epoch of the slave trade: many of them are transformed into concentration camps, where slaves awaiting the ships that will carry them to America, Europe, and Asia are imprisoned.

The slave trade: it lasts approximately three hundred years. It begins in the middle of the fifteenth century, and ends—when? Officially, in the second half of the nineteenth, but in some instances significantly later. In northern Nigeria, for example, it ends only in 1936. The trade occupies a central position in African history. Millions (the estimates differ—fifteen to thirty million people) were captured and shipped under horrendous conditions across the Atlantic. It is thought that in the course of such a journey (which lasted two to three months) nearly half the slaves routinely died of hunger, asphyxiation, or thirst; sometimes all of them perished. Those who survived were later put to work on sugar and cotton plantations in Brazil, in the Caribbean, in the United States, building the riches of that hemisphere. The slave traders (mainly the Portuguese, the Dutch, English, French, Americans, Arabs, and their African partners) depopulated the continent and condemned it to a vegetative apathy: up to the present day, large stretches remain desolate, transformed into desert. To this day Africa has not recovered from this misfortune, from this nightmare.

The slave trade also had disastrous psychological consequences. It poisoned interpersonal relations among Africa's inhabitants, propagated hatred, inflamed wars. The strong would try to overpower the weak and sell them in the marketplace, kings traded their subjects, conquerors their prisoners, courts of law those they had condemned.

On the psyche of the African this trade left the deepest and most painfully permanent scar: the inferiority complex. I, a black man or woman: i.e., the one whom the white merchant, occupier, torturer can abduct from house or field, put in irons, herd aboard ship, sell, then drive with a whip to ghastly toil.

The ideology of the slave traders was based on the belief that the black man is not human, that mankind is divided into humans and subhumans, and that with the latter one can do as one will—preferably, exploit their labor and then dispose of them. In the notes and records maintained by these traders is laid out (although in a primitive form) the entire later ideology of racism and totalitarianism, with its core thesis that the Other is the enemy; worse—subhuman. The philosophy that inspired the construction of Kolyma and Auschwitz, one of obsessive contempt and hatred, vileness and brutality, was formulated and set down centuries earlier by the captains of the *Martha* and the *Progresso*, the *Mary Ann* and the *Rainbow*, as they sat in their cabins gazing out the portholes at groves of palm trees and sun-warmed beaches, waiting aboard their ships anchored off the islands of Sherbro, or Zanzibar, for the next batch of black slaves to be loaded.

In this trade—a worldwide enterprise, really, for Europe, both Americas, and many countries of the Near East and Asia participated in it—Zanzibar is a sad, dark star, a grim address, a cursed isle. Toward it, for years—no, centuries—drew caravans of slaves freshly seized in the interior of the continent, in Congo and Malawi, in Zambia, Uganda, and the Sudan. Frequently tied together with ropes, to make escape more difficult, they served at the same time as porters, carrying to the harbor and onto ships valuable mechandise: tons of ivory, gallons of palm oil, the skins of wild animals, precious stones, ebony.

Transported on boats from the continent's coast to the island, they were then exhibited for sale in the marketplace. It was called Mkunazini, and it occupied the square near my hotel upon which today stands the Anglican cathedral. The prices varied: from one dollar for a child, to twelve for a young, beautiful girl. Rather expensive, since in Senegambia for one horse the Portuguese could get twelve slaves.

The healthiest and strongest were then driven from Mkunazini to the port: it is close by, several hundred meters. From here, on ships specially designed for the transport of slaves, they would sail to America, or to the Near East. The seriously ill, for whom no one wanted to pay even a few cents, were thrown upon the rocky shore after the day's activity in the marketplace ended; here they would be devoured by prowling bands of wild dogs. Those among the weak who managed in time to get better and regain their strength would remain on Zanzibar and work as slaves to the Arabs—the proprietors of the enormous plantations of clove trees and coconut palms. Many who took part in the revolution were the grandsons of these slaves.

In the early morning, when the breeze from the sea was still crisp and the temperatures relatively cool, I set out for town. Two young men with machetes follow me. Protectors? Guards? Police? I don't try to engage them in conversation. Their simple, poorly made machetes clearly present a problem for them. How should they carry them? Proudly and fiercely, or shyly and discreetly? The machete has always been the tool of the laborer, of the pariah, a sign of low status; now, since a few days ago, it has become prestigious, a symbol of power. Whoever has one on him has to belong to the victorious class, for the conquered walk around empty-handed, weaponless.

Immediately upon leaving the hotel one enters the narrow streets typical of old Arab towns. I cannot say why these people built in such a cramped and crowded fashion, why they pressed together this way, practically one atop another. Was it so that they would never have far to walk? Or to be better able to defend the town? I don't know. But one thing is certain: this mass of piled stone, this accretion of walls, this layering of balconies, recesses, eaves, and rooftops, somehow secured, as though in an icy treasury, a corner of shade, a tiny breeze, and a bit of coolness during the most terrifying noontime heat.

The streets were constructed with similar foresight and ingenuity. They are so situated and arranged that whichever one you take, and in whichever direction, you will ultimately arrive at the seashore, at a wide boulevard where it is more spacious and pleasant than in the congested center.

The city is now deserted and lifeless. What a contrast with how it looked just a few days ago! For Zanzibar was the place where you could meet half the world. Centuries ago, Muslim refugees from Shiraz, Iran, settled on this island already inhabited by indigenous people. With time, they mingled with the local population, nevertheless retaining a certain separateness: they did not come from Africa, after all, but from Asia. Later, Arabs from the Persian Gulf started to arrive. They conquered the island's Portuguese rulers and seized power, which they then exercised for 260 years. They filled the leading positions in the most lucrative lines of business: the trade in slaves and ivory. They became the proprietors of the best stretches of land and the largest plantations. They commanded a great fleet of ships. With time, Indians and Europeans—mainly the British and the Germans—also came to play key roles in the trade.

Formally, the island was ruled by a sultan, the descendant of Arabs from Oman. In reality, it was a British colony (officially a protectorate).

The lush, fertile plantations of Zanzibar lured people from the continent. They found work here harvesting cloves and coconuts. With increasing frequency, they remained here and settled. In this climate and with the pervading poverty, moving from place to place is not difficult: in just a few hours, you can erect a shelter and stash all your possessions inside—a shirt, a pot, a water bottle, a piece of soap, and a mat. A man can quickly have a roof over his head and, most importantly, his own place on earth; he can now start looking around for something to eat. This presents more of a problem. In practice, he can get work only on an Arab plantation—everything is in their hands. For years, the newcomer from the continent treated this order of things as normal—until, that is, a leader and agitator showed up in the neighborhood and told him that this Arab was someone Other, and that there was something ominous, satanic, about this Other: he was not only a stranger, but a bloodsucker and an enemy. The universe that the immigrant had perceived as preordained once and for all by the gods and the ancestors, he now saw as an injurious and degrading order, which, if he was to continue living, must be changed.

Herein lies the attractiveness of ethnic agitation: its ease and accessibility. The Other is visible, everyone can recognize and remember his image. One doesn't have to read books, think, discuss: it is enough just to look.

On Zanzibar, this racial dichotomy, increasingly fraught, is created on the one hand by the ruling Arabs (20 percent of the population), and on the other by their subjects, black Africans from the island and the continent—small farmers and fishermen, an indeterminate and fluid mass of laborers, house servants, donkey drivers, porters.

These tensions mount at the very moment when the Arab world and black Africa are both setting out on their respective roads to independence. What does this mean on Zanzibar? The Arabs are saying, We want independence (meaning: we want to stay in power). The Africans are saying the same thing: we want independence. But they imbue this slogan with another meaning: because we are the majority, power should be transferred into our hands.

Those are the states and the essence of the conflict. And the British then add fuel to the fire. Because they have good relations with sultans of the Persian Gulf (from whom the sultan of Zanzibar traces his descent), and because they fear an Africa in revolt, they announce that Zanzibar is part of the Arab world, not of the African, and by granting it independence they simultaneously ratify Arab power. The African party—the Afro-Shirazi Party, whose leader is Abeid Karume—protests against this, but it protests legally, observing the law, because although it consitutes the opposition, it is a parliamentary opposition.

Meantime, a young man from Uganda turns up in Zanzibar—John Okello. He has just turned twenty-five. As is frequently the case in Africa, he has, or he pretends to have, many professions—he is a stonecutter, a bricklayer, a house painter. A semi-illiterate, but endowed with charisma, a self-made man with a sense of mission. He is animated by several simple ideas, which come to him as he is cutting stone or laying bricks:

- *God gave Zanzibar to Africans, and he promised me that the island will now revert back to them.*
- *We must conquer and throw out the Arabs, otherwise they will not step aside and will continue oppressing us.*
- *We must understand on which side our bread is buttered: there is no point counting on the support of those who are employed; only the hungry can support the cause.*
- *We will not draw politicians like Karume and others into the fray. They are great people, and it would be a shame if they were killed, in the event that we lose.*
- *We will wait until the British are gone. We couldn't manage against the British. The day only the Arabs are left is the day we strike.*

These thoughts so absorb and consume him that he has to spend a lot of time alone in the forest, because it is only there that he can fully surrender to them. At the same time, already a year prior to Zanzibar's independence, Okello single-handedly begins organizing his underground army. Driving around the island, through villages and towns, he sets up divisions, which in the end will number more than three thousand. Their education begins immediately. For some, this consists of training in the use of bows and arrows, knives, sticks, and spears. Other divisions practice fighting with axes, machetes, chains, and hammers. Additional courses include instruction in wrestling, boxing, and throwing stones.

On the eve of the uprising Okello appoints himself field marshal and gives the rank of army general to several of his closest aides, most of them plantation workers and former policemen.

Three hours after Prince Philip, in the name of Queen Elizabeth, transfers Zanzibar into Arab hands, Field Marshal John Okello makes his move, and in the course of a single night seizes power on Zanzibar.

Before noon, Felix, Arnold, and I drive with our escort to the field marshal's headquarters. The courtyard of an Arab house is teeming with people. The women are cooking cassava and vegetables over fires, roasting chickens and lamb kebabs. Our guides push us through the crowd, which parts unwillingly and eyes us with suspicion but also with some curiosity: in these hours, all the white people are in hiding. In a large oriental foyer, on an ebony armchair, sits Okello, smoking a cigarette. He has very dark skin, and a massive head with heavy features. He is wearing a policeman's cap: his units had seized the police storehouses and found some rifles and uniforms inside. A piece of blue fabric is tied around the band of his cap (I don't know what the color signifies). Okello seems absent, as if he is in shock; he appears not to see us. People are crowding in around him, pushing, shoving, everyone is saying something, gesticulating; the disorder is cosmic, and no one is trying to control it. A conversation, of course, is out of the question. At this point, we are after only one thing: that he give us permission to remain on the island. Our guides address him. Okello nods his consent. A moment later, something occurs to him, and he decides to accompany us out. He throws an old rifle over his shoulder and grabs another in his hand. With his first hand he first adjusts the pistol stuck in his belt, then picks up another one. Thus armed to the teeth, he pushes us ahead of him and out into the courtyard, as if to our own execution.

One of the symptoms of the illness consuming me is a constant, exhausting fever. It flares up in the evening, and then I have the odd sensation that it is my bones that are radiating this high temperature. As if someone had replaced the bone marrow with high-resistance metal coils and hooked them up to an electric current. The coils become white-hot, and the entire skeleton, engulfed in an invisible, internal fire, burns.

It is impossible to sleep. On evenings like this in Dar es Salaam, I lie in my room and watch the lizards hunting. Those that usually prowl around the apartment are small, extremely animated, with a pale gray or brick-colored skin. Graceful, agile, they scurry effortlessly over the walls and ceiling. They never move at a considered, calm pace. First they stand motionless, paralyzed—then, suddenly, they dash off, reach some goal known only to themselves, and again freeze. Only by their rapidly pulsating abdomens can you tell that this sprint, this flinging of their bodies at an invisible finish line, has so exhausted them that it is now absolutely necessary for them to catch their breath, rest, and regain their strength—before the next lightning-fast run.

They begin hunting in the evening, after the lights have been turned on in the room. The objects of their interest and attack are various types of insects: flies, beetles, moths, dragonflies, and, most important, mosquitoes. The lizards appear suddenly, as if someone had sling-shot them onto the walls. They look around without moving their heads: their eyes are capable of 180-degree rotation within their sockets, like the telescopes of astronomers, thanks to which they can see everything both in front of and behind them.

A lizard has suddenly spotted a mosquito. It sets off in that direction. The mosquito sees the danger, starts up, and begins escape maneuvers. Interestingly it never flees downward, into the abyss above the floorboards, but rises into the air, circles nervously and angrily, and then, spiraling upward, lands on the ceiling. It doesn't yet see, and it certainly does not understand, that this decision will have fatal consquences. For once it has attached itself to the ceiling, and its head is hanging down, it becomes disoriented, confused. As a result, instead of swiftly removing itself from the field of danger—which the ceiling represents—it behaves as if it had fallen into a hopeless trap.

Now the lizard can rejoice and lick its chops; victory is at hand. It takes nothing for granted, however—it remains focused, alert, and determined. It jumps onto the ceiling and begins to make smaller and smaller orbits around the mosquito, running all the while. Magic must play some role here, or witchcraft, or hypnosis, for the mosquito, although it could save itself simply by fleeing into empty space where no predator could reach it, permits itself to be encircled tighter and tighter by the lizard, which moves in its usual rhythm: a jump, then immobility; a jump, then immobility. The moment comes when the mosquito notices with terror that it has no more room to maneuver, that the lizard is close upon it, and this realization only stuns and disables it further, until, utterly resigned and defeated, it lets itself be swallowed without putting up the slightest resistance.

All attempts to befriend the lizards are futile. They are highly distrustful and skittish creatures, walking (or rather, scampering) along their own paths. This failure of ours also has a certain metaphorical value: individuals can live together, under one roof, without ever understanding one another, with no common language whatsoever.

On Zanzibar I cannot watch the forays of the lizards, because power is shut off every evening and I must wait patiently in the darkness for daylight. These long and empty hours, spent drowsily awaiting the break of day, are difficult.

Yesterday at dawn (which is never pale here, but instantly colorful, purple, fiery) the peal of a small bell resounded in the street. At first distant and muffled, it drew nearer and nearer, becoming clear, strong, and high-pitched. I looked out the window. An Arab was making his way down the narrow street—a vendor of hot coffee. He had on the embroidered cap Muslims wear, and a loose white djellabah. In one hand he carried a conical metal pot with a spout and in the other a basket full of porcelain cups.

The drinking of morning coffee is an age-old ritual here, with which—along with prayers—Muslims begin their day. The bell of the coffee seller, who each day at dawn walks up and down the streets of his district, is their traditional alarm clock. They jump up and wait in front of their houses, until the man bearing the fresh, strong, aromatic brew appears. The morning's first cup is an occasion of greetings and salutations, of mutual assurances that the night passed happily, and of expressions of faith that this promises to be—Allah willing—a good day.

When we first arrived here, there was no coffee seller. And now, barely five days later, he was back: life was resuming its old course, normality and dailiness were returning. It is a beautiful and heartening thing, this obstinate, heroic human striving for normality, this almost instinctive searching for it—no matter what. Ordinary people here treat political cataclysms—coups d'état, military takeovers, revolutions, and wars—as phenomena belonging to the realm of nature. They approach them with exactly the same apathetic resignation and fatalism as they would a tempest. One can do nothing about them; one must simply wait them out, hiding under the roof, peering out from time to time to observe the sky—has the lightning ceased, are the clouds departing? If yes, then one can step outside once again and resume that which was momentarily interrupted—work, a journey, sitting in the sun.

The return to normal is relatively easy in Africa, and can even be accomplished quite rapidly. Because so much here is makeshift, impermanent, light, and shabby, it is possible instantly to destroy a village, a field, or a road—and just as quickly to rebuild them.

We usually went to the post office before noon to send our dispatches. There were already ten of us, for seven more foreign correspondents had been allowed in. The small post office building, adorned with arabesques, had a history: great travelers—Livingstone and Stanley, Burton and Speke, Cameron and Thomson—had sent their telegrams from here. The teleprinters inside reminded me of those long-ago days. Their exposed innards, with all their little wheels, cogs, gears, and levers, looked like the mechanisms of the huge old clocks in the towers of medieval city halls.

John, from UPI, a tall and eternally perplexed-looking blond-haired fellow, grabbed his head after reading the telegram he had just received. As we left the post office, he took me aside and showed me the alarming piece of paper. His editors were informing him that military revolts had erupted overnight in Kenya, Tanganyika, and Uganda, and that he must get to those countries at once. "At once!" John exclaimed. "At once, but how?"

The news was startling. Army coups! It looked serious, although we had no details. Barely a week ago—Zanzibar. Today already, the whole of East Africa! Clearly, the continent was entering a period of disturbances, revolts, takeovers. And we, the residents of the Zanzibar Hotel, now had a new problem: how to leave here? A longer stay made no sense in any event—Okello's people would not let us travel beyond the town and into the countryside, where battles had raged earlier and, apparently, many were being held prisoner. As for the town itself it was peaceful, sleepy; the days passed uneventfully.

We had a meeting after returning to the hotel, during which John informed everyone about his telegram. We all wanted to get back to the mainland, but no one knew how. Zanzibar was still cut off from the rest of the world. To make matters worse, it looked as if the locals, still afraid of intervention, were holding us hostage. Karume, the only one who could help us, was elusive, spending most of his time at the airport, and of late he hadn't been seen there, either.

There was really only one possibility: to try the sea route. Someone read in a guidebook that it is seventy-five kilometers from here to Dar es Salaam. It is a pleasant journey by ship—but where do we get a ship? A boat was out of the question. We couldn't take the local boat owners into our confidence, because, even supposing they were still alive, they would be either in jail, or afraid to help, or they might inform against us. And the greatest danger of all was that Field Marshal Okello's inexperienced, casually recruited people, scattered as they now were along the entire coastline, would begin shooting were they to spot a boat—after all, no one really controlled them.

As we were conferring, a messenger brought a new telegram together with our mail. His editors were once again ordering John to act quickly: the military had already seized airports and government buildings, and the prime ministers of the three countries had disappeared; perhaps they were in hiding, but it was uncertain if they were still alive. We listened to this sensational bulletin in helplessness and anger. Our little conference came to nothing. There was only one thing to do: wait.

The two Englishmen—Peter from Reuters and Aidan from Radio Tanganyika—had gone to look for their compatriots in the city, hoping with their help to find some way out. When they returned near evening they called another meeting. They had found an elderly Englishman who had decided to leave at the earliest opportunity and wanted to sell a motorboat in good condition. "The boat is moored nearby, in the port, in a secluded, out-of-the-way bay. He will take us there in the evening, along side paths and under cover of darkness. Hidden in the boat, we will wait until late at night, until the guards fall asleep. The Englishman, an old colonialist, said: 'A negro is a negro. Be what may, he has to sleep.' When midnight passes, we will start the motor and begin our escape. The nights are so dark now, that even if they did try to shoot, it is doubtful they could hit us."

They finished, and silence descended. Then, the first voices were heard. As always, there were supporters and opponents of the idea. Questions were posed; a discussion began. Had there been other possibilities, this flight by boat would doubtless have seemed too risky and foolhardy. But there were none. The ground was burning beneath our feet, and time was of the essence. Zanzibar? With the same determination that we had tried to get here, we would now struggle to get out. Only Felix and Arnold were opposed. Felix deemed the plan idiotic, and considered himself too old for such adventures, while Arnold simply had too much valuable photographic equipment he was afraid to lose. They nevertheless agreed to pay our hotel bills when we were already out at sea, so as not to arouse suspicion.

A slight, gray-haired man arrived in the evening, dressed in the traditional costume of British colonial administrators: a white shirt, wide white shorts, and white kneesocks. We followed him. The darkness was so profound that his silhouette ahead of us appeared and disappeared like a phantom. Finally, we sensed boards beneath our feet—it was probably the pier. The old man whispered that we should walk down the steps to the boat. What steps? What boat? We couldn't see anything. But he insisted, his words now resounding like commands. And we knew the field marshal's men could be lurking somewhere close by. Mark, the Australian, a massive man with a wide, good-hearted face, climbed down first; during our earlier deliberations, he had maintained that he knew how to sail and could navigate the boat. He also had the key to the lock on the chain with which the boat was secured to the pier, and knew how to start the engine. When Mark's foot reached the bottom of the boat, there was a splash, and everyone hissed for quiet! Quiet! We were now descending one after the other: the Englishmen, Peter and Aidan; the German, Thomas; the American, John; the Italian, Carlo; the Czech, Jarek; and I. Each tried to feel for the shape and location of the boat, where the side was and how the bulkheads were spaced, and then groped for a spot somewhere on the little bench, or failing that on the boat's bottom.

The old Englishman disappeared and we were left alone.

There were no lights anywhere. The silence was ever more penetrating. Only now and then could we hear a wave hitting the pier, and from somewhere far, very far away, the roll of the invisible ocean. So as to not give ourselves away, we honored the silence, uttering not a word. John's watch had a phosphorescent dial, and he passed it around from time to time—the miniature glowing dot circulating from hand to hand: 22:30, 23:00, 23:30. We stayed this way, in the deepest darkness, half-asleep, numbed, and anxious, until John's watch indicated two in the morning. Mark pulled on the line activating the engine. The motor, like a wild animal unexpectedly goaded, roared and howled. The boat rocked, lifted its bow, and took off straight ahead.

The Zanzibar port is on the western side of the island, the one closest to the continental coast. Logically, therefore, one would have to travel due west to reach the mainland, and southwest if the goal was Dar es Salaam. But for now we cared about one thing only: to gain as much distance as possible from the port. Mark set the controls to maximum speed, and the boat, shuddering ever so slightly, skimmed the calm, smooth surface. The darkness was still absolute, and no shots came from the direction of the island. The escape had succeeded; we were safe. This realization pulled us out of our torpor and our spirits rose. We motored along blissfully for more than an hour, then suddenly everything began to change. The hitherto glassy surface of the water started to move restlessly and violently. Waves reared up, crashing against the side of the boat, with increasing force, relentless. It was if a mighty fist were pounding with angry regularity at the hull. Strangely it seemed a force of blind savage cry and at the same time of cool, systematic calculation. A strong wind arose, and rain, the kind of downpour that comes only in the tropics: rain like a waterfall, rain like a wall of water. Because it was still dark, we lost our bearings completely; we no longer knew where we were, or in which direction we were headed. But soon even this became unimportant, for we

were being hurled about by ever larger waves, by now so dangerous and frenzied, we couldn't tell what would happen to us the
next minute, the next second. The boat would heave and groan
upward, freezing for a moment on the wave's invisible summit,
and then plunge abruptly from the precipice into a roaring abyss,
a rumbling darkness.

Then the engine, flooded with water, stopped. Now the real
hell. The disabled boat was tossed in every direction, spinning
helplessly in a circle, while we waited, in terror, for the next wave
to flip it over. Someone was shouting hysterically, someone else
was calling to God for help, someone else still was lying on the
bottom, moaning and vomiting. Everyone was desperately holding on to the sides. The squall drenched us over and over, seasick-
ness tore out our insides, and if there was anything left of us, it
was only an ice-cold animal fear. We had no inner tubes or life
jackets, and death loomed with each approaching wave.

The engine was dead; we couldn't restart it. Suddenly, Peter
yelled through the gale: "Oil!" It had occurred to him that an
engine of this type needs not only gasoline but also oil, mixed in
with its fuel. He and Mark began rummaging through the storage
places. They found a can and added the oil to the tank. Mark
yanked a few times on the line; the engine sputtered, then roared.
Our joyful shouts pierced the wind; the storm was still raging, but
at least there was a hope now.

The dawn was gloomy, the clouds hung low in the sky, but the
rain was breaking, and it was finally growing light. Where were
we? All around was water, vast, dark, still agitated. In the distance,
the horizon, rising and falling, undulating, in a measured, cosmic
rhythm. Later, when the sun was high, we spotted a dark line on
the horizon. Land! We headed in that direction. Before us was a
flat shoreline, palm trees, a group of people, and in the background—huts. It turned out that we were back on Zanzibar, but
far beyond the town. Not knowing the sea, we didn't realize that

we had been caught by the monsoon, which blows at this time of year, and which luckily spit the boat up here—it could well have carried us to the Persian Gulf, Pakistan, or India. No one would have survived such a journey—we would have died of thirst, or eaten one another from hunger.

We got out of the boat and fell, half-dead, on the sand. I couldn't calm down, though, and began asking the assembled people how to get to town. One of them had a motorcycle and agreed to take me. We sped along through fragrant green tunnels, between banana trees, mangoes, and clove trees. The rush of hot air dried my shirt and pants—they were white and salty from the seawater. An hour later we reached the airport, where I was hoping to find Karume—and hoping he would help me get to Dar. Suddenly, I spotted a small plane standing on the runway, and Arnold loading his gear inside. In the shade of a wing stood Felix. When I ran up to him, he looked up, greeted me, and said:

"Your place is empty. It's waiting for you. Get in."

The Anatomy of
a Coup d'État

From a notebook I kept in Lagos in 1966:

On Saturday, January 15, the army staged a coup d'état in Nigeria. At one o'clock in the morning, an alarm sounded in all the military units across the country. The various divisions set about carrying out their designated tasks. The difficulty of the coup lay in its needing to be implemented in five cities at once: in Lagos, which is the capital of the federation, as well as in the capitals of Nigeria's four regions—in Ibadan (Western Nigeria), Kaduna (Northern Nigeria), Benin (Central-Western Nigeria), and Enugu (Eastern Nigeria). In a country with a surface area three times that of Poland, inhabited by fifty-six million people, the coup was executed by an army numbering barely eight thousand soldiers.

Saturday, 2 a.m.

Lagos: Military patrols (soldiers in helmets, battle dress, and carrying automatic weapons) seize control of the airport, the radio station, the telephone exchange, and the post office. By orders of the military, the electrical plant cuts power to the African neighborhoods. The city sleeps, the streets are empty. Saturday night is very dark, hot, and airless. Several jeeps stop near

King George V Street. It is a small street at one tip of the island of Lagos (for which the whole city is named). On one side is the stadium. On the other—two villas. One is the residence of the prime minister of the federation, Sir Abubakar Tafawa Balewa. In the other lives the minister of finance, Chief Festus Okotie-Eboh. The soldiers surround both villas. A group of officers enters the prime minister's residence, wakes him, and leaves with him. A second group arrests the minister of finance. The cars drive off. Several hours later, an official government communiqué will state that the prime minister and his appointee "were taken to an unknown destination." Balewa's subsequent fate is unknown. Some say he is imprisoned in the military barracks; many believe he has been killed. People maintain that Okotie-Eboh was also killed. He was not shot, they say, but rather "bludgeoned to death." This version may be less a reflection of reality than an expression of public opinion about the man. He was a deeply repugnant individual, brutal, greedy, large, even grotesquely fat. Through corruption, he managed to amass an indescribably large fortune. He behaved with the utmost contempt toward the people he ostensibly served. Balewa was his opposite—likable, modest, calm. A tall, thin, almost ascetic Muslim.

The army seizes the harbor and surrounds Parliament. Patrols circulate through the streets of the sleeping city.

It is 3 a.m.

Kaduna: On the outskirts of the capital of Northern Nigeria, surrounded by high walls, stands the one-story residence of the region's prime minister, Ahmadu Bello. In Nigeria, the titular head of state is Dr. Nnamdi Azikiwe. The head of the government, Tafawa Balewa. But the actual ruler of the country is Ahmadu Bello. All Saturday long Bello receives guests. The last visit, at 7 p.m., is paid him by a group of Fulani. Six hours later, in the bushes across from the residence, a group of officers sets up two mortars. The group's commander is Major Chukuma

Nzeogwu. At three o'clock in the morning, a shot is fired from a mortar. The shell explodes on the roof of the residence. A fire erupts. It is the signal to attack. The officers first storm the palace's guardhouse. Two of them die in the struggle with the prime minister's security force, the rest make it into the flaming building. In the hallway they encounter Ahmadu Bello, who has run out of his bedroom. He is felled by a bullet, which hits him in the temple.

The city sleeps, the streets are empty.

It is 3 a.m.

Ibadan: The palace of the prime minister of Western Nigeria, Chief Samuel Akintola, stands on one of the gentle hills over which sprawls this single-storied city-village, "the largest village in the world," with 1.5 million inhabitants. For three months now, bloody battles have been waged in the region, a police curfew is in effect in the city, and Akintola's palace is heavily guarded. The troops begin their assault, a gun battle ensues, and then outright hand-to-hand combat. A group of officers finally forces its way into the palace. Akintola dies on the verandah, hit by thirteen bullets.

It is 3 a.m.

Benin: The army commandeers the radio station, the post office, and other important targets. It closes all exits from the city. Several officers disarm the policemen guarding the residence of the region's prime minister, Chief Dennis Osadebay. Not a shot is fired. From time to time, a green jeep carrying soldiers passes down the street.

It is 3 a.m.

Enugu: The residence of the prime minister of Eastern Nigeria, Dr. Michael Okpara, is silently and discreetly surrounded.

Inside, in addition to the prime minister, sleeps his guest, the president of Cyprus, Archbishop Makarios. The commander of the insurgents guarantees both dignitaries their freedom of movement. In Enugu, the revolution is polite. Other army units seize the radio station, the post office, and close off all roads exiting the city, which continues to sleep.

The coup was successfully carried out in five Nigerian cities simultaneously. In the space of several hours, the small army became the de facto ruler of this enormous country—Africa's superpower. In the course of a single night, death, arrest, or flight into the bush ended hundreds of political careers.

Saturday—morning, afternoon, and evening.

Lagos awakes, knowing nothing about anything. A normal city day begins—the shops open, people are on their way to work. There is no visible army presence downtown. But at the post office we are told that all lines of communication with the outside world have been severed. You cannot send a telegram. The first bits of gossip start to circulate around the city. That Balewa was arrested. That the army staged a coup d'état. I drive to the barracks in Ikoyi (a Lagos neighborhood). Jeep patrols are coming out of the gates, armed with automatic weapons, with machine guns. A crowd has gathered across from the gate, motionless, silent. Women who eke out a living cooking and selling simple dishes on the street are already spreading out in a smoky encampment.

At the other end of town, Parliament convenes. There are many soldiers in front of the building. They search us at the entrance. Out of the 312 members of Parliament, only 33 have arrived. Only one minister appears—R. Okafor. He proposes that the deliberations be postponed. The representatives who are present demand explanations: What has happened? What is happening? At this, a military patrol enters the chamber—eight soldiers, who disperse the assembled.

The radio broadcasts only music. There are no announcements. I go to see the AFP correspondent, David Laurell. We are both close to tears. These are frustrating moments for journalists: we have news of world import, and we cannot transmit it. We set off together for the airport. It is guarded by a division of the navy and appears deserted—no passengers, no airplanes. On the way back we are stopped at a military checkpoint: they will not let us back into town. A long discussion ensues. The soldiers are polite, courteous, calm; an officer arrives and eventually waves us through. We return through dark neighborhoods: there is still no electrical power. The sidewalk vendors are burning candles or oil lamps near their stalls, as a result of which the streets look from a distance like cemetery alleyways on the Day of the Dead. Even at night it is humid, and so airless that it is difficult to breathe.

Sunday—new rulers.

Helicopters buzz over the city, but otherwise the day is peaceful. Such a revolt (and they are more and more frequent) is usually orchestrated by a small group of officers living in barracks inaccessible to civilians. They act with the utmost secrecy. The country learns of everything after the fact, and then most often has to rely on gossip and conjecture.

This time, however, the situation is quickly clarified. Just before midnight, the new head of state—Major General Johnson Aguiyi-Ironsi, the forty-one-year-old army commander—goes on the radio. He says that the military "consented to take power," that the constitution and the government are being suspended. Power will now lie with the Supreme Military Council. Law and order will be restored in the country.

. . .

Monday—the reasons for the coup.

Rejoicing in the streets. My Nigerian friends, meeting me, slap me on the back, laugh; they are in excellent spirits. I walk through the square—the crowds are dancing, a boy beats out a rhythm on an aluminum barrel. A month ago, I witnessed a similar coup d'état in Dahomey—there, too, the street was cheering the army. The latest wave of military revolts is very popular in Africa; reaction is enthusiastic.

The first expressions of support and of allegiance to the new government arrive in Lagos: "The day of January 15," says the resolution of one of the local parties, the UPGA (United Progressive Grand Alliance), "will pass into the history of our great republic as the day when we first achieved true liberty, although Nigeria has been independent for five years now. The mad rush of our politicians toward self-enrichment disgraced Nigeria's name abroad. . . . A ruling caste had arisen in our country, which based its power on the sowing of hatred, on pitting brother against brother, on liquidating everyone who held a view different from theirs. . . . We salute the new regime as if it had been sent down by God to liberate the nation from black imperialists, from tyranny and intolerance, from the deceptions and destructive ambitions of those who claimed to represent Nigeria. . . . Our Motherland cannot be a stomping ground for political wolves, who plunder the country."

"The widespread anarchy and the disillusion of the masses," states the resolution of the youth organization, Zikist Movement, "made this revolution necessary. In the years since independence, fundamental human rights were brutally violated by the government. People were denied the right to live in freedom and with mutual respect. They were not allowed to have their own opinions. Organized political gangsterism and the politics of falsehood turned all elections into a farce. Instead of serving the nation, politicians were busy stealing. Unemployment and exploitation were on the rise, and in their sadism toward the population, the small clique of feudal fascists in power knew no bounds."

. . .

Thus many African nations are already living through a second phase of their short postwar history. The first phase was a rapid decolonization, the gaining of independence. It was characterized by a universal optimism, enthusiasm, euphoria. People were convinced that freedom meant a better roof over their heads, a larger bowl of rice, a first pair of shoes. A miracle would take place—the multiplying of loaves, fishes, and wine. Nothing of the sort occurred. On the contrary. There was a sudden increase in the population, for which there was not enough food, schools, or jobs. Optimism quickly turned to disenchantment and pessimism. The people's bitterness, fury, hatred was now directed against their own elites, who were rapidly and greedily stuffing their pockets. In a country without a well-developed private sector, where plantations belonged to foreigners and the banks to foreign capital, the political career was the only road to riches.

In short—the poverty and disillusion of those on the bottom rungs, coupled with the cupidity and gluttony of those on the top, create a poisoned, unstable atmosphere, which the army senses; presenting itself as the champion of the injured and the humiliated, it emerges from the barracks and reaches for power.

Tuesday—the tom-toms call to war.

A report from Eastern Nigeria that appeared in today's edition of the Lagos newspaper, the *Daily Telegraph*:

Enugu.—When news of the arrest of the prime minister of Eastern Nigeria, Dr. Michael Okpara, reached his native region of Bende, in all the local villages—in Ohuku, Ibeke, Igbere, Akyi, Ohafia, Abiriba, Abam, and Nkporo—the war drums began to beat, convening the tribal warriors. They were told that their compatriot, Dr. Okpara, had been kidnapped. At first, the warriors believed this was the work of the agents of the ruling coalition, and decided to go

to war. Anyone who owned a wagon put it at their disposal. In the
course of a few hours, Enugu, the capital of Eastern Nigeria, was
overrun by fighters armed to the teeth with swords, spears, bows,
and shields. The warriors chanted war songs. Tom-toms pounded
throughout the town. As this was going on, it was explained to
the tribal commanders that it was the army that had seized power,
and that Dr. Okpara was alive, although under house arrest. When
the warriors heard this, they expressed joy and began returning to
their villages.

Thursday, January 20—the journey to Ibadan.

I went to Western Nigeria to find out what people were saying about the revolution. At the Lagos tollgates, soldiers and policemen inspect cars and baggage. It is 150 kilometers from Lagos
to Ibadan, along a green-lined road running between gentle hills.
In recent months, during the civil war, many people died here.
You still never know whom you will meet around the next curve.
In the ditches lie burned-out cars, most often large limousines
with governmental license plates. I stopped near one of them—
there were still charred bones inside. All the towns along the road
bear the signs of battle: the skeletons of houses incinerated, or
leveled; furniture broken, trucks turned upside down, smoldering
ruins. Every place is deserted, the people have run away, scattered
who knows where.

I reach Akintola's villa. It is on the outskirts of Ibadan, in a
residential, wooded ministerial neighborhood, now completely
abandoned. The palaces of the ministers, imposing, luxurious,
and kitschy, stand ruined and empty. Even the servants are gone.
Some of the ministers have died, others fled to Dahomey. There
are several policemen in front of Akintola's place. One of them
grabs a gun before giving me a tour. The villa is large, new. A
puddle of blood has congealed on the marble floor at the entrance. A bloodied djellabah is still lying next to it. There is a pile
of scattered, torn letters, and two plastic machine guns, smashed

to pieces, perhaps belonging to Akintola's grandsons. The walls are pockmarked by bullet holes, the courtyard full of shattered glass, the window screens ripped out by soldiers during the assault on the villa.

Akintola was fifty years old, a heavyset man with a wide, baroquely tattooed face. In the past several months he had not left his residence, which was under heavy police guard—he was afraid. Five years ago he had been a middle-class lawyer. After a year of premiership, he already had millions. He simply poured money from the government accounts into his private ones. Wherever you go in Nigeria, you come across his houses—in Lagos, in Ibadan, in Abeokuta. He had twelve limousines, largely unused, but he liked to look at them from his balcony. His ministers also grew rich quickly. We are here in a realm of absolutely fantastical fortunes, all made in politics, or, more precisely, through political gangsterism—by breaking up parties, falsifying election results, killing opponents, firing into hungry crowds. One must see this wealth against the background of desperate poverty, in the context of the country over which Akintola ruled—burned, desolate, awash in blood.

I returned to Lagos in the afternoon.

Saturday, January 22—Balewa's funeral.

The announcement by the Federal Military Government about the death of the former prime minister of Nigeria, Sir Abubakar Tafawa Balewa:

"On Friday morning peasants from the region of Otta, near Lagos, said that they had found in the bush a corpse resembling Tafawa Balewa. It was in a sitting position, its shoulders leaning against a tree. The body was covered by an ample white djellabah, and a round cap was lying at its feet. That same day the body was transported by special plane to Balewa's native town of Bauchi (in Central Nigeria). Besides the pilot and the radio operator, there were only soldiers on board. The body of Tafawa Balewa was buried in the Muslim cemetery in the presence of a large number of people."

The daily *New Nigerian* states that the inhabitants of Northern Nigeria do not believe in the death of their leader, Ahmadu Bello. They are convinced that he escaped under Allah's coat to Mecca.

Today a friend, a Nigerian student named Nizi Onyebuchi, told me: "Our new leader, General Ironsi, is a supernatural man. Someone was shooting at him and the bullet changed course, not so much as grazing the general."

My Alleyway, 1967

The apartment that I rent in Lagos is constantly broken into. It happens not only when I am away for a longer stretch of time—in Chad, or Gabon, or Guinea. Even if I am going on a short trip to a nearby town, to Abeokuta or to Oshogbo, I know that upon my return I will find the window popped out of its frame, the furniture turned upside down, the cupboards emptied.

The apartment is located in the center of town, on the island of Lagos. The island was once a staging area for slave traders, and these shameful, dark origins of the city have left traces of something restless and violent in its atmosphere. You are made constantly aware of it. For instance, I may be riding in a taxi and talking with the driver, when suddenly he falls silent and nervously surveys the street. "What's wrong?" I ask, curious. "Very bad place!" he answers, lowering his voice. We drive on, he relaxes and once again converses calmly. Some time later, we pass a group of men walking along the edge of the road (there are no sidewalks in the city), and at the sight of them the driver once again falls silent, looks about, accelerates. "What's going on?" I ask. "Very bad people!" he responds. It's another kilometer before he is calm enough to resume our conversation.

Imprinted in such a driver's head must be a map of the city resembling those that hang on the walls of police stations. Little multicolored warning lights are constantly lighting up on it, flashing, pulsating, signaling places of danger, sites of attacks and other crimes. These warning lights are especially numerous on the map of the downtown, where I live. I could have chosen to live in Ikoyi, a safe and luxurious neighborhood of rich Nigerians, Europeans, diplomats, but it is too artificial a place, exclusive, closed, and vigilantly guarded. I want to live in an African street, in an African building. How else can I get to know this city? This continent?

But it is far from simple for a white man to move into an African neighborhood. To start with, the Europeans are outraged. Someone with my intentions must be deranged, not in complete possession of his mental faculties. So they try to dissuade me, warn me: It is certain that you will perish, and the only thing still in doubt is the precise way this will happen—either you will be killed, or you will simply die of your own accord, because living conditions are so dreadful there.

But the African side also regards my plan with scant enthusiasm. First of all, there are the technical difficulties—live where, exactly? This kind of neighborhood is all poverty and overcrowding, wretched little houses, clay huts, slums; there is no fresh air, and often no electricity; it is dust, stench, and insects. Where can you go? Where can you find a separate corner? How do you get around? What do you do? Take, for instance, something as basic as water. Water must be brought from the other end of the street, because that's where the pump is. Children do this. Sometimes—women. Men? Never. And here's a white gentleman standing with the children in the line for the pump. Ha! Ha! Ha! This is impossible! Or let's say that you have found a small room somewhere, and you want to shut the door to work. Shut the door? This is unthinkable. We all live together in a family, in a group—children, adults, old people; we are never apart, and even after death our spirits remain among the living, with those who are still in this world. Shut yourself alone in a room, in such a way that no one can enter? Ha! Ha! Ha! This is impossible! "And besides," the natives explain gently to me, "it is dangerous in our neighborhood. There are many bad people around here. The worst are the *boma* boys—gangs of debauched hoodlums, who attack, mug, and rob—a dreadful swarm of locusts that ravages everything. They will quickly sniff out that a lone European has come to live here. And to them, a European is a rich man. Who will protect you then?

But I held firm. I didn't listen to the warnings. My mind was made up—perhaps in part because so often I had felt irritated with people who arrived here, lived in "little Europe" or "little America" (i.e., in luxury hotels), and departed, bragging later that they had been to Africa, a place that in reality they had never seen.

And suddenly, an opportunity arose. I met an Italian, Emilio Madera, who in a back alley not far from Massey Street owned a little warehouse of farm implements. Like many whites who were gradually liquidating their enterprises here, he had closed his business. The two-room service apartment above it was now vacant, and he was all too happy to rent it to me. He drove me there one evening in his car and helped me carry up my things (the metal stairs were attached to the building's exterior walls). It was pleasantly cool inside, for Emilio had turned on the air conditioner that morning. There was also a working refrigerator. Emilio wished me a good night and quickly departed. He was flying to Rome early the next morning—after the latest military coup, he was afraid of further unrest and wanted to take some of his money out of the country.

I began to unpack.

An hour later the lights went out.

I didn't have a flashlight. Worse still, the air conditioner had stopped, and in addition to it being completely dark, it now quickly became hot and stuffy. I opened the window. In swept the stench of rotten fruit, burnt oil, soap, and urine. Although the sea was somewhere nearby, you could detect no breeze in this enclosed and congested alley. It was March, a month of crushing heat, when the nights often seemed hotter and more stifling than the days. I looked out the window. Up and down the street below me, on woven mats or directly on the ground, lay half-naked people. The women and children were asleep; several men, their backs leaning against the walls of the clay houses, stared at me. I didn't know what their gazes meant. Did they want to meet me? Help me? Kill me?

I decided that I could not endure until dawn in these sweltering rooms, and went down. Two men rose; the others watched, motionless. We were all sweaty, deadly tired; merely existing in this climate is an extraordinary effort. I asked them if this kind of electrical outage happened often. They didn't know. I asked if something could be done about it. They conversed among themselves in a language I did not understand. One of them disappeared. Minutes passed—fifteen, thirty, forty-five. Finally he returned, bringing two young men with him. They said that they could fix the problem for ten pounds. I agreed. Soon, the lights were back on inside the apartment, and the air conditioner was working. Several days later—another outage, another ten pounds. Then fifteen, twenty.

And the thefts? In the beginning, I was filled with rage each time I returned to my ransacked apartment. To be robbed is, first and foremost, to be humiliated, to be made a fool of. But with time I came to understand that seeing a robbery as a humiliation and an affront is an emotional luxury. Living amid the poverty of my neighborhood, I realized that theft, even a petty theft, can be a death sentence. To steal is to commit manslaughter, murder. A solitary woman had her little corner in my street, and her sole possession was a pot. She made a living buying beans for credit from the vegetable vendors, cooking them, seasoning them with a sauce, and selling them to passersby. For many, this bowl of beans was the only daily meal. One night, a piercing cry awoke us. The entire alleyway stirred. The woman was running around in a circle, despairing, frenzied: thieves had snatched her pot, and she had lost the one thing she depended on for her livelihood.

Many of my neighbors here have just the one thing. Someone has a shirt, someone a panga, someone a pickax. The one with a shirt can find a job as a night watchman (no one wants a half-naked guard); the one with a panga can be hired to cut down weeds; the one with the pickax can dig a ditch. Others have only their muscles to sell. They count on someone needing them as porters or messengers. In all these instances, the chances of employment are slim, because competition is enormous. And further, these are frequently only odd jobs—for one day, for several hours.

Thus my alley, the adjacent streets, and the entire neighborhood are full of idle people. They wake in the morning and search for some water with which to wash their faces. Then, those with a bit of money buy themselves breakfast: a glass of tea and stale roll. But many people don't eat anything. Before noon still, the heat is difficult to bear—one must look for a shady spot. The shade moves hourly with the sun, and man moves with the shade—following the shade, crawling after it to hide in its dark, cool interior, is each day his only real occupation. Hunger. One badly wants to eat, but there is nothing to be had. Making matters worse, the smell of roasting meal wafts from a nearby bar. Why don't these people storm the bar? After all, they are young and strong.

One of them, apparently, was unable to control himself, for suddenly, a cry resounds: it's one of the street vendors shouting—a boy snatched a bunch of bananas from her stand. The victim and her neighbors set off in pursuit and eventually catch him. The police appear out of nowhere. Policemen here carry large wooden clubs, with which they brutally beat offenders, striking them with all their might. The boy is lying in the street now, cringing, curled up, trying to shield himself from the blows. A crowd has gathered, which occurs here in the blink of an eye, since these legions of the unemployed have little to do besides waiting for some event, some commotion, some excitement—anything to distract them, to help pass the time. They press closer and closer, as if the dull thud of the clubs and the moans of the victim afforded them genuine pleasure. With shouts and screams they encourage and incite the policemen. Here, if a thief is caught, people immediately want to tear him apart, lynch him, chop him into pieces. The boy is groaning, already he has let go of the bananas. Those standing closest throw themselves on the fruit, tear the bunch apart.

Then everything returns to normal. The vendor still complains and curses, the policemen leave, the battered, tortured boy drags himself to some hiding place—sore and hungry. The onlookers disperse, returning to their places under walls, under roofs—to the shade. They will stay there until evening. After a day of heat and hunger, one is weak and listless. But a certain stupor, an internal numbness, has its benefits: man could not survive here without it, for otherwise the biological, animal part of his nature would bite to death everything that is still human in him.

In the evening, the alleyway comes ever so slightly to life. Its residents gather. Some of them have spent the whole day here, tormented by attacks of malaria. Others are just returning from the city. Some have had a good day: they found work somewhere, or else they met one of their kinsmen, who shared his pennies with them. They will be eating supper tonight, a bowl of cassava with a hot paprika sauce, perhaps even accompanied by a boiled egg or a piece of lamb. Some of this will go to the children, who watch the men greedily as they swallow each bite. Every bit of food disappears immediately and without a trace. Everything is eaten, down to the last crumb. No one has any supplies, for even if someone did have extra food, he wouldn't have anywhere to keep it, no place to shut it. You live in the immediate, current moment;

each day is an obstacle difficult to surmount, and the imagination does not reach beyond the present, does not concoct plans, does not dream.

Whoever has a shilling goes to the bar. The bars are numerous—in the back streets, at intersections, in the squares. Sometimes these are humble places, with walls cobbled together from corrugated iron, and calico curtains instead of doors. Even so, we are meant to feel as if we have entered an amusement park, found ourselves at a carnival. Music is coming from the old radio, a red lightbulb dangles from the ceiling. Glossy photographs of film actresses cut out from magazines adorn the walls. Behind the counter stands the usually fat, powerfully built madame: the proprietress. She sells the only thing available in the bar: a home-brewed beer. The beers can be various—banana, corn, pineapple, palm. Generally, each of these women specializes in one kind. A glass of such a beverage has three merits: (a) it contains alcohol, (b) being a liquid, it quenches thirst, and (c) because the solution at the bottom of the glass is thick and dense, it constitutes for the hungry an ersatz nourishment. Therefore, if someone has earned only a shilling in the course of a day, he will most probably spend it in a bar.

It is rare for someone to settle for long in my alleyway. The people who pass through here are the city's eternal nomads, wanderers along the chaotic and dusty labyrinth of its streets. They move away quickly and vanish without a trace, because they never really had anything. They go, either tempted by the mirage of employment, or frightened by an epidemic that has suddenly broken out nearby, or evicted by the owners of the clay huts and verandas, whom they were unable to pay for the space they occupied. Everything in their life is temporary, fluid, and frail. It exists and it doesn't exist. Even if it does exist—then for how long? This eternal uncertainty causes my neighbors to live in a perpetual state of alert, of unabating fear. They fled the poverty of the countryside and made their way to the city in the hope that life would be better for them here. Those who succeeded in tracking down a cousin could count on some support, some help getting started. But many of these former peasants did not find any of their relations, or any fellow tribesmen. Often, they didn't even understand the language being spoken in the streets, didn't know how to ask about anything. Still, the force of the city absorbed them, its life became their only world, and by the next day already they were unable to extricate themselves from it.

They started to build a roof over their heads, some little corner, a nook of their own. Because these arrivals had no money—having come here to make some from traditional villages where money is not commonly used—they could look for a place only in the slum neighborhoods. It is an extraordinary sight, the construction of such a neighborhood. Most often, the municipal authorities designate the worst land for this purpose: marshes, quagmires, or barren desert sands. Someone erects the first shack there. Next to it, someone else puts up another one. And then another. Thus, spontaneously, a street is formed. Nearby, another street is advancing. Eventually they will meet, and create an intersection. Now both streets will start to spread, divide, branch out. And a neighborhood will come into being. But first, people collect building material. It is impossible to figure out where they get it. Do they dig it out of the earth? Do they pull it down from the clouds? The one thing is certain: this penniless throng is not buying anything. On their heads, on their backs, under their arms, they bring pieces of corrugated iron, boards, plywood, plastic, cardboard, metal automobile parts, crates, and all this they assemble, erect, nail, and glue into something halfway between a cabin and a lean-to, whose walls configure themselves into an improvised, colorful collage. Because the floor of the hut often consists of swampy ground, or sharp rocks, they line it with elephant grass, banana leaves, raffia, or rice straw, so as to have somewhere to sleep. These neighborhoods, these monstrous African papier-mâché creations, are made up of everything and anything, and it is they, and not Manhattan or the Parisian La Défense, that represent the highest achievement of human imagination, ingenuity, and fantasy. An entire city erected without a single brick, metal rod, or square meter of glass!

Like many other elemental "happenings," the slum neighborhoods have a short life span. It suffices that they spread too far, or that the city decides to build something on the same site. I once witnessed a slum extermination, not far from my alleyway. The shacks had reached down to the shore of the island. The military government deemed this unacceptable. Trucks carrying policemen arrived in the morning. A crowd gathered instantly. The police started to move on the settlement, driving out the inhabitants. A cry went up; there was turmoil. At this the bulldozers materialized, enormous bright-yellow Caterpillars. A moment later, clouds of dust and debris gusted upward as the machines advanced, demolishing street after street and leaving in their wake trampled, bare earth. That day, the alley filled up with refugees. It was crowded and noisy for a while, and even more stifling.

One day I had a visitor. He was a middle-aged man in a white djellabah. His name was Suleiman, and he hailed from Northern Nigeria. He had once worked for my Italian landlord as a night watchman. He knew the street and the entire surrounding neighborhood. He acted shy and didn't want to sit in my presence. He asked if I didn't need a night watchman, for he had just lost his job. I said I didn't, but he made a good impression on me and I gave him five pounds. A few days later he came again. This time he sat down. I made him some tea, and we started to talk. I told him about how I was being continually robbed. Suleiman considered this to be something completely normal. Theft is a method—admittedly unpleasant—of lessening inequality. It is good that they rob me, he declared. It can even be seen as a friendly gesture on the part of the perpetrators—their way of letting me know that I am useful, and, therefore, that they accept me. Basically, I can feel safe. Have I ever felt threatened here? No, I had to admit. Well, there you go! I will be safe here as long as I let myself be freely robbed.

The moment I inform the police, and they start to pursue the thieves, is the moment I would be advised to move away.

He came again a week later. I gave him tea. He drank, and then said in a mysterious tone that he would take me to the Jankara Market, where we would make an appropriate purchase. Jankara Market is where witch doctors, herbalists, fortune tellers, and exorcists sell all manner of amulets, talismans, divining rods, and magical medicines. Suleiman walked from table to table, looking, asking. Finally, he indicated that I should buy a bunch of white rooster feathers from a certain woman. They were expensive, but I didn't resist. We returned to the alley. Suleiman arranged the feathers, tied them together with a piece of thread, and hung them from the top of my door frame.

From that moment on, nothing ever disappeared from my apartment.

Salim

In the darkness, I suddenly spotted two glaring lights. They were far away and moved about violently, as if they were the eyes of a wild animal thrashing about in its cage. I was sitting on a stone at the edge of the Ouadane oasis, in the Sahara, northeast of Nouakchott, the Mauritanian capital. For an entire week now I had been trying to leave this place—to no avail. It is difficult to get to Ouadane, but even more difficult to depart. No marked or paved road leads to it, and there is no scheduled transport. Every few days—sometimes weeks—a truck will pass, and if the driver agrees to take you with him, you go; if not, you simply stay, waiting who knows how long for the next opportunity.

The Mauritanians who were sitting beside me stirred. The night chill had set in, a chill that descends abruptly and, after the burning hell of the sun-filled days, can be almost piercingly painful. It is a cold from which no sheepskin or quilt can adequately protect you. And these people had nothing but old, frayed blankets, in which they sat tightly wrapped, motionless, like statues.

A black pipe poked out from the ground nearby, a rusty and salt-encrusted compressor-pump mechanism at its tip. This was the region's sole gas station, and passing vehicles always stopped here. There is no other attraction in the oasis. Ordinarily, days pass uneventfully and unchangeably, resembling in this the monotony of the desert climate: the same sun always shines, hot and solitary, in the same empty, cloudless sky.

At the sight of the still-distant headlights, the Mauritanians began talking among themselves. I didn't understand a word of their language. It's quite possible they were saying: "At last! It's finally coming! We have lived to see it!"

It was recompense for the long days spent waiting, gazing patiently at the inert, unvarying horizon, on which no moving object, no living thing that might rouse you from the numbness of hopeless anticipation, had appeared in a long time. The arrival of a truck—cars are too fragile for this terrain—didn't fundamentally alter the lives of the people. The vehicle usually stopped for a moment and then quickly drove on. Yet even this brief sojourn was vital and important to them: it injected variety into their lives, provided a subject for later conversation, and, above all, was both material proof of the existence of another world and a bracing confirmation that that world, since it had sent them a mechanical envoy, must know that they existed.

Perhaps they were also engaged in a routine debate: will it—or won't it—get here? For traveling in these corners of the Sahara is a risky adventure, an unending lottery, perpetual uncertainty. Along these roadless expanses full of crevices, depressions, sinkholes, protruding boulders, sand dunes and rocky mounds, loose stones and fields of slippery gravel, a vehicle advances at a snail's pace—several kilometers an hour. Each wheel has its own drive, and each one, meter by meter, turning here, stopping there, going up, down, or around, searches for something to grip. Most of the time, these persistent efforts and exertions, which are accompanied by the roar of the straining and overheated engine and by the bone-bruising lunges of the swaying platform, finally result in the truck's moving forward.

But the Mauritanians also knew that sometimes a truck could

get hopelessly stuck just a step away from the oasis, on its very threshhold. This can happen when a storm moves mountains of sand onto the track. In such an event, either the truck's occupants manage to dig out the road, or the driver finds a detour—or he simply turns around and goes back where he came from. Another storm will eventually move the dunes farther and clear the way.

This time, however, the electric lights were drawing nearer and nearer. At a certain moment, their glow started to pick out the crowns of date palms that had been hidden under the cover of darkness, and the shabby walls of mud huts, and the goats and cows asleep by the side of the road, until, finally, trailing clouds of dust behind it, an enormous Berliet truck drew to a halt in front of us, with a clang and thud of metal. Berliets are French-made trucks adapted for roadless desert terrain. They have large wheels with wide tires, and grilles mounted atop their hoods. Because of their great size and the prominent shape of the grille, from a distance they resemble the fronts of old steam engines.

The driver—a dark-skinned, barefoot Mauritanian in an ankle-length indigo djellabah—climbed down from the cab using a ladder. He was, like the majority of his countrymen, tall and powerfully built. People and animals with substantial body weight endure tropical heat better, which is why the inhabitants of the Sahara usually have a magnificently statuesque appearance. The law of natural selection is also at work here: in these extremely harsh desert conditions, only the strongest survive to maturity.

The Mauritanians from the oasis immediately surrounded the driver. A cacophony of greetings, questions, and well-wishings erupted. This went on and on. Everybody was shouting and gesticulating, as if haggling in a noisy marketplace. After a while they began to point at me. I was a pitiful sight—dirty, unshaven, and, above all, wasted by the nightmarish heat of the Saharan summer. An experienced Frenchman had warned me earlier: it will feel as if someone were sticking a knife into you. Into your back, into your head. At noon, the rays of the sun beat down with the force of a knife.

The driver looked at me and at first said nothing. Then he motioned toward the truck with his hand and called out to me: *Yalla!* (Let's go! We're off!)" I climbed into the cab and slammed the door shut. We set off immediately.

I had no sense of where we were going. Sand flashed by in the glow of the headlights, shimmering with different shades, laced with strips of gravel and shards of rock. The wheels reared up on granite ledges or sank down into hollows and stony fissures. In the deep, black night one could see only two spots of light— two bright, clearly outlined orbs sliding over the surface of the desert. Nothing else was visible.

Before long, I began to suspect that we were driving blind, on a shortcut to somewhere, because there were no demarcation points, no signs, posts, or any other traces of a roadway. I tried to question the driver. I gestured at the darkness around us and asked: "Nouakchott?"

He looked at me and laughed. "Nouakchott?" He repeated this dreamily, as if it were the Hanging Gardens of Semiramis that I was asking him about—so beautiful but, for us lowly ones, too high to reach. I concluded from this that we were not headed in the direction I desired, but I did not know how to ask him where, in that case, we were going. I desperately wanted to establish some contact with him, to get to know him even a little. "Ryszard," I said, pointing at myself. Then I pointed at him. He understood. "Salim," he said, and laughed again. Silence fell. We must have come upon a smooth stretch of desert, for the Berliet began to roll along more gently and quickly (exactly how fast, I don't know, since all the instruments were broken). We drove on for a time without speaking, until finally I fell asleep.

A sudden silence awoke me. The engine had stopped, the truck stood still. Salim was pressing on the gas pedal and turning the key in the ignition. The battery was working—the starter too—but the engine emitted no sound. It was morning, and already light outside. He began searching around the cab for the lever that opens the hood. This struck me as at once odd and suspicious: a driver who doesn't know how to open the hood? Eventually, he figured out that the latches that need to be released were on the outside. He then stood on a fender and began to inspect the engine, but he peered at its intricate construction as if he were seeing it for the first time. He would touch something, try to move something, but his gestures were those of an amateur. Every now and then he would climb into the cab and turn the key in the ignition, but the engine remained dead silent. He located the toolbox, but there wasn't much in it. He pulled out a hammer, several wrenches, and screwdrivers. Then he started to take the engine apart.

I stepped down from the cab. All around us, as far as the eye could see, was desert. Sand, with dark stones scattered about. Nearby, a large black oval rock. (In the hours following noon, after being warmed by the sun, it would radiate heat like a steel-mill oven.) A moonscape, delineated by a level horizon line: the earth ends, and then there's nothing but sky and more sky. No hills. No sand dunes. Not a single leaf. And, of course, no water. Water! It's what instantly comes to mind under such circumstances. In the desert, the first thing man sees when he opens his eyes in the morning is the face of his enemy—the flaming visage of the sun. The sight elicits in him a reflexive gesture of self-preservation: he reaches for water. Drink! Drink! Only by doing so can he ever so slightly improve his odds in the desert's eternal struggle—the desperate duel with the sun.

I resolved to look around for water, for I had none with me. I found nothing in the cab. But I did discover some: attached with ropes to the bed of the truck, near the rear, underneath, were four goatskins, two on the left side and two on the right. The hides had been rather poorly cured, then sewn together in such a way that they retained the animal's shape. One of the goat's legs served as a drinking spout.

I sighed with relief, but only momentarily. I began to calculate. Without water, you can survive in the desert for twenty-four hours; with great difficulty, forty-eight or so. The math is simple. Under these conditions, you secrete in one day approximately ten liters of sweat, and to survive you must drink a similar amount of water. Deprived of it, you will immediately start to feel thirsty. Genuine, prolonged thirst in a hot and dry climate is an exhausting, ravaging sensation, harder to control than hunger. After a few hours of it you become lethargic and limp, weak and disoriented. Instead of speaking, you babble, ever less cogently. That same evening, or the next day, you get a high fever and quickly die.

If Salim doesn't share his water with me, I thought, I will die today. Even if he does, we will have only enough left for one more day—which means we will both die tomorrow, the day after at the latest.

Trying to stop these thoughts, I decided to observe him closely. Covered with grease and sweating, Salim was still taking the engine apart, unscrewing screws and removing cables, but with no rhyme or reason, like a child furiously destroying a toy that won't work. On the fenders, on the bumper, lay countless springs, valves, compression rings, and wires; some had already fallen to the ground. I left him and went around to the other side of the truck, where there was still some shade. I sat down on the ground and leaned my back against the wheel.

Salim.

I knew nothing about the man who held my life in his hands. Or, at least, who held it for this one day. I thought, if Salim chases me away from the truck and the water—after all, he had a hammer in his hand and probably a knife in his pocket, and, on top of that, enjoyed a significant physical advantage—if he orders me to leave and march off into the desert, I won't last even until nightfall. And it seemed to me that was precisely what he might choose to do. He would thereby extend his life, after all—or, if help arrives in time, he might even save it.

Clearly Salim was not a professional driver, or at any rate, not a driver of a Berliet truck. He also didn't know the area well. (On the other hand, can one really know the desert, where successive storms and tempests constantly alter the landscape, moving mountains of sand to ever different sites and transposing features of the landscape with impunity?) It is common practice in these parts for someone with even a small financial windfall to immediately hire another with less money to carry out his tasks for him. Maybe the rightful driver of this truck had hired Salim to take it in his stead to one of the oases. And hereabouts no one will ever admit to not knowing or not being capable of something. If you approach a taxi driver in a city, show him an address, and ask him if he knows where it is, he will say yes without a second's hesitation. And it is only later, when you are driving all over the city, round and round, that you fully realize he has no idea where to go.

The sun was climbing higher and higher. The desert, that motionless, petrified ocean, absorbed its rays, grew hotter, and began to burn. The hour was approaching when everything would become a hell—the earth, the sky, us. The Yoruba are said to believe that if a man's shadow abandons him, he will die. All the shadows were beginning to shrink, dwindle, fade. The dread afternoon hours were almost upon us, the time of day when people and objects have no shade, exist and yet do not exist, reduced to a glowing, incandescent whiteness.

I thought that this moment had arrived, but suddenly I noticed before me an utterly different sight. The lifeless, still horizon—so crushed by the heat that it seemed nothing could ever issue forth from it—all at once sprang to life and became green. As far as the eye could see stood tall, magnificent palm trees, entire groves of them along the horizon, growing thickly, without interruption. I also saw lakes—yes, enormous blue lakes, with animated, undulating surfaces. Gorgeous shrubs also grew there, with wide-spreading branches of a fresh, intense, succulent, deep green. All this shimmered continuously, sparkled, pulsated, as if it were wreathed in a light mist, soft-edged and elusive. And everywhere—here, around us, and there, on the horizon—a profound, absolute silence reigned: the wind did not blow, and the palm groves had no birds.

"Salim!" I called. "Salim!"

A head emerged from under the hood. He looked at me.

"Salim!" I repeated once more, and pointed.

Salim glanced where I had shown him, unimpressed. In my dirty, sweaty face he must have read wonder, bewilderment, and rapture—but also something else besides, which clearly alarmed him, for he walked up to the side of the truck, untied one of the goatskins, took a few sips, and wordlessly handed me the rest. I grabbed the rough leather sack and began to drink. Suddenly dizzy, I leaned my shoulder against the truck bed so as not to fall. I drank and drank, sucking fiercely on the goat's leg and still staring at the horizon. But as I felt my thirst subsiding, and the madness within me dying down, the green vista began to vanish. Its colors faded and paled, its contours shrank and blurred. By the time I had emptied the goatskin, the horizon was once again flat, empty, and lifeless. The water, disgusting Saharan water—warm, dirty, thick with sand and sludge—extended my life but took away my vision of paradise. The crucial thing, though, was the fact that Salim himself had given me the water to drink. I stopped being afraid of him. I felt I was safe—at least, until the moment when we would be down to our last sip.

We spent the second half of the day lying underneath the truck, in its faint, bleached shade. In this world circled all about with flaming horizons, Salim and I were the only life. I inspected the ground within my arm's reach, the nearest stones, searching for some living thing, anything that might twitch, move, slither. I remembered that somewhere on the Sahara there lives a small beetle which the Tuareg call Ngubi. When it is very hot, according to legend, Ngubi is tormented by thirst, desperate to drink. Unfortunately, there is no water anywhere, and only burning sand all around. So the small beetle chooses an incline—this can be a sloping fold of sand—and with determination begins to climb to its summit. It is an enormous effort, a Sisyphean task, because the hot and loose sand constantly gives way, carrying the beetle down with it, right back to where he began his toils. Which is why, before too long, the beetle starts to sweat. A drop of moisture collects at the end of his abdomen and swells. Then Ngubi stops climbing, curls up, and plunges his mouth into that very bead.

He drinks.

Salim has several biscuits in a paper bag. We drink the second goatskin of water. Two remain. I consider writing something. (It occurs to me that this is often done at such moments.) But I don't have the strength. I'm not really in pain. It's just that everything is becoming empty. And within this emptiness another one is growing.

Then, in the darkness, two glaring lights. They are far away and move about violently. Then the sound of a motor draws near, and I see the truck, hear voices in a language I do not understand. "Salim!" I say. Several dark faces, resembling his, lean over me.

Lalibela, 1975

Central Ethiopia is a vast, open plateau transversed by numerous ravines and valleys. During the rainy season, rapid, turbulent rivers flow along the bottoms of these chasms. In the summer months, some of them dry up and disappear, revealing parched, cracked beds over which the wind raises black clouds of dust—mud desiccated by the sun. In places, mountains of three thousand meters loom above the plateau; they bear no resemblance whatsoever to the snow-covered granitic Alps, Andes, or Carpathians. These are mountains of weathered stone, the color of copper and brass, their summits so flat and smooth they could serve as natural airfields. Flying over them, one can see wretched mud shacks, without water or electricity. Questions instantly spring to mind: How do these people live? What do they eat? Why are they there? In such places, at noon the ground must burn the soles of your feet, turn everything to ash. Who condemned them to such a ghastly, subcelestial exile? Why? For what trespasses? I never had an opportunity to climb up to those solitary settlements and search for the answers. And no one down here, on the plateau, was able to tell me anything about the people up there, those wretches of the stratosphere vegetating somewhere on the margins of humanity. Born in obscurity, they would then vanish, no doubt quickly—unknown, anonymous beings. But this is not to say the lives of those at the foot of the mountains were easy or good.

"Go to Wollo," said Teferi, "go to Haragwe. Here you will see nothing. There, you will see everything."

We were sitting on the veranda of his house in Addis Ababa. Before us lay a garden encircled by a high wall. Lush growths of hot-pink bougainvillea and bright-yellow forsythia surrounded a softly splashing fountain. The places mentioned by Teferi were several hundred kilometers away. They were the provinces whose inhabitants were dying in a mass famine. Here, on this veranda, with the smells of grilling meat wafting from the kitchen, it was impossible to even imagine this. But how can one really imagine mass death? A human being always dies alone; the moment of death is the loneliest moment of his life. "Mass death" means that, somewhere, a man is dying alone; but at the same time, another man, also alone, is dying as well, and, equally alone, another one still. It means that by coincidence—most frequently against his will—each of them, experiencing in solitude his own, singular death, finds himself in proximity to many others experiencing the same thing.

It was the mid-seventies. Africa had just entered its two darkest decades. Civil wars, revolts, coups d'état, massacres, and hunger, such were some of the symptoms of the crisis from which millions of people inhabiting the Sahel (western Africa) and eastern Africa (especially the Sudan, Chad, Ethiopia, and Somalia) began to suffer. The epoch of the fifties and sixties, full of promise and hope, had come to an end. While it lasted, the majority of the continent's countries freed themselves from colonialism and began their development as independent states. The dominant political and economic theories of the time held that freedom would automatically bring prosperity, would instantly, with one stroke, transform regions that were poor and wretched into lands flowing with milk and honey. So maintained the wisest men of these times, and it seemed there was no reason not to believe them—especially as the prophecies were so intoxicating!

But things turned out otherwise. Power struggles erupted within the new African states, with the opponents resorting to, and exploiting, all means possible: tribal and ethnic conflicts, military might, corruption, murder. At the same time, the new states proved to be weak, incapable of performing their most basic functions. And all this was occurring during the Cold War, which the East and the West transplanted onto the terrain of Africa. A salient characteristic of this war was that the problems and interests of weaker, dependent countries were utterly ignored, their affairs and dramas treated as strictly subordinate to superpower interests, with no independent significance or weight whatsoever. This was compounded by the traditional Eurocentric haughtiness and arrogance toward nonwhite cultures and societies. Thus, whenever I returned from Africa, I was asked not "How are the Tanzanians?" but rather "How are the Russians in Tanzania?" And instead of being asked about Liberians, I was asked "How are the Americans in Liberia?" (Still, this is better than what faced the German traveler H. C. Buch, who complained to me that after a grueling expedition to the most distant societies of Oceania, he always heard but one question: "What in the world did you eat there?") Nothing upsets Africans more than this kind of dismissive, supercilious treatment. They find it humiliating, degrading, a slap in the face.

Teferi was the owner of a trucking company. He had several vehicles, antiquated, rattly Bedfords, in which he transported cotton, coffee, and skins. They journeyed both to Wollo and to Haragwe, so he agreed to my going to both with one of his drivers. It was my only chance of doing so, because buses did not run to either place, airplanes did not fly.

Traveling the roads of Ethiopia is arduous and often risky. In the dry season, the car skids over gravel on a narrow shelf cut into the flank of a steep mountain; the road runs along the edge of a precipice several hundred meters deep. In the rainy season, the mountain roads are impassable. Those on level ground turn into muddy quagmires, in which one can get stuck for days.

In the summer, after several hours of driving on the plateau, you are black with dust. Because it is hot and you are dripping with sweat, at the end of a day on the road you are encased in a thick, crusty armor of dirt. The dust, composed as it is of microscopic particles, is in essence a kind of thick hot mist, penetrating clothing and pushing its way into every bodily cranny and crevice imaginable. It takes a long time to get clean. The eyes are the most afflicted. Truck drivers have permanently swollen and reddened eyes, complain of headaches, and go blind at an early age.

One can travel only by day. Between dusk and dawn, the roads are controlled by swift-footed, prowling bands, called shifts, who will rob you of everything. A group of these young bandits will operate until their first bad break. Those captured used to be hanged straightaway by the side of the road. In these more enlightened times, they are dealt with less publicly. In any encounter with them, life hangs in the balance. If a shift abandons its victim somewhere on an uninhabited and waterless expanse, the poor wretch will simply die from dehydration. Hence there are guardposts at all exits from the city. The policeman on duty looks at his watch, or simply at the sun, and calculates whether you will be able to reach the next town (or the next policeman) by dusk. If he decides that you will not, he will make you turn back.

I set off in a truck that Teferi was sending from Addis Ababa north, toward Desē and Lalibela, for a shipment of skins. Does it make sense to calculate the length of this route in kilometers? Here, one measures distances according to the number of hours and days necessary to traverse from point A to point B. For example, it is 120 kilometers from Desē to Lalibela, but it will take me eight hours along this road—if, that is, I manage to secure a good all-terrain vehicle, which is doubtful.

More than likely, it will take me a day, or two days, or more to reach my destination. The local trucks—usually rusted, dilapidated pieces of junk—are constantly breaking down on these roads through the middle of nowhere, in this dust and heat, and for spare parts one must go all the way back to Addis Ababa. The journey is always an unknown: you set out, you are rolling along, but when (and whether) you will get there, or when (and whether) you will be forced to turn around, this you can never anticipate.

There has been a long drought in the place we are headed to, and cattle are dying from a lack of grazing lands and water. The nomads are selling for pennies the skins pulled off the carcasses. They manage with this money to survive for a while yet, and then, if they do not find their way to an international relief center, they perish without a trace in the parched wastelands.

At dawn, we left the city behind us, its surrounding pale-green groves of eucalyptus, the roadside gas stations and police guard-posts, and here we were on the sun-drenched plateau, on the highway, which would be paved with asphalt for the first hundred kilometers. The driver's name was Sahlu—a trustworthy, calm man, Teferi assured me. Sahlu was silent and serious. To create a more friendly atmosphere, I nudged him in the arm, and smiled when he turned toward me. Sahlu smiled back, sincerely but a little shy, seemingly uncertain as to whether this sort of reciprocal grinning didn't put us on an unduly equal footing.

The farther we were from the city, the more sparsely inhabited and desolate was the countryside. Some children were driving a few skinny cows; some women, bent in half, were carrying heaps of dry branches on their backs. The houses we passed looked empty; we saw no one near them, no people, no movement of any kind. The landscape was immobile, unchanging, as if it were drawn this way once and for all.

Suddenly, two men stepped out onto the highway in front of us, automatic rifles in hand. They were young, strong. I noticed Sahlu turning ashen. His face was frozen, his eyes fearful. He brought the vehicle to a stop. The men jumped onto the truck bed and tapped on the roof of the cab, signaling us to start driving again. I cowered in my seat, trying not to show that I was frightened to death. I stole glances at Sahlu: he was holding the steering wheel stiffly, and looked scared, grim. We drove like this for maybe an hour. Nothing happened. It was sunny, hot, and, inside the cab, dark with dust. Suddenly, banging on the roof. Obediently, Sahlu stopped. The men jumped down without uttering a word, walked to the rear of the truck, where we could not see them, and vanished into the fields.

In the afternoon we reached the small town of Debre Sina. Sahlu stopped on the side of the road, and a group of people instantly surrounded us. Ragged, emaciated, barefoot. Many young boys, many children. A policeman—in torn black uniform, the jacket fastened with the one remaining button—quickly pushed his way toward us. He knew a little English and immediately said, "Take everything with you. Everything! They are all thieves here!" And he began pointing at those standing all around us, one by one: "This is a thief! And this is a thief!" I followed with my eyes the policeman's finger as it moved clockwise, pausing momentarily at each new face. "This is a thief!" he continued, and when he came to a tall, good-looking boy, his hand began to tremble: "This is a very big thief, sir!" he cried in warning.

The people of whom he spoke regarded me with curiosity. They smiled. Their faces showed neither anger nor cynicism, only a kind of embarrassment and, even, humility. "I have to live with them, sir," the policeman complained self-pityingly. And, as if he were searching for even the slightest compensation for his cursed fate, he stretched out his hand to me and said: "Can you help me, sir?" Then, to further justify his request, he added: "We are all poor here, sir." He pointed at himself, at his thieves, at the crooked mud houses of Debre Sina, at the shabby road, at the world.

We walked to the center of the town, to the market. On the square stood stalls with barley, millet, and beans, ones with lamb, and beside them others selling onions, tomatoes, and red peppers. Elsewhere, bread and goat cheese, sugar and coffee, cans of sardines, biscuits and wafers. A market is usually a crowded, bustling, and noisy place, but here all was silent. The vendors stood motionless and idle, now and then only swatting halfheartedly at flies. There were flies everywhere. Dark, thick, churning clouds of them, irritated, frenzied, furious. We fled to the side streets to escape them, for they had instantly thrown themselves at us, and there we encountered a different world—empty, in final agony. On the ground, in the filth and the dust, lay emaciated people. They were the inhabitants of neighboring villages. The drought had deprived them of water, and the sun had scorched their crops. They had come here, to the town, in the desperate hope that they would be given a sip of water and would find something to eat. Weak and no longer capable of any exertion, they were dying of hunger, which is the quietest and most docile kind of death. Their eyes were half-closed, lifeless, expressionless. I could not tell if they saw anything, whether they were even looking at anything in particular. Right beside where I was standing two women lay, their wasted bodies shaking with malaria. Their trembling was the only movement on this little street.

I pulled the driver by his sleeve. "Let's go," I said. We returned by way of the market, with its sacks of flour, slabs of meat, and bottles of mineral water: for the great famine was the result not of a shortage, but of inhumane relations. There was food in the country, but when the drought came, the prices went up and the poor peasants were unable to purchase any. The government could, of course, have intervened, or allowed the rest of the world to do so, but for reasons of prestige the regime did not want to admit that there was hunger in the land, and refused aid. A million people died in Ethiopia during this time, a fact concealed first by the emperor Haile Selassie, and then by the one who took his throne and his life, Major Mengistu Haile Mariam. They were divided by their struggle for power, united in their lies.

A mountainous and empty road. Neither cars nor herds of cattle. Skeletons of cows on the gray, parched, ashlike earth. Women with immense clay vats sit waiting in the shade of an acacia—what if a truck carrying water to the city passes by and the driver takes pity on them, stops, and briefly turns on the tap?

By evening we are in Desē. Ahead there is a day's driving to Lalibela. The whole way, mountain gorges heated like the insides of smelting furnaces, the land empty, devoid of people or vegetation. But we need only stop for a moment, and swarms of flies instantly surround us. It is as if they had been waiting here for us specifically! Their buzzing is deafening, triumphant, victorious: "There you are! We've got you!" Why are there so many flies here? How can there be any life whatsoever?

At last—Lalibela. It is one of the eight wonders of the world. And if it isn't, it should be. Seeing it, however, is not easy. In the rainy season, there is no passable road, and getting here in the dry season is barely less difficult. One can arrive by airplane—if they happen to be flying.

You cannot see anything from the road. More strictly speaking, all you see is an ordinary village. Boys run out to meet you, each begging that you choose him as a guide—it is their only chance to earn something. My guide's name was Tadesse Mirele and he was a schoolboy. His school was closed, everything was closed—there was famine. People were constantly dying in the village. Tadesse said that he hadn't eaten anything in several days, but there was water, and so he drinks that. Did he maybe get a handful of grain somewhere? A piece of flat bread? Yes, he admitted, a handful of grain. "But," he added sadly, "nothing else." And immediately asked: "Sir?" "Yes, Tadesse?" I replied, "I'm listening." "Be my helper, please! I need a helper!" He looked at me, and I saw then that he had only one eye. A single eye in the haggard, frightened face of a child.

A while later Tadesse suddenly grabbed me by the arm. I thought that he wanted to ask me for something, but then realized he was only preventing me from falling into a chasm. For just below was a church carved out of stone. A three-story-high structure cut into the massive mountain beneath our feet, inside it, as it were. And farther on, in the same mountain, also invisible at ground level, was carved another church, and another. All together, eleven great churches. This architectural wonder was constructed in the twelfth century by the saint Lalibela, ruler of the Amhara kingdom, whose inhabitants were (and are) Eastern Orthodox Christians. He carved them out of the mountain itself so that Muslims invading these lands could not spot them from afar. And even if they did, they could neither demolish them nor move them, because these churches constitute an integral part of the mountain. There is a Church of the Virgin Mary here, of the Savior of the World, of the Holy Cross and St. George, of Mark and Gabriel, all of them connected by underground tunnels.

"Look, sir!" said Tadesse, pointing down to the courtyard in front of the Church of the Savior of the World. But I had already noticed the sight myself. A dozen or so meters below where we stood, in the yard and on the steps of the church, surged a crowd of lame beggars. It is odd to say "surged" when speaking of discrete human beings, but that word best describes the scene. The people below were so tightly squeezed together, their crippled limbs, stumps, and crutches so tightly interwined, that they formed a single crawling mass, out of which dozens of arms stretched upward like tentacles, and, where there were no limbs, innumerable gaping mouths extended upward, waiting for something to be thrown into them. As we walked from one church to another, this gnarled, moaning, expiring creature below crept after us, and from it dropped every now and then an inert, already lifeless member, abandoned by the rest.

There had been no pilgrims here in a long while, to throw down their alms, and these cripples were unable to get out of the stony chasms.

"Did you see, sir?" Tadesse asked me as we made our way back to the village. And he said it as though to suggest he thought this the only thing really worth seeing.

Amin

I once considered writing a book about Amin, because he is such a glaring example of the relation between crime and low culture. I was in Uganda many times, saw Amin more than once; I have a small library of books about him, and stacks of my own notes. He is the most well known dictator in the history of contemporary Africa and one of the most famous in the twentieth century the world over.

Amin belongs to a small ethnic group called the Kakwa, whose territory encroaches on three countries: Sudan, Uganda, and Zaire. The Kakwa do not know to which country they belong, although they view this question with indifference, preoccupied as they are with something else: how to survive despite the poverty and hunger that prevail in this remote region without roads, cities, electricity, and cultivable land. Anyone with some initiative, wits, and luck runs as far away from here as possible. But not every direction is a propitious one. Whoever goes west will only worsen his circumstances, because he will stumble upon the thickest jungles of Zaire. Those setting off northward also err, because they will arrive at the sandy, rock-strewn threshold of the Sahara. Only the southerly direction holds promise: there the Kakwa will find the fertile lands of central Uganda, the lush and splendid garden of Africa.

It is there, after giving birth to her son, that Amin's mother makes her way, the infant on her back. She comes to the second-largest city (or, rather, town) in Uganda after Kampala—Jinja. Like thousands of others at that time, and millions upon millions today, she arrives in the hope of surviving, in the hope that life here will be better. She has no skills, no contacts, and no money. But one can make a living in a variety of ways: through petty trade, brewing and selling beer, or operating a portable sidewalk eatery. Amin's mother has a pot and cooks millet in it. She sells portions on banana leaves. Her daily earnings? A serving of millet for herself and her son.

This woman, who made her way with her child from a poor village in the north to a town in the wealthier south, became part of the population that today constitutes Africa's biggest problem. It is composed of the tens of millions who have abandoned the countryside and migrated to the monstrously swollen cities without securing adequate housing or employment. In Uganda they are called *bayaye*. You will notice them at once, because it is they who form the street crowds, so different from ones in Europe. In Europe, the man on the street is usually heading toward a definite goal. The crowd has a direction and a rhythm, which is frequently characterized by haste. In an African city, only some of the people behave this way. The others are not going anywhere: they have nowhere to go, and no reason to go there. They drift this way and that, sit in the shade, stare, nap. They have nothing to do. No one is expecting them. Most often, they are hungry. The slightest street spectacle—a quarrel, a fight, the apprehension of a thief—will instantly draw large numbers of them. For they are everywhere around here, idle, awaiting who knows what, living who knows how—the gapers of the world.

The principal characteristic of their status is rootlessness. They will not return to the countryside, and there is no place for them in the city. They endure. Somehow, they exist. Somehow: that is how best to describe their situation, its fragility, its uncertainty. Somehow one lives, somehow one sleeps, somehow, from

time to time, one eats. This unreality and impermanence of existence cause the *bayaye* to feel himself in continuous danger, and so
he is unceasingly tormented by fear. His fear is amplified by his
condition as a stranger, an unwanted immigrant from another
culture, religion, language. A foreign, extraneous competitor for
the contents of the cooking pot, which is empty anyway, and for
work, of which there isn't any.

Amin is a typical *bayaye*.

He grows up in the streets of Jinja. The town housed a battalion of the British colonial army, the King's African Rifles. The
model for this army was devised toward the end of the nineteenth
century by General Lugard, one of the architects of the British
Empire. It called for divisions composed of mercenaries recruited
from tribes hostile toward the population on whose territory they
were to be garrisoned: an occupying force, holding the locals on a
tight rein. Lugard's ideal soldiers were young, well-built men from
the Nilotic (Sudanese) populations, which distinguished themselves by their enthusiasm for warfare, their stamina, and their
cruelty. They were called Nubians, a designation that in Uganda
evoked a combination of distaste and fear. The officers and noncommissioned officers of this army, however, were for many years
exclusively Englishmen. One day, one of them noticed a young
African with a Herculean physique hanging around the barracks.
It was Amin. He was quickly enlisted. For people like him—without a job, without possibilities—military service was like winning
the lottery. He had barely four years of elementary schooling, but
because he was deemed obedient and eager to anticipate the
wishes of his commanders, he began advancing rapidly through
the ranks. He also gained renown as a boxer, becoming the Ugandan heavyweight champion. During colonial times, the army was
dispatched on countless expeditions of oppression: against the
Mau Mau insurgents, against the warriors of the Turkana tribe, or
against the independent people of the Karimojong. Amin distinguished himself in these campaigns: he organized ambushes and
attacks, and was merciless toward his adversaries.

. . .

It is the fifties, and the era of independence is fast approaching. Africanization has arrived, even in the military. But the British and French officers want to remain in control for as long as possible. To prove that they are irreplaceable, they promote the third-rate from among their African subordinates, those not too quick, but obedient, transforming them in a single day from corporals and sergeants into colonels and generals. Bokassa in the Central African Republic, for example, Soglo in Dahomey, Amin in Uganda.

When in the fall of 1962 Uganda becomes an independent state, Amin is already, because of promotions by the British, a general, and deputy commander of the army. He takes a look around him. Although he has high rank and position, he comes from the Kakwa, a small community and one, moreover, that is not regarded as native Ugandan. Meantime, the preponderance of the army comes from the Langi tribe, to which Prime Minister Milton Obote belongs, and from the related Acholi. The Langi and the Acholi treat the Kakwa superciliously, seeing them as benighted and backward. We are navigating here in the paranoid, obsessive realm of ethnic prejudice, hatred, and antipathy—albeit an intra-African one: racism and chauvinism emerge not only along the most obvious divides, e.g., white versus black, but are equally stark, stubborn, and implacable, perhaps even more so, among peoples of the same skin color. Indeed, most whites who have died in the world have died at the hands not of blacks, but of other whites, and likewise the majority of black lives taken in the past century were taken by other blacks, not by whites. And so it follows, for example, that on account of ethnic bigotry, no one in Uganda will care whether Mr. XY is wise, kind, and friendly, or the reverse, evil and loathsome; they will care only whether he is of the tribe of Bari, Toro, Busoga, or Nandi. This is the sole criterion by which he will be classified and evaluated.

For its first eight years of independence, Uganda is ruled by Milton Obote, an extraordinarily conceited man, boastful and sure of himself. When it is exposed in the press that Amin has misappropriated the cash, gold, and ivory given him for safekeeping by anti-Mobutu guerrillas from Zaire, Obote summons Amin, orders him to pen an explanation, and, confident that he himself is in no danger, flies off to Singapore for a conference of prime ministers of the British Commonwealth. Amin, realizing that the prime minster will arrest him as soon as he returns, decides on a preemptive strike: he stages an army coup and seizes power. Theoretically at least, Obote in fact had little to worry about: Amin did not represent an obvious threat, and his influence in the army was ultimately limited. But beginning on the night of January 25, 1971, when they took over the barracks in Kampala, Amin and his supporters employed a brutally efficient surprise tactic: they fired without warning. And at a precisely defined target: soldiers from the Langi and Achole tribes. The surprise had a paralyzing effect: no one had time to mount a resistance. On the very first day, hundreds died in the barracks. And the carnage continued. Henceforth, Amin always used this method: he would shoot first. And not just at his enemies; that was self-evident, obvious. He went further: he liquidated without hesitation those he judged might one day develop into enemies. Over time, terror in Amin's state also came to depend on universal torture. Before they died, people were routinely tormented.

All this took place in a provincial country, in a small town. The torture chambers were located in downtown buildings. The windows were open—we are in the tropics. Whoever was walking along the street could hear cries, moans, shots. Whoever fell into the hands of the executioners vanished. A category soon emerged, then grew and grew, of those who in Latin America are called *desaparecidos:* those who have perished, disappeared. He left his house and never returned. *"Nani?"* the policemen routinely replied, if a family member demanded an explanation. *"Nani?"* (In Swahili the word means "who"; the individual reduced to a question mark.)

Uganda started to metamorphose into a tragic, bloody stage

upon which a single actor strutted—Amin. A month after the coup Amin named himself president, then marshal, then field marshal, and finally field marshal for life. He pinned upon himself ever more orders, medals, decorations. But he also liked to walk about in ordinary battle fatigues, so that soliders would say of him, "You see, he's one of us." He chose his cars in accordance with his outfits. Wearing a suit to a reception, he drove a dark Mercedes. Out for a spin in a sweat suit? A red Maserati. Battle fatigues? A military Range Rover. The last resembled a vehicle from a science-fiction movie. A forest of antennas protruded from it, all kinds of wires, cables, spotlights. Inside were grenades, pistols, knives. He went about this way because he constantly feared attempts on his life. He survived several. Everyone else died in them—his aides-de-camp, his bodyguards. Amin alone would brush off the dust, straighten his uniform. To cover his tracks, he also rode in unmarked cars. People walking down a street would suddenly realize that the man sitting behind the wheel of that truck was Amin.

He trusted no one, therefore even those in his innermost circle did not know where he would be sleeping tonight, where he would be living tomorrow. He had several residences in the city, several more on the shores of Lake Victoria, still others in the countryside. Determining his whereabouts was both difficult and dangerous. He communicated with every subordinate directly, decided whom he would speak with, whom he wished to see. And for many, such a meeting would prove the last. If Amin became suspicious of someone, he would invite him over. He would be pleasant, friendly, treat his guest to a Coca-Cola. Executioners awaited the visitor as he left. Later, no one could determine what had happened to the man.

Amin usually telephoned his subordinates, but he also used the radio. Whenever he announced changes in the government or in the ranks of the military—and he was constantly instituting changes—he would do so over the airwaves.

Uganda had one radio station, one small newspaper (*Uganda Argus*), one camera, which filmed Amin, and one photojournalist, who would appear for ceremonial occasions. Everything was directed exclusively at the figure of the marshal. Moving from place to place, Amin in a sense moved the state with him; outside of him, nothing happened, nothing existed. Parliament did not exist, there were no political parties, trade unions, or other organizations. And, of course, no opposition—those suspected of dissent died painful deaths.

Amin's support was the army, which he created according to the colonial model, the only one he knew. Most of the men came from small communities inhabiting Africa's remote peripheries, lands on the border of Uganda and Sudan. They spoke Sudanese languages, in contrast to the country's native population, which is Bantu-speaking. Simple and uneducated, they were unable to communicate. But that was the intention—they felt alien, isolated, and wholly dependent on Amin. Whenever a truckful of them arrived, panic would erupt, the streets would empty, the villages grow deserted. Savage, enraged, most often drunk, the soldiers would pillage what they could, beat whomever they could. Randomly, indiscriminately. In the market, they would seize the sellers' goods. (If there were any, that is, for the Amin years were a time of empty shelves. As I was leaving for Kampala once, someone advised me to take along a lightbulb—there would be power in the hotel, but no bulbs.) The soldiers stole the peasants' crops, cattle, chickens. One constantly heard them shouting, *"Chakula! Chakula!"* (in Swahili, food, eat). Only copious amounts of food— a side of beef, an entire bunch of bananas, a large bowl of beans— would appease them and then for only a brief moment.

Amin was in the habit of visiting garrisons scattered across the country. On such occasions, a rally would be organized in the square. The marshal would speak. He liked to speak for hours on end. As a surprise, he would bring with him some notable person, a civilian or a military man, whom he suspected of treason, of conspiracy, of a coup attempt. The accused, bound with ropes, earlier already roughed up and scared out of his wits, was hauled to the dais. The crowd, excited by the sight, would fall into a trance and start to howl. "What shall I do with him?" Amin would try to make himself heard above the din. And the throng would shout: "Kill him! Kill him!"

The troops were in constant battle readiness. Amin, who had earlier given himself the title Conqueror of the British Empire, decided that he would liberate those among his brethren still languishing in the chains of colonial slavery. He began a series of onerous and costly military maneuvers. His troops practiced liberating the Republic of South Africa. Battalions attacked "Pretoria" and "Johannesburg," the artillery strafed enemy positions in "Port Elizabeth" and "Durban." Amin observed the hostilities through a pair of binoculars from the terrace of a villa dubbed the Command Post. Irritated by the slowness of the battalion from Jinja to capture "Cape Town," he would jump into a car and, agitated, in a lather, drive from one command point to the other, berating the officers, inciting the rank and file to battle. The shells plunged into Lake Victoria, sending up plumes of water and terrifying the fishermen.

He was a man of inexhaustible energy, perpetually excited, always in motion. When, as president, he occasionally convened a session of government, he was able to participate in it only briefly. He would soon grow bored, leap up from his chair, and leave. His thoughts came fast and furiously; he spoke chaotically, did not complete his sentences. He read English with difficulty, and was not proficient in Swahili. He had a solid command of his Kakwa dialect, although few Ugandans spoke it. Yet it is precisely these shortcomings that made him popular among the *bayaye:* he was like them, blood of their blood, bone of their bone.

Amin had no friends, and did not allow anyone to know him for long or intimately, fearful that such a relationship might enable others to organize a conspiracy or a coup. In particular, he frequently changed the heads of the two secret police units, the Public Safety Unit and State Research Bureau, which he had created for the express purpose of terrorizing the country. In the latter served *bayaye* from related Sudanese peoples—the Kakwa, the Lugabra, the Madi, and their kinsmen, the Nubians. The SRB sowed fear in Uganda. Its strength stemmed from the fact that each of its members had direct access to Amin.

One day I was wandering around the market in Kampala. It was somewhat empty, many stalls were broken, abandoned. Amin had stripped and ruined the country. There was no traffic in the streets, and the shops, which Amin had earlier confiscated from their Indian owners, gaped with musty emptiness or were simply boarded up with wooden planks, plywood, or sheets of tin. Suddenly, a band of children came up the street that led up from the lake, calling, *"Samaki! Samaki!"* (fish in Swahili). People gathered, joyful at the prospect that there would be something to eat. The fishermen threw their catch onto a table, and when the onlookers saw it, they grew still and silent. The fish was fat, enormous. These waters never used to yield such monstrously proportioned, overfed specimens. Everyone knew that for a long time now Amin's henchmen had been dumping the bodies of their victims into the lake, and that crocodiles and meat-eating fish must have been feasting on them. The crowd remained quiet. Then, a military vehicle happened by. The soldiers saw the gathering, as well as the fish on the table, and stopped. They spoke for a moment among themselves, then backed up to the table, jumped down, and opened the tailgate. Those of us who were standing nearby could see the corpse of a man lying on the truck bed. We saw the soldiers heave the fish onto the truck, throw the dead, barefoot man onto the table for us, and quickly drive away. And we heard their coarse, lunatic laughter.

. . .

Amin's rule lasted eight years. According to various sources, the field marshal for life murdered between 150,000 and 300,000 people. Finally, he provoked his own downfall. One of his obsessions was his hatred for the president of neighboring Tanzania, Julius Nyerere. Toward the end of 1978, he attacked Tanzania. The Tanzanian army responded. Nyerere's troops entered Uganda. Amin escaped to Libya, before he was allowed to settle in Saudi Arabia, as a reward for services in propagating Islam. Amin's army dispersed, some of his troops returning to their homes, others taking up banditry. The losses suffered by the Tanzanian army? One tank.

The Ambush

We were driving north from Kampala, toward Uganda's border with Sudan. At the head of the motorcade was a truck with a heavy machine gun protruding above the cab, followed by a truck carrying a platoon of soldiers, then several passenger cars, and, at the rear, an open-backed Japanese pickup, in which we three journalists were seated. It had been a long while since I had traveled in such comfort, protected by a military unit, and, moreover, one armed with a heavy machine gun! But all this, of course, was not on my account. The escort was for three ministers from President Yoweri Museveni's government, on a peace mission to the rebels marauding in the country's northern regions. Museveni, in power for two years now (it is 1988), had just proclaimed an amnesty for those who surrendered and voluntarily turned in their arms. The fighters in question were soldiers from the armies of Idi Amin, Milton Obote, and Tito Okello, three successive Ugandan dictators who in recent years had fled abroad, leaving their troops behind. The armed men were now robbing and murdering, burning villages and stealing cattle, decimating and terrorizing the northern provinces—for all intents and purposes, half the country. Museveni's divisions were too weak to control the rebels. Therefore, the president had extended an olive branch to them. He was the first

Ugandan leader in twenty-five years to turn to his enemies with words of accord, understanding, and peace.

There are three soldiers in our pickup in addition to the two local reporters and myself. They have swung their Kalashnikovs over bare shoulders (it is hot, and they have removed their shirts). Their names are Onom, Semakula, and Konkoti. The eldest among them, Onom, is seventeen. I sometimes read stories about a child in America or Europe shooting at another child. A child killing one of his contemporaries, or an adult. Such news is usually accompanied by expressions of horror and outrage. In Africa, children kill children in enormous numbers, and have been doing so for years. In fact, modern wars on this continent have been, and still are, largely wars of children.

In those places where conflict has lasted decades (as in Angola or Sudan), the majority of older people were killed long ago, or perished from hunger and disease; children remain, and it is they who are doing the fighting. The bloody chaos in which various African countries are plunged has spawned tens of thousands of orphans, hungry and homeless. They look for anyone who might feed and shelter them, and it is easiest to find food where the troops are, because soldiers have the best chances of obtaining it: weapons in these countries are not only for waging war, but are a means of survival—sometimes the only means.

Abandoned, lonely children gravitate to where troops are garrisoned, where they have their barracks and camps. They help out, work, become part of the army, "sons of the regiment." They are given weapons and quickly undergo a baptism by fire. Their older companions (also children) often laze about, and when a confrontation with the enemy is pending, send the little ones to the front lines, into the thick of battle. These armed encounters between youngsters are particularly fierce and bloody, because a child does not have the instinct for self-preservation, does not feel dread or comprehend death, does not experience the fear that only maturity will evoke.

The wars of children have also been made possible by technological developments. Today, handheld automatic weapons are short and light, the newer models increasingly resembling children's toys. The old Mauser was too long, too big, and too heavy for a child. A child's small arm could not reach freely for the trigger, and he had difficulty taking aim. Modern design has solved these problems, eliminated the inconveniences. The dimensions of weapons are now perfectly suited to a boy's physique, so much so that in the hands of tall, massive men, the new guns appear somewhat comical and childish.

Because the child is capable only of using handheld, short-range weapons (he cannot conduct long-range artillery fire, or pilot a bomber), clashes in these children's wars take the form of savagely unmediated collisions, of close, almost physical contact; the children fire at one another separated by just a step. The toll, typically, is frightful. And it is not only those killed then and there who perish. In the conditions under which these wars are fought, the wounded will also die—from loss of blood, from infection, from lack of medicines.

After a whole day of driving we reached the town of Soroti. Along the way we had passed burned-out villages and settlements—all of them plundered practically into nonexistence. The soldiers had taken everything they possibly could—not only what the inhabitants had on their backs, not only their furniture and household effects, the tools with which they worked and the dishes from which they ate, but all pipes, wires, and nails, all windows, doors, and even roofs. Like ants working on a bone, leaving behind not the tiniest trace of meat, so the successive waves of marauders in predatory flight had stripped the countryside of everything and anything that could be moved and transported. Soroti, too, was in ruins, the gas station wrecked, the pumps missing, the school benches carried off. Many of the houses had been reduced to mere skeletons, but some had survived, among them the hotel in which we stopped for the night. A group of local notables was already waiting for us—merchants, teachers, army men—surrounded by a crowd of curious onlookers. A round of greetings began, of shoulder slapping and laughter.

Soroti is the capital of a region inhabited by the Iteso, a handsome Nilo-Hamitic people. They are more than a million strong, divided into numerous tribes and clans. Their main occupation is raising cattle. The cow is their greatest treasure. It is not only a measure of wealth, but is also thought to possess mystical attributes. Its existence, the mere fact of its presence, connects the human being to an invisible higher world. The Iteso give their cattle names, and believe that each one has its own personality, its own character. At a certain age, an Iteso boy is given a cow to take care of. During a special ceremony, he also assumes its name—from then on he will be called what it is called. The child plays with his cow, spends his free moments with it, is responsible for it.

Among those greeting us was an acquaintance of mine from the sixties, the then-minister Cuthbert Obwanor. I was happy at this encounter, and we fell immediately into conversation. I wanted him to show me around, because it was my first time in these parts. We set out for a walk, though I quickly found it a somewhat disconcerting experience. It is the local custom for women, when they see a man walking toward them, to move to the side, kneel, and wait on their knees until he approaches. He greets them, and in response to this they inquire whether there is anything they can do for him. If he answers "Nothing," they wait until he passes, and only then rise and go on their way. Similar scenes were repeated later, as I sat with Cuthbert on a bench in front of his house: passing women came up to us, knelt, and silently waited. Sometimes my host, busy talking, failed to notice them. They would continue to wait, motionless, until he finally greeted them and wished them farewell, at which point they would get up and walk away. Despite its being evening already, it was still hot, and the atmosphere was stifling, warm and heavy. Hidden in the deep recesses of the night, crickets chirped loudly and insistently.

In the end, we were invited by the local authorities to the one bar still operating. It was called Club 2000. On the second floor was a little salon for important guests, where we were seated at a long table. The waitresses came in, young, tall girls. Each knelt down before her designated guest and said her name. Then they walked out, and returned carrying an enormous steaming clay pitcher filled with *marva,* a hot local beer made out of millet seeds. You drink *marva* through a long, hollowed-out reed called an *epi.* This reed now started to circulate among the guests. Each drew a few sips and passed it to his neighbor. As this was going on, the waitresses poured into the pitcher either more water or more *marva:* this—what they pour in and how quickly the *epi* circulates—determines the revelers' degree of drunkenness. Soroti, like this entire region, has one of the highest incidences of AIDS in the world, and this drinking session took place in the days when it was still believed that HIV could be transmitted through saliva. Each time you reached for the *epi,* you were bidding your life farewell. But what could you do? Refuse? That would have been considered a great insult, a sign that you held your hosts in contempt.

In the morning, before we set off, two Dutch missionaries arrived, Albert and Johan. Exhausted, covered in dust, they had trudged to Soroti to "see people from the big world": for them, living as they had for more than a decade in this outback, Kampala had become the great world. They did not travel to Europe, did not want to leave the church and the mission buildings (they lived somewhere near the Sudanese border), afraid that upon their return they would find only bare, scorched walls. The area where they worked is a vast, hot savannah, dry in the summer, green during the rainy season, the endless, remote stretches of north-eastern Uganda, inhabited by the people who so fascinate many anthropologists, the Karimojong. The residents of Kampala speak of their kinsmen from Karimojong (it is at once the name of a place, a people, and a person) with distaste and embarrassment. The Karimojong walk around naked, and insist upon this custom, seeing the human body as beautiful (and in fact they are magnificently built, tall and slender). Their intransigence on this score has yet another basis: most of the Europeans who reached them in the early years of African exploration rapidly fell ill and died, from which the Karimojong deduced that clothing causes illness, and getting dressed is tantamount to sentencing yourself to death. (In their system of belief, furthermore, suicide is the greatest sin imaginable.) That is why they were always desperately afraid of clothing. Amin, who believed that going about naked demeans Africans, issued a decree against the custom, and his troops executed on the spot anyone they caught without clothes. The terrified Karimojong would obtain wherever they could a piece of fabric, a shirt, or pants, roll this up into a little bundle, and carry it around with them. Upon hearing that army vehicles were nearby, or that a government agent had been seen nosing about, they would get dressed, and with great relief remove everything again as soon as the coast was clear.

The Karimojong are cattle breeders, and milk is their main source of nourishment. Related to the Iteso, they too regard cows as mystical beings and their greatest treasure. They believe that God gave to them, and to them alone, all the cattle in the world, and that it is their historical mission to recover these creatures. With this goal in mind, they relentlessly organize armed incursions against neighboring tribes. These cattle raids are part pillaging expeditions, part patriotic missions, and part religious duty. A young boy must take part in a cattle raid to attain the status of a man. The forays are the principal subject of native legends, tales, myths. They have their heroes, their histories, their mystical themes.

Father Albert described such an expedition. The Karimojong walk single file, he said, at an even pace, in tight formation. They move along well-trodden paths of war. Each division numbers two hundred, three hundred men. They sing songs or emit loud, rhythmic cries. Their reconnaissance having earlier established the location of grazing herds belonging to another people, their objective is to abduct these herds. When they reach their destination, there is a battle. The Karimojong are well-trained, fearless fighters, which is why they usually triumph and succeed in making off with the spoils.

"The thing is," said Father Albert, "that in times past these columns were armed with spears and arrows. During a skirmish, several people died, and the rest either surrendered or fled. And today? There are still these columns of naked men, but now they are armed to the teeth with automatic weapons. They start firing right away, massacre the local population, destroy villages with grenades, sow death. These are still the traditional tribal conflicts, the same ones as centuries ago, only now they claim an incomparably greater number of victims. Modern civilization has not reached us," he concludes. "There are no electric lamps here, no telephones, no television. The only aspect of it that has penetrated is automatic weapons."

I asked the missionary what their work entails, what kinds of problems they face.

"This is a very difficult terrain," Father Johan admitted. "These people ask us how many gods there are in our religion, and whether we have a special god for cattle. We explain to them that there is only one god. This disappoints them. Our religion is better, they say; we have a special god who takes care of cattle. After all, cows are the most important thing!"

We set off, before noon, heading deeper north, our pickup again bringing up the rear, but we had not gone far before we heard an explosion, shots, and then terrifying screams. We were on a narrow laterite road, full of holes and ruts, running between two walls of dense, three-meter-high elephant grass.

We had fallen into an ambush.

We cowered inside the truck, not knowing what to do. Stay inside? Jump out?

In Africa, the ambush is the most frequently used form of combat. It has many advantages for those setting it. First of all, the benefit of surprise: people driving along a road are incapable of maintaining their alertness and readiness for an entire day; in this climate, on these roads, they tire quickly and become drowsy. Secondly, the attackers are invisible to those approaching, and so are safe themselves. Thirdly, the successful ambush not only defeats an adversary, but also yields invaluable material conquests—cars, uniforms, provisions, weapons. The technique of the ambush also suits those for whom heat, hunger, and thirst (the permanent state of the local rebels and soldiers) make long marches and rapid regroupings difficult. A group of armed men can occupy a shady, comfortable place in the bush and calmly lounge about until their victim falls into their hands.

They apply two different tactics. The first is called hit and run, and this still gives those being ambushed some chance of collecting themselves and fighting back. The second, hit and hit (i.e., shoot, and shoot again), usually ends in death for the ambushed.

In the end, we jumped out of the car and ran to the front of the column. The attackers had hit the truck with a missile. A dead soldier lay on the truck bed, and two others were wounded. The front window had shattered; blood was seeping from under the sleeve of one man's uniform. There was chaos, disorder, people running along the length of the convoy, here and there, without rhyme or reason. No one knew what would happen the very next moment, the very next second. Were our enemies close by, hidden behind the thick, tall grasses, observing our hysterical commotion, pointing their guns at us, calmly taking aim? We had no idea what awaited us, into whose hands we had fallen. Instinctively I started to scrutinize the walls of green, trying to make out the shapes of gun barrels pointed in our direction.

Eventually, the truck went back to Soroti, in reverse gear, because the road was too narrow for it to turn around. We pushed on ahead. However, the officers decided that we should not ride in the cars, but proceed slowly on foot, walking behind the soldiers who, guns at the ready, headed up the procession.

There Shall Be a Holiday

I pleaded with Godwin, a journalist from Kampala, to take me to his village. It was relatively close by: fifty kilometers outside the city. For half the way, you can follow the main highway, which heads east toward Kenya along the shore of Lake Victoria. Both sides of the road teem with life—shops, bars, little hotels open day and night. It is usually bustling and noisy, with the activity not stopping altogether even at noon. On verandas, under overhangs, or beneath umbrellas sit tailors stooped over their machines, shoemakers repairing shoes and sandals, barbers cutting and styling. Women are beating manioc; others, next to them, are cooking bananas on a grill, or selling dried fish, juicy papayas, or homemade soap made out of ashes and sheep lard. Every few kilometers there is a car and bicycle repair shop, a tire-repair establishment, or a place to purchase fuel (depending on where you are, this is either an actual gas station with a pump, or simply a table with bottles or jars of gasoline awaiting the customer).

If you stop even for a moment somewhere along the way, the car is surrounded at once by a crowd of children, as well as by women selling everything and anything a traveler might need: bottles of Coca-Cola and of the local moonshine called *waragi,* tea biscuits and ladyfingers (in packages and individually), cooked rice and sorghum pancakes. They are the competitors of their friends farther away, who are unable to approach since they have stalls to guard—there are thieves everywhere.

These roads are also places of ecumenical diversity and tolerance. We pass an ornate mosque, whose costly construction was financed by Saudi Arabia; farther on, a considerably more humble little church; farther still, tents of the Seventh-Day Adventists, who wander across the continent warning about the coming end of the world. And this structure with the conical roof woven from rice straw? It is the temple of the highest god of the Ganda people, Katonda.

Every now and then we come to a roadblock (this can consist simply of a piece of wire or string) and a police or army guardpost. Even if you are far from the capital and, moreover, have not been listening to the radio (newspapers do not penetrate here, and there is no television), the behavior of the policemen and soldiers on guard will tell you a lot about the situation within the country. If, the minute you have come to a stop, and without so much as asking you a single question, they begin shouting and punching, it means that the country is under a dictatorship, or that there is war, but if they walk up to you, smile, extend their hands, and politely say, "You probably know that we earn very little," it means that you are driving through a stable, democratic country, in which elections are free and human rights are observed.

The master of African roads and trails is the truck driver. Passenger cars are too weak to manage the ruts and the potholes. Half of them would get stuck somewhere along the way (especially during the rainy season), and the others, even if they had completed a route, would at the end of it be fit only for the junkyard. Whereas the truck can go almost anywhere. It has a powerful engine and wide tires, and a suspension as strong as the Brooklyn Bridge. The drivers of these vehicles understand well the treasure they possess, and therein lies their power. You can pick them out instantly in a roadside crowd by the manner in which they move. They have a positively regal bearing. Often, they do not even deign to descend from their lofty perches in the cabs—they know that everything will be brought to them. If a truck stops in a small settlement, a group of exhausted, pleading people will rush toward it—they are trying to get somewhere and do not have the means to do so. Therefore they camp by the roadside, hoping for an opportunity, for someone who will take them along for a fee. No one expects compassion. The truck drivers certainly are unfamiliar with this emotion. On the roads along which they travel, in the scorching heat and fire of the tropics, they see, day in and day out, women loaded down with packages, walking single file. If a driver had even an ounce of pity in his heart and wanted to help them, he would have to stop constantly, and would never reach his destination. That is why the relationship between the drivers and the women moving along the shoulders of the road is characterized by absolute coolness—they do not notice each other, they pass with indifference.

Godwin works until evening, therefore we cannot see this time the full spectacle that is the road east out of Kampala. It is late, nighttime already, when we set out, and the road looks completely different from how it appears by day.

Everything is plunged in the deepest darkness. The only thing visible are glowing lines of weak, wavering flames along both sides of the road—the lamps and candles in front of the vendors' stalls. Most often, these aren't even proper stalls, just a few measly odds and ends set directly on the ground, in the most bizarre combinations: a little pyramid of tomatoes next to a tube of toothpaste, mosquito spray next to a pack of cigarettes, a box of matches next to a metal tea can. Godwin says that earlier, in the years of dictatorship, it was preferable to camp outside near such candles than to spend time in brightly lit interiors. Seeing troops approaching, a man could instantly blow out the candle and vanish into the darkness. By the time the soldiers arrived, there wouldn't be a soul left. A candle is good, because you can see everything, while remaining invisible yourself. Whereas in an illuminated interior, it is the other way around, and therefore more dangerous.

Finally we turned off the main highway onto an uneven, unpaved country road. All you could see in the glow of the headlights was a narrow dirt tunnel between two walls of dense, succulent, saturated greenery. This is the Africa of the humid tropics—lush, riotously overgrown, endlessly germinating, multiplying, and seething. We traveled along this tunnel, actually an intricate and confusing labyrinth of forks and turns, until suddenly the wall of a house loomed directly in our path. This was the end of the road. Godwin stopped the car and turned off the engine. A deep silence descended. It was so late already that even the crickets were quiet, and there seemed to be no dogs in the vicinity. One could hear only the mosquitoes, angry and impatient, as if they could stand waiting for us no longer. Godwin knocked on the door. It opened, and a dozen sleepy, half-naked children spilled out. Then a tall, serious woman emerged, her gestures full of dignity and joyous welcome: Godwin's mother. After some preliminary greetings, she gathered all the children in one room, and in the other spread out sleeping mats for us on the floor.

When I peered out the window in the morning, I felt I was in a boundless tropical garden. All around grew palm trees, banana trees, tamarind trees, coffee bushes—the house was drowning in thick, tangled growth. Tall grasses and billowing shrubs were pushing in from everywhere, so rampant that there was little room left for people. Godwin's yard was small; I saw no road anywhere (other than the one we had arrived on), and most important, I didn't notice any other houses, although Godwin had told me we were going to a village. In this densely jungled region of Africa, villages are laid out not along the road (which often does not even exist), but scattered over a large area, with houses at some distance from one another, joined only by paths submerged in the thickets, invisible to the untrained eye. One has to be an inhabitant of the village, or at least know it well, in order to understand the layout of these paths, their course and connections.

I set off with the children for water; getting it is their responsibility. Maybe two hundred meters from the house ran a small, barely moving stream, overgrown with burdock and bulrushes, in which slowly and with great difficulty the boys filled their buckets. Then they carried these buckets back on their heads, trying their best not to spill a single drop. They walked with great concentration, carefully balancing their slight, childish bodies.

One of the buckets is designated for morning ablutions. You wash your face in such a way as not to waste too much water. You scoop a handful from the bucket and then spread it over your face—attentively and not too energetically, so that it doesn't run off between your fingers. A towel is unnecessary, because the sun shines fiercely from early morning and skin dries rapidly. Next, you break off a small twig from a bush and crush one end with your teeth until you have created a kind of wooden brush. Now you clean your teeth, long and meticulously. Some people do this for hours; it is a pastime for them like gum chewing is for others.

Next, because this is a double holiday (it is Sunday, and guests have arrived from the city), Godwin's mother prepares breakfast. Normally one eats once a day in the village, in the evening; in the dry season, once every two days—if one doesn't simply starve. For breakfast there is tea and a piece of cornmeal pancake, as well as a bowl of matoke, a dish made of boiled green bananas. The children behave like nestlings: they stare greedily at the bowl of matoke, and when their mother finally allows them to eat, they gulp everything down in a second.

All the while, we are outside in the yard. Lying in the middle, and calling immediate attention to itself, is a rectangular stone slab: it is the grave of the ancestors, the *masiro*. In Africa, burial customs vary greatly. Certain forest tribes just lay down their deceased in the bush, to be devoured by wild animals. Others bury corpses in specially designated places, in simple, unadorned cemeteries. There are those who bury the dead beneath the floors of inhabited houses. But most frequently they are laid to rest in close proximity to the house—in yards, in gardens, where they can be close, where we can feel their fortifying presence. Belief in the ghosts of ancestors, in their ministering power, in their vigilant attention, encouragement, and goodwill is very much alive and constitutes a source of comfort and confidence. Having them near us, we feel more secure; when we are at a loss as to what to do, they will hasten to give us advice and—what is immeasurably important—will stop us from taking a false step or the wrong road altogether. Therefore each home, each household, has two dimensions: the visible, palpable one and the hidden, mysterious, sacred one. Every person tries, if he can, to visit regularly his family home, the ground of his ancestors—there he gains strength and shores up his identity.

The yard's second focal point, besides the ancestral grave, is the kitchen. This consists of a hole in the ground surrounded on three sides by clay walls, and in it lie three blackened stones arranged in a triangle. You place the pot on top of them, and light a wood fire beneath. It is the simplest of appliances, invented during neolithic times but still useful.

Because it was morning and the heat was still relatively tolerable, Godwin went off to greet the neighbors, having agreed earlier that I could accompany him. People here live in simple clay houses covered with corrugated tin, which by noon radiates heat like a fired-up oven. Windows are mere openings in the walls, and the doors are most often made out of plywood or tin, loosely fitted, without frames—symbolic, really, because they do not even have knobs or locks.

Someone arriving here from the city is considered a great gentleman, a Croesus, a lord. Although the city is not far away, it nevertheless belongs to another, better world, a planet of plenty.

Both sides, those from the city and those from the country, understand this, which is why the person from the city knows he cannot arrive here empty-handed. Consequently, preparations for a trip to the countryside cost people from the city much time and money. When my friend in Kampala purchases anything, he immediately explains, "I have to take this to the country." He walks the streets, inspects the merchandise, and deliberates: "This would be good for a present, when I go to the country."

Presents, presents. This is a culture of constant gift-giving. But because Godwin did not have time to shop, he gave his neighbors twists of Ugandan shillings, slipping them discreetly into their pockets.

First we visited Stone Singevenda and his wife, Victa. Stone is twenty-six years old and works on construction projects, although he has been unable to find a job for some time. Victa works: she cultivates a little field of manioc, from which they live. Victa gives birth every year. They have been married four years and have four children, with a fifth on the way. It is the custom here to offer a guest something, but Victa and Stone do not give us anything—they have nothing to give.

It is different with their neighbor, Simon; he straightaway sets a plate of peanuts before us. But Simon is a wealthy man: he has a bicycle, and thanks to this he has a job. Simon is a bicycle trader. There are few major roads in the country. Trucks are scarce. Millions of people inhabit villages to which no roads lead and which trucks cannot reach. These people have it the hardest, and are the poorest. They live far from the marketplace, too far to carry there on their heads the few bulbs of cassava or yams, the bunch of green bananas or sack of sorghum—the vegetables and fruit native to this region. Because they cannot sell them, they have no money, and therefore they cannot buy anything—the desperate, closed circle of poverty. But, suddenly, Simon appears with his bicycle. He has fitted it out with myriad devices—trunks, bags, clips, brackets. The contraption serves more for transport than for riding. On this bike, for a slight fee (slight, for we are here always in the realm of a subsistence economy), Simon (and there are thousands like him in these parts) carries produce to the market for the village women (women, because this kind of small trade is their bailiwick). Simon says that the farther one goes from a major road, from the truck and the market, the greater the poverty. "And because people from Europe spend their time here only in the cities," Simon observes, "and drive along the major roads, they cannot even imagine what our Africa looks like."

One of Simon's neighbors is Apollo—a man of indeterminate age, skinny and taciturn. He stands in front of his house pressing his shirt on a board. He has a charcoal-heated iron, enormous, rusted, and old. His shirt is older still. To describe it one must resort to the vocabulary of art critics, capricious postmodernists, scholars of suprematism, of abstract expressionism. It is a masterpiece of patchwork, of collage and pop art, a testament to the heights of imagination attained by those hardworking tailors whose little shops we passed driving here along the road from Kampala. For this shirt has had its holes patched so many times, there are so many bits and pieces of the most varied fabrics, colors, and textures sewn onto it, that it is no longer possible to ascertain the color and material of that original, primary, ancestral shirt, the one that had set into motion the long process of alterations and transfigurations, the effect of which now lies before Apollo on his ironing board.

The Buganda take enormous care with their grooming and their attire. In contrast to their fellow countrymen the Karimojong, who disdain clothing, the Buganda dress neatly and carefully, covering their arms down to the wrists, and their legs down to the ankles.

Apollo says that things are good because the civil war has ended, but bad because the price of coffee has fallen (it's the 1990s) and they grow coffee here; it is the main source of livelihood. No one wants to buy it, no one comes for it. The coffee goes to waste, the bushes grow wild, and the people have no money. He sighs, and carefully guides the iron among the patches and seams, like a sailor navigating his boat between treacherous reefs.

As we stand talking, a cow emerges from a thicket of banana trees, followed by several playful little shepherds, then a stooped old man—Lule Kabbogozza. In 1942, Lule fought in Burma—he refers to this as the only event in his life. The rest of it was spent in this village. Now he laments the same as the others: "What do I eat?" he asks. "Cassava. Day and night cassava." But he has a sunny disposition, and gestures toward the cow with a smile. At the beginning of the year several families get together, save their pennies, and purchase a cow at market. The cow grazes in the countryside, there is plenty of grass. When Christmas comes, it is slaughtered. Everyone gathers for the occasion. They make certain that everything is equitably divided. They offer most of the blood as a sacrifice to the ancestors (there is no more precious offering than cow's blood). The rest of the beast they immediately roast and cook. It is the one and only time in the year when the village eats meat. Later they will buy another cow, and in a year's time there will be another feast.

If I find myself somewhere nearby, I am told, I will be welcome. There will be *pombe* (banana beer), there will be *waragi*. And I will get as much meat as I want!

A Lecture on Rwanda

L adies and gentlemen.
        Our subject is Rwanda. It is a small country,
so small that on certain maps of Africa it is marked with only a
dot. You must read the accompanying explanatory notes to discover that this dot, at the continent's very center, indicates
Rwanda. It is a mountainous country. Plains and plateaus are
more characteristic of Africa, whereas Rwanda is mountains and
more mountains. They rise two thousand, three thousand meters,
even higher. That is why Rwanda is frequently called the Tibet of
Africa—although it earned this moniker not only because of its
mountains, but also on account of its singularity, distinctness, difference. It is extraordinary not only geographically, but also
socially. As a rule, the populations of African states are multitribal
(Congo is inhabited by 300 tribes, Nigeria by 250, and so on),
whereas only one group inhabits Rwanda, the Banyarwanda, a
single nation divided into three castes: the Tutsi cattle owners (14
percent of the population), the Hutu farmers (85 percent), and
the Twa laborers and servants (1 percent). This caste system (bearing certain analogies to India's) took shape centuries ago; because
no written sources exist on the subject, there is ongoing disagree-
ment as to whether this occurred in the twelfth century, or as late
as the fifteenth. Suffice it to say that a kingdom has existed here

for hundreds of years, ruled by a monarch called *mwami,* who was Tutsi.

This mountain kingdom was a closed state, maintaining relations with no one. The Banyarwanda initiated no conquests, and, like the Japanese at one time, they did not allow foreigners into their territory (which is why, for example, they had no experience of the slave trade, the bane of other African peoples). The first European to enter Rwanda, in 1894, was a German traveler and officer, Count G. A. von Götzen. It is worth noting that eight years prior to this, at the Berlin Conference that partitioned Africa, the colonial powers awarded Rwanda to the Germans, a development about which no Rwandan, including the king, was so much as informed. For a number of years, the Banyarwanda lived as a colonized people, without knowing it. Later, too, the Germans took little interest in the colony, and after World War I they lost it to Belgium. The Belgians also were not exceedingly active here. Rwanda was distant from the coasts, more than 1,500 kilometers away, and, most important, it was of little value, no significant raw materials having ever been discovered there. The Banyarwanda's social system, shaped centuries ago, was thus able to endure unaltered in its mountainous stronghold until the second half of the twentieth century.

This system had several characteristics reminiscent of European feudalism. The country was ruled by a monarch surrounded by a group of aristocrats and a throng of noblemen. Together, they constituted the ruling caste: the Tutsis. Their greatest, and really sole wealth was cattle: the zebu cows, a breed characterized by long, beautiful, swordlike horns. These cows were never killed—they were sacred, untouchable. The Tutsis nourished themselves with their milk and blood (the blood, drawn from arteries in the neck cut with the point of a spear, was collected in vessels that had been washed with cow's urine). All these actions were performed by men, for women were forbidden to have contact with cattle.

The cow was the measure of everything: wealth, prestige,

power. The more cattle one had, the richer one was; the richer one was, the more power one had. The king owned the most cattle, and his herds were under special protection. The main focus of the festivities marking the yearly national holiday was the parade of cattle. A million of them would pass before the monarch. This lasted hours. The animals raised clouds of dust that hung over the kingdom for a long time. The dimensions of these clouds attested to the health of the monarchy, and the ceremony itself was endlessly and emotionally extolled in Tutsi poetry.

"The Tutsi?" I often heard in Rwanda. "The Tutsi sits on the threshold of his house and watches his herds grazing on the mountainside. The sight fills him with pride and happiness."

The Tutsis are not shepherds or nomads; they are not even breeders. They are the owners of the herds, the ruling caste, the aristocracy.

The Hutus, on the other hand, constitute the much more numerous and subordinate caste of farmers (in India they are called Vaisyas). The relations between the Tutsis and the Hutus were authentically feudal—the Tutsi was the lord, the Hutu his vassal. The Hutus lived by cultivating land. They gave a portion of their harvest to their master in exchange for protection and for the use of a cow (the Tutsis had a monopoly on cattle; the Hutus could only lease them from their seigneurs). Everything according to the feudal order—the dependence, the customs, the exploitation.

Gradually, toward the middle of the twentieth century, a dramatic conflict arises between the two castes. The object of the dispute is land. Rwanda is small, circumscribed, and densely populated. As often in Africa, a battle erupts between those who make their living raising cattle and those who cultivate the land. Usually, however, the spaces on the continent are so great that one side can move onto unoccupied territory and the sparks of war are extinguished. In Rwanda, such a solution is impossible—there is no place to go, nowhere to retreat to. Meantime, the Tutsis' herds increase and need ever more grazing land. There is but one way to create new pastures: by taking land from the peasants, i.e., by ejecting the Hutus from their territories. But the Hutus are already cramped. Their numbers have been swelling rapidly for years. Making matters worse, the lands they farm are poor, for all intents and purposes infertile. The mountains of Rwanda are covered with a very thin layer of soil, so thin that when the rainy season comes each year, the downpours wash away large stretches of it, and in many places where the Hutus had their little fields of manioc and corn, naked rock now glistens.

So, on the one side, the powerful, expanding herds of cattle—the symbol of Tutsi wealth and strength; and on the other the squeezed, huddled, increasingly displaced Hutus. There is no room, there is no land. Someone must leave, or perish. Such is the situation in Rwanda in the fifties, when the Belgians enter the picture. They have suddenly become highly involved: Africa is just then at a critical juncture, there is a surging wave of liberation, of anticolonialism, and there is pressure to act, to make decisions. Belgium is among those powers whom the independence movement has caught most by surprise. Thus, Brussels has no game plan, its officials do not really know what to do. As is usual in these circumstances, their response is to delay finding real solutions, to stall. Until now, the Belgians ruled Rwanda through the Tutsis, leaning on them and using them. But the Tutsis are the most educated and ambitious sector of the Banyarwanda, and it is they who now are demanding freedom. And they want it immediately, something for which the Belgians are utterly unprepared. So Brussels abruptly switches tactics: it abandons the Tutsis and begins to support the more submissive, docile Hutus. It begins to incite them against the Tutsis. These politics rapidly bear fruit. The emboldened, encouraged Hutus take up arms. A peasant revolt erupts in Rwanda in 1959.

In Rwanda, alone in all of Africa, the liberation movement assumed the form of a social, antifeudal revolution. In all of Africa, only Rwanda had its siege of the Bastille, its dethronement of the king, its Gironde and its terror. Groups of peasants, enraged, inflamed Hutus armed with machetes, hoes, and spears, moved against their masters-rulers, the Tutsis. A great massacre began, such as Africa had not seen for a long time. The peasants set fire to the households of their lords, slit their throats, and crushed their skulls. Rwanda flowed with blood, stood in flames. A massive slaughter of cattle began; the peasants, often for the first time in their lives, could eat as much meat as they wished. At the time, the country had a population of 2.6 million, including 300,000 Tutsis. It is estimated that tens of thousands of Tutsis were murdered, and as many fled to neighboring states—to the Congo, Uganda, Tanganyika, and Burundi. The monarchy and feudalism ceased to exist, and the Tutsi caste lost its dominant position. Power was now seized by the Hutu peasantry. When Rwanda gained its independence in 1962, it was members of that caste who formed the first government. At its head was a young journalist, Grégoire Kayibanda. I was visiting Rwanda for the first time then. My memories of Kigali, the capital, are of a small town. I was unable to find a hotel; perhaps there wasn't one. Some Belgian nuns finally took me in, letting me sleep in the maternity ward of their neat little hospital.

The Hutus and the Tutsis awoke from such a revolution as from a bad dream. Both had lived through a massacre, the former as its perpetrators, the latter as its victims, and such an experience leaves a painful and indelible mark. The Hutus have mixed emotions. On the one hand, they vanquished their masters, cast off the feudal yoke, and for the first time attained power; on the other hand, they did not defeat their lords in an absolute way, did not annihilate them, and this consciousness, that the enemy was painfully wounded but still lives and will seek vengeance, sowed in their hearts an insuppressible and mortal fear (let us remember that fear of revenge is deeply rooted in the African mentality, that the immemorial right of reprisal has always regulated interpersonal, private, and clan relations here). And there is a lot to be afraid of. For although the Hutus seized the mountainous fortress of Rwanda and established their rule there, a Tutsi fifth column, numbering around 100,000, remains within its borders; further-more, and perhaps even more dangerously, the fortress is encircled by the encampments of Tutsis expelled from it yesterday.

The image of the fortress is not poetic license. Whether you enter Rwanda from Uganda, Tanzania, or Zaire, you will always have the same impression of stepping through the gates of a stronghold that rises up before you, fashioned from immense, magnificent mountains. And so it is now for the Tutsi, a freshly exiled and homeless vagabond; when he awakens in the morning in a refugee camp and walks out in front of his shabby tent, he beholds the mountains of Rwanda. In those early hours of the day, they are a startlingly beautiful sight. I myself often jumped up at dawn just to look. High yet gentle peaks stretch before you into infinity. They are emerald, violet, green, and drenched in sun-light. It is a landscape devoid of the dread and darkness of rocky, windswept peaks, precipices, and cliffs; no deadly avalanches, falling rocks, or loose rubble are lying in wait for you here. No. The mountains of Rwanda radiate warmth and benevolence, tempt with beauty and silence, a crystal clear, windless air, the peace and exquisiteness of their lines and shapes. In the mornings, a transparent haze suffuses the green valleys. It is like a bright veil, airy, light and glimmering in the sun, through which are softly visible the eucalyptus and banana trees, and the people working in the fields. But what the Tutsi sees there above all else are his graz-ing herds. Those herds, which he no longer possesses yet which were for him the foundation of existence and the reason for liv-ing, now swell in his imagination into myth and legend, become his fondest desire, dream, obsession.

That is how the Rwandan drama is engendered, the tragedy of the Banyarwanda nation, born of an almost Israeli-Palestinian inability to reconcile the interests of two social groups laying claim to the same scrap of land, too small and confined to accom-modate them both. Within this drama is spawned the temptation, at first weak and vague, but with the passing of years ever more clear and insistent, of the *Endlosung*—a final solution.

But this is still a long way off. We are in the sixties, Africa's most promising and optimistic years. The great expectations and euphoria reigning on the continent ensure that no one pays much attention to the bloody events in Rwanda. There is no communication or newspapers, and besides—Rwanda? Where is that? How does one get there? The country appears forgotten by God and men alike. It is quiet here, lifeless, and—as can be quickly ascertained—boring. No major road runs through Rwanda, there are no big cities, it is rare for anyone to pass this way. Years ago, when I told a friend of mine, a reporter from the *Daily Telegraph*, Michael Field, that I had been to Rwanda, he asked: "And did you see the president?" "No," I answered. "So what did you go there for?" he exclaimed, astounded.

It is true that what strikes you most in a place like Rwanda is its deep provincialism. Our world, seemingly global, is in reality a planet of thousands of the most varied and never intersecting provinces. A trip around the world is a journey from backwater to backwater, each of which considers itself, in its isolation, a shining star. For most people, the real world ends on the threshold of their house, at the edge of their village, or, at the very most, on the border of their valley. That which is beyond is unreal, unimportant, and even useless, whereas that which we have at our fingertips, in our field of vision, expands until it seems an entire universe, overshadowing all else. Often, the native and the newcomer have difficulty finding a common language, because each looks at the same place through a different lens. The newcomer has a wide-angle lens, which gives him a distant, diminished view, although one with a long horizon line, while the local always employs a telescopic lens that magnifies the slightest detail.

For the natives, however, the dramas are real, and the tragedies painful and not exaggerated. So it was in Rwanda. The revolution of 1959 divided the Banyarwanda nation into two opposing camps. From now on, the passage of time would serve only to strengthen the mechanisms of discord, sharpen the conflict, lead again and again to bloody collisions and, finally, to apocalypse.

The Tutsis, who have spread out in the camps along the borders, conspire and contract. In 1963 they strike from the south, from neighboring Burundi, where their kinsmen, the Tutsis of Burundi, hold power. Two years later—another Tutsi invasion. The Hutu army stops it, and in retaliation organizes a great massacre in Rwanda. Twenty thousand Tutsis die, hacked to pieces by Hutu machetes. (Other estimates put the figure at fifty thousand.) No outside observers are present, no international commissions, no media. I remember that a group of us, foreign correspondents, tried to get into Rwanda but were refused entrance by the authorities. We were reduced to gathering what information we could in Tanzania, from escapees—mainly women with children, terrified, wounded, hungry. The men were usually killed first, did not return home from expeditions. Many wars in Africa are waged without witnesses, secretively, in unreachable places, in silence, without the world's knowledge, or even the slightest attention. And thus it was with Rwanda. The border skirmishes, pogroms, massacres go on for years. Tutsi partisans (called "cockroaches" by the Hutus) burn villages and slaughter the locals. The Hutu villagers, in turn, supported by their army, organize rapes and massacres.

Living in such a country is difficult. There are still many villages and towns with a mixed population. Tutsis and Hutus live side by side, pass each other on the roads, work in the same place. And, privately, they conspire. Such a climate of suspicion, tension, and fear is fertile breeding ground for the old, tribal African tradition of underground sects, secret associations, and mafias. Real and imaginary. Everyone secretly belongs to something— and is convinced that everyone else, the Others, also belongs to something. And, naturally, the thing they belong to is a hostile, enemy organization.

. . .

Rwanda's twin country is its southern neighbor, Burundi. The two have a similar geography and social structure, and a common history going back centuries. Their destinies diverged only in 1959: in Rwanda, the peasant revolution of the Hutus was triumphant, and its leaders assumed power, whereas in Burundi the Tutsis maintained and even strengthened their rule, expanding the army and creating something akin to a feudal military dictatorship. Nevertheless, the preexisting, almost organic connections between the twin countries continued to function, and the massacre of Tutsis by Hutus in Rwanda evoked a retaliatory massacre of Hutus by Tutsis in Burundi, and vice versa.

In 1972, the Hutus from Burundi, emboldened by the example of their brothers in Rwanda, attempted to stage an insurrection, slaughtering, for starters, several thousand Tutsis, who, in response, killed more than a hundred thousand Hutus. It was not the fact of the massacre alone, for these occurred regularly in both countries, but its staggering proportions that created an uproar among the Hutus of Rwanda, who decided to react. They were further inspired by the fact that during the pogrom, several hundred thousand (a million, they sometimes say) Hutus from Burundi sought shelter in Rwanda, creating an enormous problem for this poor country already periodically beset by food shortages.

Taking advantage of this crisis (they are murdering our kinsmen in Burundi; we do not have the wherewithal to support a million immigrants), the commander in chief of the Rwandan military, General Juvénal Habyarimana, staged a coup d'état in 1973 and declared himself president. The coup exposed the profound rifts and conflicts within the Hutu community. The defeated president Grégoire Kayibana (who would later be starved to death) represented a moderately liberal Hutu clan from the country's central region. The new ruler, on the other hand, hailed from a radical, chauvinistic branch inhabiting Rwanda's northwest. (Habyarimana, one can say, is the Radovan Karadžić of the Rwandan Hutus.)

Habyarimana will rule for twenty-one years, until his death

in 1994. Massively built, powerful, energetic, he focuses all his attention on erecting an iron-clad dictatorship. He institutes a one-party system. He names himself party leader. All the country's citizens must be party members from the time of birth. The general now improves upon the all-too-simple scheme of enmity: Hutu versus Tutsi. He will enrich this formula by adding another dimension, a further division—those in power versus those in the opposition. If you are a loyal Tutsi, you can become the head of a hamlet or a village (although not a minister); if you criticize the authorities, however, you will end up behind bars or on the scaffold, even if you are 100 percent Hutu. The general was absolutely correct to proceed this way: Tutsis were not the only ones hostile to his dictatorship; there were also large numbers of Hutus who genuinely hated him and resisted him in every way they could. Finally, the conflict in Rwanda was not only a quarrel between castes, but also a violent clash between tyranny and democracy. In this sense the language of ethnic categories, and the mind-set it stems from, is terribly deceptive and misleading. It blurs and neglects the more profound truths—good versus evil, truth versus lies, democracy versus dictatorship—limiting one to a single, and indeed superficial and secondary dichotomy, a single contrast, a single set of oppositions: He is of infinite worth because he is Hutu; or he is worthless because he is Tutsi.

While strengthening the dictatorship was the first task to which Habyarimana devoted himself, gradual advances were also being made on a parallel front: the privatization of the state. With each passing year, Rwanda was increasingly becoming the private property of the clan from Gisenyi (the general's small hometown), or, more strictly speaking, the property of the president's wife, Agathe, and of her three brothers, Sagatawa, Seraphin, and Zed, as well as of a bevy of their cousins. Agathe and her brothers belonged to the clan called Akazu, and this name became the password that could open many doors within Rwanda's mysterious labyrinths. Sagatawa, Seraphin, and Zed had luxurious palaces around Gisenyi, from which, together with their sister and her husband, the general, they ruled over the army, the police, the banks, and the bureaucracy of Rwanda. So, a little nation somewhere in the mountains of a distant continent, ruled by a greedy family of voracious, despotic petty chieftains. How did it come to acquire such tragic worldwide renown?

I have already mentioned how in 1959 tens of thousands of Tutsis fled the country to save their lives. For years after, thousands upon thousands of others followed. Their camps stretched along Rwanda's borders in Zaire, Uganda, Tanzania, and Burundi, communities of unhappy and impatient exiles living with only one thought: to return home, to their (already mythic) herds. Life in such camps is listless, wretched, and hopeless. But there are people who are born in such places, reach adulthood, and still retain the desire to accomplish something, who try to fight for something. So it was with the Tutsis. Their main objective, of course, was returning to the lands of their ancestors. The ancestral ground is a sacred concept in Africa, a deeply desired and magnetic place, the source of life. But leaving a refugee camp is no simple matter; doing so is often forbidden by the local authorities. The one exception is Uganda, where a civil war has been raging for years, and disorder and confusion prevail. In the eighties, the young activist Yoweri Museveni starts a guerrilla war against the horrific regime of the psychopath and butcher Milton Obote. Museveni needs fighters. And he quickly finds them, because in addition to his Ugandan brethren, the young men from Rwandan refugee camps are volunteering: militant, battle-hungry Tutsis. Museveni gladly accepts them. They undergo military training in Uganda's forests, under the direction of professional instructors, and many of them go on to finish officer-training schools abroad. In January 1986, Museveni enters Kampala at the head of his divisions and seizes power. Many of these divisions are commanded by, or include in their ranks, Tutsis born in the refugee camps—sons of the fathers who had been driven out of Rwanda.

For a long time no one notices that there has arisen in Uganda a well-trained and battle-tested army of Tutsi avengers, who think of one thing only: how to revenge themselves for the disgrace and injury inflicted upon their families. They hold secret meetings, create an organization called the Rwandan Patriotic Front, and make preparations to attack. During the night of September 30, 1990, they disappear from the Ugandan army barracks and from the border camps, and at dawn enter Rwandan territory. The authorities in Kigali are completely surprised. Surprised and terrified. Habyarimana has a weak and demoralized army, and the distance from the Ugandan border to Kigali is not much more than 150 kilometers: the guerrillas could march into Kigali in a day or two. That is what would certainly have happened, for Habyarimana's troops offered no resistance, and maybe it would never have come to that hecatomb and carnage—the genocide of 1994—were it not for one telephone call. This was the call for help General Habyarimana made to the French president, François Mitterrand.

Mitterrand was under strong pressure from the French pro-African lobby. Whereas the majority of European capitals had radically broken with their colonial past, Paris had not. French society still includes a large, active, and well-organized army of people who made their careers in the colonial administration, spent their lives (quite well!) in the colonies, and now, as foreigners in Europe, feel useless and unwanted. At the same time, they believe deeply that France is not only a European country but also the community of all people partaking of French culture and language; that France, in other words, is also a global cultural and linguistic entity: *Francophonie*. This philosophy, translated into the simplistic language of geopolitics, holds that if someone, somewhere in the world, is attacking a French-speaking country, it is almost as if he were striking at France itself.

Moreover, the bureaucrats and generals of the pro-African lobby still suffered acutely from the Fashoda complex. A few words about this. In the nineteenth century, when European countries were dividing Africa among themselves, London and Paris were obsessed by a bizarre (although then quite understandable) notion: that their possessions on this continent be arranged in a straight line with territorial continuity. London wanted to have such a line stretching north to south, i.e., from Cairo to Cape Town, and Paris wanted it from west to east, i.e., from Dakar to Djibouti. Now, if we take a map of Africa and draw two perpendicular lines on it, they will cross in southern Sudan, in a place along the Nile where a small fishing village lies—Fashoda. Europe at the time was convinced that whoever first secured Fashoda would realize his expansionist ideal of an uninterrupted colonial empire. A race began between London and Paris. Both capitals sent military expeditions toward Fashoda. The French got there first. On July 10, 1898, covering on foot the difficult track from Dakar, Captain J. B. Marchand reached Fashoda and planted the French flag. Marchand's division consisted of 150 Senegalese—brave and devoted men. Paris went wild with joy. The French were bursting with pride. Two months later, however, the British arrived in Fashoda. The commander of that expedition, Lord Kitchener, realized with astonishment that the village was already occupied. Ignoring this, he raised the British flag. London went wild with joy. The British were bursting with pride. A fever of nationalist euphoria engulfed both countries. At first, neither side wanted to back down. There were many indicators that World War I might erupt then and there, in 1898—over Fashoda. In the end (for this is a long story), the French had to withdraw. England was victorious. Among old French colonials, the Fashoda episode would remain a painful wound, and they would instantly go on the attack at the news that somewhere, anywhere, the *Anglophones* were making a move on something.

And so it was this time, when Paris learned that the English-speaking Tutsis, from the territories of English-speaking Uganda, had invaded French-speaking Rwanda, and thus violated the borders of *Francophonie*.

The divisions of the Rwandan Patriotic Front were already closing in on the capital, and Habyarimana's government and clan were packing their bags, when airplanes deposited French paratroopers at the airport in Kigali. Officially, there were only two companies of them. But that was enough. The guerrillas wanted to fight Habyarimana's regime, but they preferred not to risk war with France, against which they wouldn't have stood a chance. They called off the offensive on Kigali but remained in Rwanda, permanently occupying its northeastern territories. The country was de facto partitioned, although both sides considered this to be a temporary, provisional situation. Habyarimana counted on being strong enough in time to expel the guerrillas, and they in turn believed the French would withdraw one day, and that the regime, together with the entire Akazu clan, would fall on the very next.

There is nothing worse than this state of being neither at war nor at peace. One group went on the attack hoping to enjoy the fruits of victory; but now this dream is dying—the offensive must be suspended. The mood is even darker among those who were attacked: yes, they survived, but they saw before their eyes the specter of defeat, realized that the end of their rule was possible. They now want to save themselves at all cost.

Three and a half years will pass from the 1990 fall offensive to the slaughter of April 1994. Violent disputes erupt within Rwanda's government between those favoring compromise through the creation of a national ruling coalition (Habyarimana's people plus the guerrillas) and members of the fanatical, despotic Akazu clan directed by Agathe and her brothers. Habyarimana himself hedges, hesitates, does not know what to do, and increasingly loses his influence over events. A radical branch of the

Akazu clan seizes the upper hand, rapidly and resolutely. The clan has its ideologues: they are the intellectuals, scholars, professors of history and philosophy from the Rwandan university in Butare— Ferdinand Nahimana, Casimir Bizimungu, Leon Mugesira, and several others. It is they who formulate the ideology that will legitimize genocide as the only possible solution, the only means of ensuring Hutu survival. The theory developed by Nahimana and his colleagues holds that the Tutsis are simply a foreign race. They are Nilotic people, who arrived in Rwanda from some- where along the Nile; conquered this land's indigenous inhabi- tants, the Hutus; and started to exploit, enslave, and destroy them from within. The Tutsis seized everything that is valuable in Rwanda: land, cattle, markets, and, with time, the state itself. The Hutus were relegated to the role of a conquered people, con- demned for centuries to live in poverty, hunger, and humiliation. But the Hutu nation must take back its identity and dignity, resume its place as an equal among the other nations of the world.

But what—Nahimana reflects, in dozens of speeches, articles, and brochures—does history teach us? Its experiences are tragic, and fill us with dispiriting pessimism. The entire history of Hutu- Tutsi relations is a dark passage of unceasing pogroms and massa- cres, of mutual extermination, forced migrations, furious hatred. There is not room enough in tiny Rwanda for two nations so for- eign and mortally at odds with each other. Moreover, Rwanda's population is growing at a dizzying rate. By mid-century, the country had two million inhabitants; now, fifty years later, close to nine million live here. So what is the way out of this cursed circle, what escape is there from this cruel fate, for which the Hutus themselves, as Mugesira admits self-critically, are respon- sible: "In 1959 we committed a fatal error, allowing the Tutsis to escape. We should have acted then: erased them from the surface of the earth." The professor believes that now is the last opportu- nity to correct this mistake. The Tutsis must return to their real native land, somewhere along the Nile. "Let us send them back there," he exhorts, "alive or dead." That is what the scholars from

Butare envision as the only answer, the final solution: someone must die, must permanently cease to exist.

Preparations begin. The army, which numbered five thousand, is expanded to thirty-five thousand. The Presidential Guard is honed to become a second strike force, elite units heavily armed with modern weaponry (arms and materiel are sent by France, South Africa, and Egypt; France also provides instructors). But the greatest emphasis is placed on forming a paramilitary organization, Interahamwe (meaning "Let Us Strike Together"). Joining it and undergoing military and ideological training are people from villages and towns, unemployed youths and poor peasants, schoolchildren, students, office workers—a huge throng, a veritable popular movement, whose task it will be to carry out the apocalypse. Simultaneously, the prefects and deputy prefects are ordered to start drawing up lists of those in the opposition, as well as all kinds of suspicious, uncertain, ambiguous individuals, malcontents of various sorts, pessimists, skeptics, liberals. The theoretical mouthpiece of the Akazu clan is the newspaper *Kangura,* but the main organ for propaganda, as well as the principal medium through which orders are disseminated to the largely illiterate populace, is Radio Mille Collines, which later, during the slaughter, will broadcast this call several times daily: "Death! Death! Graves with Tutsi bodies are still only half full. Hurry, and fill them to the top!"

In the middle of 1993, African states compel Habyarimana to enter into an agreement with the Rwandan Patriotic Front. The guerrillas are to participate in government and in the parliament, and to make up 40 percent of the army. But such a compromise is unacceptable to the Akazu clan. They would thereby lose their monopoly on power, something they will not agree to. They declare that the hour of final reckoning has arrived.

On April 6, 1994, "unknown perpetrators" fire a rocket shooting down the plane of President Habyarimana as it is making its landing approach to Kigali. Habyarimana was returning from abroad in disgrace, having signed a pact with the enemies. The downing of his plane is the signal to begin the slaughter of the regime's opponents: the Tutsis first and foremost, but also the large Hutu opposition. The officially orchestrated massacre of the defenseless population lasts three months, until the day the RPF troops seize control of the country, forcing the adversary to flee.

Estimates of the number of victims vary. Some say half a million, others one million. No one will ever know for sure. The most terrifying fact is that people who only yesterday were guilty of nothing today were murdering other completely innocent people. And so even if the number of victims was not one million, but, let us say, just one, would it not be proof enough that the devil is among us, and that in the spring of 1994 he just happened to be in Rwanda?

Between a half million and one million murdered—that is of course a tragically high number. But, given the hellish striking power of Habyarimana's army, its helicopters, heavy machine guns, artillery, and armored vehicles, many more could have been killed in the course of three months of systematic shooting. Yet this did not happen. Most perished not on account of bombs or heavy machine guns; instead they were hacked and bludgeoned to death with the most primitive of weapons—machetes, hammers, spears, and sticks. For the leaders of the regime had more than just the ultimate goal—the final solution—in mind. On the road to the Highest Ideal, which was nothing less than the total annihilation of the enemy, it was critical that the nation be united in crime; through mass participation in the criminal act there would arise an all-unifying feeling of guilt, so that every citizen, having on his conscience another's death, would be haunted from that moment by someone else's inalienable right to retaliation, behind which he could glimpse the specter of his own end.

Whereas in the Nazi and Stalinist systems death was meted

out by executioners from specialized institutions, the SS or the NKVD, and the deed perpetrated by independent operatives in hidden locations, in Rwanda the point was for everyone to be a bearer of death, for the crime to be a mass, popular, and even elemental act—so that there would remain not a single pair of hands not steeped in the blood of those deemed by the regime to be enemies.

That is why, later, the terrified and defeated Hutus would flee in such numbers to Zaire, and once there roam from place to place, carrying their meager possessions on their heads. Those in Europe, observing the endless columns on their television screens, could not fathom what force propelled these emaciated wanderers, what power commanded these skeletons to keep walking, in punitive formations, without stopping or resting, without food or drink, without speaking or smiling, trudging humbly, obediently, and with vacant eyes along their ghastly road of guilt and anguish.

The Black Crystals of the Night

The orange ball of the sinking sun is just visible at the far end of the road along which we are driving. It will disappear at any moment behind the horizon and cease blinding us, and then night will descend, rapidly, and we will be left alone with the dark. Out of the corner of my eye I notice that Sebuya, the driver of the Toyota, is growing anxious. In Africa, drivers avoid traveling at night—darkness unnerves them. They are so afraid of it that they may flatly refuse to drive after sunset. I have observed them at times when they were nevertheless compelled to do so. Instead of keeping their eyes focused straight ahead, they begin to peer apprehensively to the sides. Their features grow tense and sharp. Beads of sweat appear on their brows. They fidget in their seats, and slide down behind the steering wheel as if someone were shooting at the car. Despite the fact that the roads are rough, full of potholes, washouts, and ruts, instead of slowing down, they accelerate, tearing carelessly along, anything just to reach a place where there are people, where one can hear the hum of human voices and where the lights are shining.

"*Kuna nini?*" I ask (in Swahili: did something bad happen?). They never answer, just careen along amid clouds of dust and the clang of metal.

—"*Hatari?*" I ask after a while (some kind of danger?). They remain silent, paying no attention.

They are afraid of something, grappling with a demon that I do not see and do not understand. For me, this night has well-defined and straightforward characteristics: it is dark, almost black, hot, windless, and, if we stop and Sebuya turns off the engine, full of silence. But according to Sebuya, I know nothing of darkness. In particular, I do not know that day and night are two distinct realities, two separate worlds. In daytime, man can cope somehow with his environment, can exist and endure, even live peacefully; the night, however, renders him defenseless, easy prey to his enemies, and conceals forces with nefarious designs upon his life. That is why fear, which during the day slumbers in a man's heart, secretive and subdued, is transformed at night into an overpowering fright, a haunting, tormenting nightmare. How important it is at that time to be in a group! The presence of others brings relief, soothes the nerves, lessens the tension.

"Hapa?" (here?) Sebuya asked me, when we caught sight of the mud shacks of a village by the roadside. We were in western Uganda, not far from the Nile, driving toward the Congo. It was getting dark and Sebuya was already very jittery. I could see that I would be unable to persuade him to keep going, so agreed to spending the night here.

The villagers took us in without enthusiasm, even reluctantly, which is strange and surprising in these parts. But Sebuya pulled out a wad of shillings, and the sight of money, so extraordinary and tempting for these people, decided things in our favor. Before long, a cleanly swept clay hut lined with fresh grasses had been prepared for us. Sebuya fell quickly into a deep sleep, but I was soon awakened by an army of bustling and aggressive insects. Spiders, cockroaches, crickets, ants, a multitude of tiny, soundless, and busy creatures, which while often invisible, could be felt slithering, clinging, tickling, pinching—sleep was impossible. For a long time I turned from side to side, until finally, exhausted and defeated, I stepped out in front of the hut and sat down, leaning my back against the wall. The moon was shining brightly and the night was clear, silvery. All around was profound silence. Cars rarely appear in these parts, and the wildlife has long been killed off and eaten.

Suddenly, I heard murmurs, steps, then the rapid patter of bare feet. Then silence once more. I looked around, but at first saw nothing. After a moment, the murmurs and steps again. Then silence again. I began to study the features of the landscape—a clump of thin shrubs, several umbrella-shaped acacias in the distance, some rocks protruding from the ground. At last, I spied a group of eight men, carrying, on a simple stretcher made of branches, another man covered with a piece of cloth. They moved in a peculiar fashion. They did not walk in a straight line, but advanced furtively, creeping in one direction, then in another, maneuvering. They crouched down behind a shrub, looked about cautiously, and then scurried to the next hiding place. They circled, swerved, stopped, and started, as if they were children playing some elaborate game of espionage. I observed their bent, half-naked silhouettes, their nervous gestures, the queer, stealthful behavior, until finally they disappeared for good behind a ridge, and the only thing around me again was the silent, clear, inviolate night.

At dawn we drove on. I asked Sebuya if he knew the name of the people in whose village we had spent the night. "They are called Amba," he said. Then, after a moment, added: *"Kabila mbaya"* (this means, roughly, "bad people"). He did not want to tell me any more—here, one avoids evil even as a subject of conversation, preferring not to step into that territory, careful not to call the wolf out of the forest. As we drove, I reflected upon the event I had inadvertently witnessed. The nocturnal drama, those puzzling zigzags and twists of the bearers, their haste and anxiety, concealed a mystery to which I had no key. Something was going on here. But what?

People like the Amba and their kinsmen believe profoundly that the world is ruled by supernatural forces. These forces are particular—spirits that have names, spells that can be defined. It is they that inform the course of events and imbue them with meaning, decide our fate, determine everything. For this reason nothing happens by chance; chance simply does not exist. Let us consider this example: Sebuya is driving his car, has an accident, and dies. Why exactly did Sebuya have an accident? That very same day, all over the world, millions of cars reached their destinations safely—but Sebuya had an accident and died. White people will search for various causes. For instance, his brakes malfunctioned. But this kind of thinking leads nowhere, explains nothing. Because why was it precisely Sebuya's brakes that malfunctioned? That very same day, all over the world, millions of cars were on the road and their brakes were working just fine— but Sebuya's were not. Why? White people, whose way of thinking is the height of naivete, will say that Sebuya's brakes malfunctioned because he failed to have them inspected and repaired in good time. But why was it precisely Sebuya who failed to do this? Why, that very same day, a million . . . etc., etc.

We have now established that the white man's way of reasoning is quite unhelpful. But it gets worse! The white man, having determined that the cause of Sebuya's accident and death was bad brakes, prepares a report and closes the case. Closes it!? But it is precisely now that the case should begin! Sebuya died because someone cast a spell on him. This is simple and self-evident. What we do not know, however, is the identity of the perpetrator, and that is what we must now ascertain.

Speaking in the most general terms, a wizard did it. A wizard is a bad man, always acting with evil intent. There are two types of wizards (although our Western languages do not differentiate adequately between them). The first is more dangerous, for he is the devil in human form. The English call him witch. The witch is a dangerous person. Neither his appearance nor his behavior betray his satanic nature. He does not wear special clothing, he does not have magical instruments. He does not boil potions, does not prepare poisons, does not fall into a trance, and does not perform incantations. He acts by means of the psychic power with which he was born. Malefaction is a congenital trait of his personality. The fact that he does evil and brings misfortune owes nothing to his predilections; it brings him no special pleasure. He simply is that way.

If you are near him, he need only look at you. Sometimes, you will catch someone watching you carefully, piercingly, and at length. It might be a witch, just then casting a spell on you. Still, distance is no obstacle for him. He can cast a spell from one side of Africa to the other, or even farther.

The second type of wizard is gentler, weaker, less demonic. Whereas the witch was born as evil incarnate, the sorcerer (for that is what this weaker sort is called in English) is a career wizard, for whom the casting of spells is a learned profession, a craft, and a source of livelihood.

To condemn you to illness or bring some other misfortune down on you, or even to kill you, the witch has no need of props or aids. All he need do is direct his infernal, devastating will to wound and annihilate you. Before long, illness will fell you, and death will not be far behind. The sorcerer does not have such destructive powers within himself. To destroy you, he must resort to various magical procedures, mysterious rites, ritual gestures. For example, if you are walking at night through thick bush and lose an eye, it is not because you accidentally impaled yourself on a protruding yet invisible branch. Nothing, after all, happens by accident! It is simply that an enemy of yours wanted to exact vengeance and went to see a sorcerer. The sorcerer fashioned a little clay figure—your likeness—and, with the tip of a juniper branch dipped in hen's blood, gouged out its eye. In this way he issued a verdict on your eye—cast a spell on it. If one night you are wending your way through dense bush and a branch pokes out your eye, it will be proof positive that an enemy of yours wanted to avenge himself, went to see a sorcerer, etc. Now it is up to you to uncover who this enemy is, go visit a sorcerer, and in turn order your own revenge.

If Sebuya dies in a car crash, then the most important thing for his family now is to ascertain not whether his brakes were bad, for that is of no consequence, but whether the spells that caused this death were cast by a wizard-devil (witch) or an ordinary wizard-craftsman (sorcerer). It is a critical question, entailing a long and intricate investigation, into which will be pressed various fortune-tellers, elders, medicine men, and so forth. The outcome of this detective work is of utmost significance! If Sebuya died as a result of spells cast by a wizard-devil, then tragedy has befallen the entire family and clan, because a curse like that affects the whole community, and Sebuya's death is merely a foretoken, the tip of the iceberg: there is nothing to do but await more illnesses and deaths. But if Sebuya perished because a wizard-craftsman wanted it thus, then the situation is far less dire. The craftsman can strike and destroy only individuals, isolated targets: the family and the clan can sleep in peace!

Evil is the curse of the world, and that is why I must keep wizards, who are its agents, carriers, and propagators, as far away from myself and my clan as possible; their presence poisons the air, spreads disease, and makes life impossible, turning it into its opposite—death. The wizard, by definition, lives and practices among others, in another village, in another clan or tribe. Our contemporary suspicion of and antipathy for the Other, the Stranger, goes back to the fear our tribal ancestors felt toward the Outsider, seeing him as the carrier of evil, the source of misfortune. Pain, fire, disease, drought, and hunger did not come from nowhere. Someone must have brought them, inflicted them, disseminated them. But who? Not my people, not those closest to me—they are good. Life is possible only among good people, and I am alive, after all. The guilty are therefore the Others, the Strangers. That is why, seeking retribution for our injuries and setbacks, we quarrel with them, enter into conflicts, conduct wars. In a word, if unhappiness has befallen us, its source is not within us, but elsewhere, outside, beyond us and our community, far away, in Others.

I had long forgotten about Sebuya, about our expedition to the Congo, and about the night spent in the Amba village, when years later, in Maputo, a book fell into my hands about magic in eastern Africa, specifically a report by the anthropologist E. H. Winter on studies he conducted among the Amba.

The Amba, Winter states, are a highly unusual social group. Like other tribes on the continent, they take seriously the existence of evil and the danger of spells, and thus fear and hate wizards, but contrary to the widely held view that wizards dwell among others, that they act from without, from a distance, the Amba maintain that the wizards are among them, within their families, within their villages, that they form an integral part of their community. This belief has resulted in the gradual disintegration of Amba society, corroded as it has become by hatred, consumed by suspicion, confounded by free-floating fear. Anyone can be a wizard, brother fears brother, son fears father, a mother fears her own children. The Amba rejected the comfortable and comforting view that the enemy is the stranger, the foreigner, the man of a different faith or skin color. No! Possessed by a peculiar kind of masochism, the Amba live in torment and distress; at this very moment, evil can be under my own roof, asleep in my bed, eating from the same dish as I. And there is an additional difficulty: it is impossible to determine what wizards look like. After all, no one has seen one. We know they exist because we see the results of their actions: they caused the drought, as a result of which there is nothing to eat, fires keep igniting, many people are sick, someone is always dying. Plainly, wizards never rest, endlessly occupied as they are with raining misfortunes, defeats, and tragedies down upon our heads.

The Amba are a homogeneous, cohesive community who live in small villages scattered in sparsely wooded bush; often they suspect a neighboring village, inhabited by their kinsmen, of harboring the wizard who has caused them misfortune. They declare war on the village they judge to be evil. The besieged community defends itself, and sometimes undertakes a war of retaliation. The unceasing wars the Amba wage among themselves leave them thoroughly weakened and defenseless against aggressors from other tribes. Nonetheless, they are so preoccupied with the internecine threat that they are oblivious to this danger. Paralyzed by the specter of an enemy within the gates, they tumble unrestrained into the abyss.

The depressing fate that has come to weigh upon them at least unites them, makes possible a paradoxical solidarity. If I become convinced, say, that a wizard hiding in my village is plaguing me, I can move to another one, and even if that village is at war with my own, I will be hospitably received. This is because all Ambas appreciate how much a wizard can torment you. Consider the paths along which you walk: he can scatter on them pebbles, leaves, feathers, little twigs, dead flies, monkey hairs, or mango peelings. It is enough merely to step on any one of those things—you will at once sicken and die. And such small nothings can be found on every trail. So, practically speaking, you cannot move? That is correct, you cannot. You are afraid even to step out of your mud house, for right there on the threshold might be a piece of the bark of a baobab, or a poisoned acacia thorn.

The wizard wants to hound us to death—that is his objective. There is no medicine against him, there is no protection. The only option is flight. That is why the people I saw that night, carrying a sick man on a stretcher, were moving so furtively: they were escaping. A wizard had cast a spell on the sick man, and the illness was a sign that the wizard was preparing the man's death. That is why the victim's relatives, under the cover of darkness, were trying to hide him, conceal him from the wizard's view, save his life.

Although no one knows what the wizard looks like, we know a lot about him. He moves only at night. He participates in ceremonies during which sentences are meted out—we are sleeping, and over there, unbeknownst to us, our demise has been decided. He can transport himself to wherever he wishes with fantastic speed, quicker than lightning. He adores human flesh, dotes on human blood. He does not speak, so we cannot recognize his voice. We do not know his facial features, the shape of his head.

But it is possible that one day a man will be born with such strength of vision and such willpower that, staring intently into the blackness, he will see the night begin to thicken, stiffen, coalesce into black crystals, and then will see these crystals compose themselves ever more clearly into the silent and dark visage of a wizard.

These People, Where Are They?

They are supposed to be here—but where are they? Rain is falling and it is cold. The clouds hang low—thick, dark, motionless. As far as the eye can see: swamps, bogs, floodwaters. The single road leading here is also flooded. Our cars, although they are powerful all-terrain vehicles, have become stuck in the mud, buried in the black, viscous goo, and are now standing tilted at the most extraordinary angles, in ruts, puddles, narrow crevices. We have had to climb down and continue on foot, getting drenched in heavy downpours. We pass a high escarpment, from whose summit a flock of peacocks surveys us carefully and anxiously. I notice a man in the grass by the roadside. He is curled up, shriveled, shivering with malaria; he does not extend his hand, does not beg, looks at us with eyes that ask for nothing, that are devoid even of curiosity.

In the distance, far away, we spot several ruined barracks. Other than that, it is desolate. And wet, for this is the rainy season.

This place is called Itang. It is located in western Ethiopia, close to the border with Sudan. For several years now a camp has stood here housing 150,000 Nuer—refugees from the Sudanese war. There were still here just a few days ago. But today the place is deserted. Where did they go? What happened to them? The only thing that disturbs the stillness of these swamps, the only thing you hear, is the croaking of the frogs, a frenzied, toadlike uproar, loud, relentless, deafening.

In the summer of 1991 the United Nations high commissioner for refugee affairs, Sadako Ogata, was going to Ethiopia to visit the camp in Itang, and I had been invited to join her. I dropped everything and went. It was a rare opportunity: camps like these are located in remote places, difficult to reach; and, more frequently than not, there is no admittance. Life in them is sheer misery, a sad vegetative existence, perpetually on the brink of death. Yet other than a group of doctors and the employees of various charitable organizations, few people know much about these camps; the world scrupulously isolates such places of collective suffering, preferring not to know.

I always thought that it would be impossible to see Itang. First, you have to get to Addis Ababa. There, you must charter (but from whom?) and pay for (but with what?) an airplane to take you five hundred kilometers to Gambēla, the only town near Itang with an airport. Since the town borders Sudan, securing permission to land would be indescribably difficult. But let us assume that you have a plane, and even permission. You arrive in Gambēla. What now? Whom should you go see in this poor little town, where a number of Ethiopians stand motionless, barefoot in torrential rain in the empty marketplace? What are they thinking about? What are they waiting for? And where in the world are you going to find a car in Gambēla, or a driver, people to help you pull the car out of the mud, ropes, and shovels? And what about provisions? But let us assume you have all these. How long would it take you to reach your destination? Would one day be enough? How many sentries at roadblocks along the way would you have to chat up, placate, bribe, to be allowed to continue? All this only to arrive at the gates, and have the guard order you to turn back—because an epidemic of cholera or dysentery has just broken out in the camp, or the commander who must give his consent is not present, or there is no one to interpret for you with the Nuer. Or, as is now happening to us, you see no one on the other side of the gate, not a single living soul.

Sudan was the first country in Africa to gain independence after World War II. Prior to that it was a British colony, distinct entities artificially, bureaucratically glued together: the Arab-Muslim North and the black-Christian (and animistic) South. A long-standing antagonism and hatred existed between these two populations, because the northern Arabs for years had invaded the South, captured its inhabitants, and sold them into slavery.

How could these two hostile worlds coexist in one independent nation? They could not—and that is exactly what the British wanted. In those years, the European powers were convinced that they could formally give up their colonies, while continuing de facto to govern them—being needed in Sudan, for example, for continual reconciliation between the Muslims of the North and the Christians and animists of the South. Before long, however, these imperial delusions lay in tatters. As early as 1962, the first North-South civil war erupted in Sudan (already preceded by earlier revolts and insurrections in the South). When I was traveling to the South for the first time in 1960, I needed in addition to a Sudanese visa another special visa, on a separate piece of paper. In Juba, the largest town in the South, a border patrol officer took it from me. "How can you do that?!" I snorted angrily. "I need it to reach the border with the Congo, which is still two hundred kilometers from here!" The officer pointed at himself and said, not without a measure of pride: "I am the border!" Indeed, beyond the town's tollgates unfolded an expanse over which the government in Khartoum exercised no significant control. It remains thus to this day: Juba is protected by an Arab garrison from Khartoum, and the province itself is in the hands of the guerrillas.

The first Sudanese war lasted ten years, until 1972. During the next ten years, a fragile, impermanent peace prevailed, but in 1983, following an attempt by the Muslim government in Khartoum to impose Islamic law, or sharia, on the entire country, a ghastly new chapter of the war began, and continues to the present day. It is the longest and largest war in the history of Africa, and probably the largest in the world right now, but because it is being waged in the most remote backwaters of our planet, and does not directly threaten anyone in, say, Europe or America, it does not arouse much interest. Moreover, the theaters of this war, its vast and tragic killing fields, are for all intents and purposes— both because of the region's inherent impediments to communication and Khartoum's draconian restrictions—inaccessible to the media. The majority of people in the world have not the slightest idea that a great war is being fought in Sudan.

It is being fought on many fronts, and also on many levels, and today the conflict between the North and the South is not even paramount. In fact, that old divide can confuse and distort the true picture. Let us begin in the north of this immense country of 2.5 million square kilometers. The North consists in large measure of the Sahara and the Sahel, which we associate with a boundlessness of sand and weathered rocky rubble. Northern Sudan is sand and rocks, but it is not only that. As one flies over this part of Africa from Addis Ababa to Europe, an extraordinary view presents itself below: passing through the golden-yellow surface of the Sahara, which stretches as far as the eye can see, is a great, shockingly green band of fields and plantations—the shores of the Nile, which flows here in wide, gentle semicircles. The border between the deep ocher of the Sahara and the emerald of these fields is as sharp as if it had been carved with a knife: there are no intermediate shades here, no gradations. Immediately beyond the last little shoots of a plantation begin the first small clods of the desert.

Once upon a time, these riverine fields supported millions of Arab fellaheen, as well as nomadic peoples who now and then stopped here. With time, however, and especially since the middle of the twentieth century and independence, the fellaheen started to be ousted by their wealthy kinsmen from Khartoum, who, together with the generals, and with the help of the army and the police, gained possession of these fertile lands along the Nile, creating on them gigantic plantations of export crops—cotton, rubber, sesame. Thus came into being a powerful class of Arab landowners, which in alliance with the generals and the bureaucratic elite seized power in 1956 and holds it to this day, waging a war against the "Negro" South, which it treats like a colony, and simultaneously oppressing its fellow ethnic countrymen, the Arabs from the North.

Dispossessed, dislodged, deprived of land and cattle, the Sudanese Arabs must find someplace to go, something to do, a means of livelihood. The Khartoum oligarchy folds some of them into its ever larger army, others into the ranks of its vast police and bureaucracy. But the rest? That multitude of the landless and uprooted? These the regime will try to direct toward the South.

The inhabitants of the North number around twenty million, those of the South around six. The latter are composed of dozens of tribes, speaking a host of languages, adhering to various religions and cults. In this multitribal ocean of the South, two groups nevertheless stand out; together they make up half the population of this part of the country. They are related (although sometimes also mutually embattled) peoples: the Dinka and the Nuer. You can mistake each for the other at a distance: they are both tall, (around the two-meter mark), slender, with very dark skin. A beautiful, well-built, dignified, and even somewhat haughty race. Anthropologists have long wondered how they came to be so tall and thin. They subsist almost exclusively on milk, sometimes supplemented by the blood of their cows, which they raise, worship, and love. Killing cattle is forbidden, and women cannot touch them. The Dinka and the Nuer have subordinated their lives to the needs and requirements of their animals. They spend the dry season with them near the rivers—most importantly, the Nile, the Ghazal, and the Sobat—and in the rainy season, when grass turns the distant plateaux green, they leave the rivers and head upcountry with their cattle. The lives of the Dinka and the Nuer pass in this immemorial rhythm, this pendulum-like, almost ritualistic wandering between the riverbanks and the pastures on the plateaux of the Upper Nile. To exist, they must have space, land without boundaries, a wide, open horizon. Hemmed in, they sicken, turn into skeletons, wane, die.

I do not know how exactly the war began, it was so long ago. Did soldiers from the government forces steal a cow from the Dinka? Did the Dinka set out to retrieve it? Did shooting break out? Were there casualties? It must have happened something like that. Of course, the cow was just a pretext. The Arab lords in Khartoum could not tolerate the shepherds from the South having the same rights as they did. The people from the South could not accept as their rulers, in an independent Sudan, the sons of slave traders. The South demanded secession, their own state. The North decided to destroy the rebels. Massacres began. The war is said to have claimed a million lives by now. For the first ten years, a spontaneous, poorly organized guerrilla movement, Anya-Nya, operated in the South. Later, in 1983, a Dinka career colonel, John Garang, organized the Sudanese People's Liberation Army (SPLA), which now controls most of the region.

The war flares up, dies down, then explodes again. Although it has gone on so many years, I have heard of no one trying to write its history. In Europe, there are shelves of books dedicated to every war, archives full of documents, special rooms in museums. Nothing of the kind exists in Africa. Here, even the longest and greatest war is quickly forgotten, falls into oblivion. Its traces vanish by the day after: the dead must be buried immediately, new huts erected on the site of burned ones.

Documents? There never were any. There are no written orders, no ordnance maps, cryptographs, leaflets, proclamations, newspapers, letters. The custom of writing memoirs and diaries does not exist (most frequently, there is simply no paper). There is no tradition of writing histories. Most important—who would do this? There are no collectors of memorabilia, curators, archivists, historians, archaeologists. It is actually just as well there are no such people nosing about the battlefields. They would be quickly spotted by the police, imprisoned, and, suspected of spying, shot. History in these parts appears suddenly, descends like a deus ex machina, reaps its bloody harvest, seizes its prey, and disappears. What exactly is it? Why has it chosen us to cast its evil eye upon? It is better not to think about it. Better not to pry.

Getting back to the Sudan. The war, which began with lofty-sounding slogans, the drama of a young state (the North: we must maintain the country's unity; the South: we are fighting for independence), with time degenerates into a war waged by various military castes against their own nation, a war of the armed against the defenseless. For all this is occurring in a poor country, a country of hungry people, where someone reaching for a weapon, for a machete or a machine gun, is doing so first and foremost in order to grab some food, to get something to eat. It is a war over a handful of corn, a bowl of rice. All thefts are easier here, in this country of enormous distances and roadless expanses, of poor communication and transportation, of a small and scattered population—conditions under which robbery, pillage, and banditry go unpunished, if only for lack of any sort of control or supervision.

There are three types of armed forces conducting this war. There is the government army—an instrument of the Khartoum elite—commanded by the president, General Omar Hassan al-Bashir. Cooperating with the army are numerous official and secret police units, Muslim brotherhoods, the private regiments of large landowners.

Opposed to this ruling force are the guerrillas of John Garang's SPLA, as well as various units in the South that have broken away from the SPLA.

The third and final category of armed combatants are the countless so-called militias: paramilitary groups of young people (often children) of tribal origins, commanded by various local or clan chieftains, who, depending on the situation and the benefit therein, will cooperate with either the army or the SPLA (African militias are a product of recent years, an anarchistic, aggressive, and expanding force, which destabilizes states, armies, organized guerrilla groups, and political movements).

Who are all these armies, divisions, legions, posses, and corps—so numerous and so long embattled—arrayed against? Sometimes, it is each other. But most frequently it is their own nation they are fighting, in other words, the defenseless—which means, in particular, women and children. But why are they against women and children? Could it be that these armed men are governed by some kind of a biological antifeminism? Of course not. They attack and rob groups of women and children because women and children are the targets of international aid: it is they for whom the sacks of flour and rice are intended, the boxes of biscuits and powdered milk, things of no consequence in Europe, but here, between the sixth and twelfth degrees of latitude, priceless. One doesn't always actually have to dispossess the women of these treasures. It suffices simply to surround the delivery plane as it lands, confiscate the sacks and boxes, and carry or drive them over to one's regiment.

For years now the regime in Khartoum has availed itself of the weapon of hunger to defeat the South's inhabitants. It is doing today with the Dinka and the Nuer what Stalin did with the Ukrainians in 1932: it is starving them to death.

People are not hungry because there is no food in the world.

There is plenty of it; there is a surplus, in fact. But between those who want to eat and the bursting warehouses stands a tall obstacle indeed: politics. Khartoum restricts the number of flights bringing supplies for the hungry. Many of the planes that reach their destination are robbed by the local chieftains. Whoever has weapons, has food. Whoever has food, has power. We are here among people who do not contemplate transcendence and the existence of the soul, the meaning of life and the nature of being. We are in a world in which man, crawling on the earth, tries to dig a few grains of wheat out of the mud, just to survive another day.

Itang:

We walked over to where some barracks stood. This must have been the hospital, now ravaged, ruined. But by whom? The beds are turned over, the tables broken, the cabinets thrown open. The new X-ray machine smashed with rocks, twisted, its levers torn off, its control panel, with its dials and clocks, crushed. It must have been the only X-ray machine within a five-hundred-kilometer radius. Now someone has turned it into useless scrap metal. But who? And why? Next to it lies an electrical generator, also battered, broken. The only technological objects (besides, of course, weapons) for endless miles in every direction, now rendered useless, turned into junk.

We walked from there along a causeway to the only dry area. Stagnant water on both sides, the smell of rot, raging mosquitoes. Marshes and more marshes, and among them a few shanties, most of them empty, but some with people sitting or lying in them. In the water, then? Yes, in the water—I saw it with my own eyes. In the end, a hundred, two hundred people were assembled for us. Someone ordered them to stand in a half circle. They did so silently, motionless. Where have the others gone, those one hundred fifty thousand? Where did they all set off to one night? Into Sudan. Why? The leaders ordered it. The residents of the camp are people who have been hungry for years, no longer able to comprehend, disoriented, without will. It is good that someone still orders them to do something, that he realizes that they exist, wants something from them. Why did they not leave with the others? It is impossible to ascertain. Do they want something? No, nothing. As long as they continue to receive aid, they will live. If aid does not come, they will die. Yesterday, they received aid. And the day before yesterday. So it really isn't so bad; there is nothing to ask for.

An older man gives them the signal to disperse. I ask if I might be allowed to take a photograph. Of course I am allowed. Here, everything is allowed.

The Well

Someone is waking me up; I feel a light, careful touch. The face that leans over me is dark, and above it I see a white turban, so bright it glows, as if it were phosphorescent. It is still night, but there is movement all around. Women are dismantling shelters, boys are placing brushwood on the fire. There is haste in this bustle, a race against time: one must accomplish as much as possible, i.e., break camp and get on the road, before the sun rises and the heat starts. These people feel no connection to the place in which they happen to be. They will soon depart, leaving no trace. In their ballads, which they sing in the evenings, is a constantly repeated refrain: "My country? My country is where the rain falls."

But it is a long way till evening. First, one must prepare oneself for the road. Most important, the camels must be watered at the well. This lasts a long time, because they are capable of swallowing great quantities, laying in reserves, as it were, something neither man nor any other beast can do. That completed, the boys milk them, filling flat, leather skins with the acidic, somewhat tart milk. Then the sheep and goats drink. There are perhaps two hundred of them. The herds are tended by women. Finally, people drink—men first, then women and children.

Now the first streak of light colors the horizon—a portent of day, and the call to morning prayer. It is the men who pray, first washing their faces with a handful of water, a ritual that requires the same concentration as prayer: not a single drop of the precious liquid, just as not a single word of God, can be wasted.

The women now offer each man a bowl of tea. The tea has been boiled with sugar and mint and is thick as honey and fortifying; in the dry season, when there is a shortage of food, it must sustain them all day, until the next bowlful—dinner.

The sun appears, it grows light, and it is high time to be on the road. First, the herd of camels, led by the men and the boys. Next, the sheep and goats mill about in clouds of dust. Immediately after them, the women and children. That is the order in which a group of animals and people customarily travels; this time, however, at the very end, walk Hamed and his donkey, and I. Hamed is a merchant from Berbera, in whose little hotel I had spent a night. When he told me that he was setting off with his cousin to visit his brother in Laascaanood, I asked if he would take me along.

But where is Berbera? Where is Laascaanood? Both lie in northern Somalia, Berbera on the Gulf of Aden, Laascaanood on the Hawd Plateau. At dawn, my companions prayed toward Mecca facing north, with the sun to their right. The geography of this region is intricate, entangled, and god forbid you go astray: in this desert climate, a mistake means death. Whoever has been here knows that these are the hottest places on earth. But only someone who has come to know them well can fully comprehend what I am saying. Daytime hours during the dry season, especially around noon, are a hell almost impossible to bear. All around, everything is burning. Even the shade is hot, even the wind is ablaze. As if a meteorite were passing in the vicinity, its thermal radiation reducing everything to ashes. People, animals, and plants grow still, stiff. Silence descends, a lifeless, overwhelming quiet.

We are at this very moment advancing across the empty trackless expanse toward that blinding phenomenon, the fiery peak of day, toward the torture of scorching heat and exhaustion, from which, moreover, there is no adequate shelter or escape. No one speaks, as if the march itself required all one's attention and energy, although it is, after all, an everyday activity, a monotonous routine, a way of life. From time to time only one can hear the sound of a stick beating the back of a lazy camel, or women shouting at the unruly goats.

Eleven o'clock approaches; the column slows, then stops and scatters. Everyone tries to hide from the sun. The only way to do so is to get beneath one of the wide, branching acacias that grow here and there, whose shallow, tattered canopies are shaped like umbrellas: there is shade there, a smidgen of hidden coolness. Aside from those trees, it's just sand and more sand, everywhere. Maybe some thorny shrubs. Bunches of burned, coarse grass. Strips of gray, brittle moss. And, very occasionally, a protruding stone or two, some weathered boulders, heaps of stony rubble.

"Wouldn't it have been better to stay there, by the well?" I ask Hamed, dead tired. We are barely on the third day of our journey, and already I feel that I cannot go on. We sit leaning against a gnarled tree trunk, in a narrow band of shade, so skimpy that in addition to us, only the donkey's head can fit, while the rest of his body broils in the sun.

"No," he replied, "because the Ogaden are approaching from the west, and we do not have the strength to resist them."

I realized in that instant that our peregrination was no mere wandering from place to place, but that as we walked we were participating in a struggle, in ceaseless and dangerous maneuvers, in collisions and clashes, which could at any moment end badly.

The Somalis are a single nation, several million strong. They share a common language, history, culture, territory, and religion: Islam. About one quarter of the population live in the south and an engaged in farming, growing sorghum, corn, beans, and bananas. But the majority are owners of herds, nomads. It is they with whom I am traveling now, on the great expanse of semi-desert somewhere between Berbera and Laascaanood. The Somalis are divided into several large clans (such as Isaaq, Daarood, Dir, Hawiye), which are each in turn subdivided into smaller clans, of which there are dozens, and further still into kinship groups, of which there are hundreds, even thousands. The arrangements, alliances, and conflicts within these familial associations and constellations make up the history of Somali society.

The Somali is born somewhere on the road, in a shack-tent or directly under the open sky. He will not know his place of birth; it will not have been written down. Like his parents, he will have no village or town he calls home. He has but a single identity—it is determined by his ties to family, to the kinship group, to the clan. When two strangers meet, they start by asking, "Who are you?" "I am Soba," the first one begins, "from the family of Ahmad Abdullah, which belongs to the Mussa Arraye group, which is from the clan of Hasean Said, which is part of the larger Isaaq clan," etc. After this recitation, the second stranger gives the particulars of his lineage, his roots. The exchange lasts a long time and is immensely important, because both individuals are trying to determine whether something unites them or divides them, whether they should embrace or attack each other with knives. Their personal rapport, their mutual sympathy or antipathy, have no meaning; their relationship, be it friendly or hostile, depends on the current state of affairs between their two clans. The human being, the singular, distinct person, does not exist—or he matters only as part of this or that bloodline.

When a boy turns eight, a great honor is bestowed upon him: with his friends, he will henceforth take care of a herd of camels, the greatest treasure of Somali nomads. To them, camels are the measure of all things—wealth, power, life. Above all, life. If Ahmed kills someone from another clan, his family must pay the damages. One hundred camels if he killed a man, fifty camels if the victim was a woman. Otherwise—war! Man is nourished by the camel's milk. He transports his house on its back. He cannot start a family without a camel: acquiring a wife requires compensating her clan—in camels.

The herd of each kinship group consists of camels, sheep, and goats. The land here cannot be cultivated. It is dry, hot sand, which brings forth nothing. The herd, therefore, is the sole source of sustenance. But the animals need water and pasturelands, both of which are scarce even in the rainy season; in the dry season, most pastures disappear entirely, and pools and wells become shallow or dry up altogether. If the drought persists, hunger ensues, animals perish, many people die.

The young Somali starts getting to know his world. He studies it. Those individual acacias, those torn-up clumps of sod, those lonely, elephantine baobabs are signals telling him where he is and which way he should go. Those tall rocks, those steep, stony faultlines, the protruding cliff edges, instruct him, indicate directions, keep him from losing his way. But just as he feels he has learned this landscape, as it starts to seem legible and familiar, it destroys his self-confidence. For he discovers that the places he thought he knew, the labyrinths and compositions of signs that surround him, look one way when scorched by a drought, and another when they are covered by lush vegetation during the rainy season; those crevices and rocky outcroppings have one shape, depth, and color in the horizontal rays of the morning sun, and altogether different ones at noon, when the rays fall perpendicularly. The youngster will then comprehend that the features of the landscape are varied and changeable, and that one must know the order of their permutations, their significance, what they are telling him, what they are warning him of.

That is his first lesson: that the world speaks, and that it speaks in many languages, which one must always continue learning. But with the passage of time, the boy is also taught another lesson: about the paths and roads traced upon the earth, their course, design, and direction. For although there is seemingly nothing about, just empty, uninhabited wilderness, in reality these lands are traversed by numerous trails and tracks, footpaths and high-ways, admittedly invisible against the sand and the rocks, yet nev-ertheless deeply etched in the memory of the people who have wandered these regions for centuries. It is here that begins the great Somali game, the game of survival, of life. For these trails lead from well to well, from pasture to pasture. As a result of age-old wars, conflicts, and negotiations, each clan, kinship group, and family has its own traditionally recognized trails, wells, and pastures. The situation is more or less ideal in a year of abundant rains and lush grasses, when the herds are not too numerous and the human population has not increased unduly. But just let there be a drought, which occurs frequently, let the grasses disappear and the wells run dry! Then the fine web of footpaths and road-ways, so painstakingly woven over the years to ensure that the clans are able to pass one another comfortably, avoiding unneces-sary contact and conflict, all at once loses its significance, gets tan-gled, loosens, and tears. A desperate search begins for wells still containing water; death-defying attempts are made to reach them at all cost. Herds are driven from everywhere toward those few places where some green still remains. The dry season becomes a time of fever, tension, fury, and wars. People's worst traits surface: distrust, deceit, greed, hatred.

Hamed tells me that their poetry often recounts the drama and destruction of clans who, walking across the desert, were ulti-mately unable to reach a well. Such a tragic journey lasts days, even weeks. First, the sheep and goats perish. They can go only several days without water. "Then the children," he says, adding nothing more. Neither the reactions of the mothers and fathers, nor what the funerals are like. "Then the children," he repeats, and again falls silent. It is so hot now that even talking is difficult.

It is just past noon, and there is nothing to breathe. "Then the women die," he continues after a while. "Those who have survived cannot stop for long. If they were to stop after each death, they would never reach the well. One death would cause another, and then another. The clan would disappear somewhere along its route." I was now meant to imagine this trail that does not exist, meaning, that is invisible, and on it a band of people and animals, ever dwindling, smaller and smaller. "The men and the camels live for a while still. The camel can survive without drinking for three weeks. And it can walk a long distance—five hundred kilometers or more. The whole way, the female will have a tiny bit of milk." Those three weeks are the upper limit of life for the man and the camel, if they are all alone on the earth. "Alone on the earth!" Hamed cries out, and there is a note of terror in his voice, for that is the one thing a Somali cannot imagine: finding himself alone in the world. The man and the camel continue on in their search for a well and water. They walk more and more slowly, with greater and greater effort, because the ground over which they are moving is aflame, there is heat everywhere, everything all around is blazing, burning—the stones, the sand, the air. "The man and the camel die together," Hamed says. "It occurs when the man can no longer find milk—the camel's udders are empty, dry and cracked. Usually, the nomad and the beast still have enough strength to drag themselves to a bit of shade. They are found later lying lifeless in that shade—or where it had seemed to the man that there was shade."

"I know about this," I interrupted Hamed. "I saw it with my own eyes in the Ogaden." We were driving around the desert in trucks, trying to find dying nomads and take them to the camp in Godē. I was shocked that whenever we found dying Somalis and their camels, they refused to be parted from the animals, even though certain death awaited them. I was accompanying a group of young volunteers from the humanitarian organization Save. They would have to forcibly tear a shepherd away from his camel—one skeleton from another—the man cursing at them all the way to camp. But he never remained there for long. These people received three liters of water daily, for everything: drinking, cooking, washing. And daily rations of a half kilogram of corn. Plus, once a week, a small sack of sugar and a piece of soap. The Somalis knew how to set even some of this aside, selling the corn and sugar to dealers hanging around the camp, putting away the money to buy a new camel, and running off into the desert again.

They were unable to live any other way.

Hamed is not surprised at this. "That is our nature," he says, without resignation, with a touch of pride even. Nature is something one cannot oppose, attempt to improve, or free oneself from. Nature is decreed by God, and is therefore perfect. Droughts, heat waves, empty wells, and death on the road also partake of that perfection. Without them, man would be unable later to appreciate the true delight of rain, the heavenly taste of water, and the life-giving sweetness of milk. A beast would not be able to rejoice in the succulent grass, or relish the smell of a meadow. Man would not know what it is to stand in a stream of cold, crystal-clear water. It would not even occur to him that this is simply to be in heaven.

It is three o'clock, the heat is beginning to subside. Hamed raises himself, wipes the sweat from his face, straightens his turban. He will go take part in a meeting of all adult men, called a *shir*. The Somalis have no hierarchical structure of governance. All decisions are made during this meeting, at which everyone can speak. The first order of business: listening to reports from children's reconnaissance missions. The children do not rest. Since morning they have been ferreting about, investigating the surrounding area: Is there a large and hostile clan nearby? Where might there be the closest well to which we have a chance of getting first?

The Shadow of the Sun

Can we continue on our way, confident that nothing threatens us? All these matters will be discussed in turn. The *shir* is all bustle, quarrels, shouts, confusion. Finally, however, the most important decision will be made: how should we proceed. Then, we will take our places in the order established centuries ago, and we will be on our way.

A Day in the Village of
Abdallah Wallo

It is the girls who rise first in the village of Abdallah
Wallo and go for water even before the sun is up.
This is a fortunate village: water is nearby. All one has to do is
climb a steep, sandy bank down to the river. The river is called the
Senegal. On its northern shore lies Mauritania, and on its southern the country with the same name as the river—Senegal. We
are where the Sahara ends; ahead of us lies the barren, semi-arid,
hot savannah known as the Sahel, which, several hundred kilometers farther south, toward the equator, will in turn give way to the
humid, malarial regions of tropical forest.

After reaching the river, the girls fill tall, metal tubs and plastic canisters with water, help one another place them on their
heads, and, chatting, climb the steep incline back to the village.
The sun rises, and its rays catch the water in the containers. The
water trembles, sways, and glitters like quicksilver.

The girls disperse to their houses, their yards. From the earliest morning, from the onset of this expedition to the river, they
are carefully and neatly dressed, always the same way: in a wide,
loose dress of flowered calico, ankle-length and concealing the
entire body. This is a Muslim village—nothing in a woman's attire
should suggest that she might wish to tempt a man.

The sounds of pots being set down and the splash of water are like the tolling of the bell in a small country church: they bring everyone to life. From the mud huts—there are only mud huts here—children tumble out. There are throngs of them, as if the village were a giant kindergarten. As soon as they step over the thresholds, the little ones start to pee, instinctively, in no particular place, to the left, to the right, some carefree and joyful, others still a bit sleepy and sulky. They finish, then rush to the buckets and canisters for a drink. Girls—and only the girls—seize the opportunity to wash their faces. It doesn't occur to the boys. The children now turn their attention to breakfast. Or, rather, that's just how I think of it; the concept of breakfast does not exist here. If a child has something to eat, he eats it. It can be a piece of bread or a biscuit, a chunk of cassava or banana. He never eats this by himself, for the children share everything; usually, the oldest girl in the group makes certain that everyone receives an equal portion, even if it's only a crumb. The rest of the day will be a continuous search for food. These children are always hungry. They instantly swallow anything that is given them, and immediately start looking for the next morsel.

Mornings in Abdallah Wallo are not accompanied by the barking of dogs or the clucking of hens or the lowing of cows. There is not a single animal in the village, not one creature that one could describe as being livestock—cattle, domestic birds, goats, or pigs. As a result, there are no barns, stables, pigpens, or henhouses.

There is also no vegetation in Abdallah Wallo, no greenery, flowers, or shrubs, no gardens or orchards. Man lives here one-on-one with the bare earth, loose sand, and crumbling clay. He is the only living creature in the hot, blazing emptiness, and is wholly preoccupied with survival, with the effort to remain above ground. There is man, and there is water. Here, water takes the place of everything else. Because there are no animals, it nourishes and sustains; because there is no shade-producing vegetation, it cools; its splashing is like the rustle of leaves, the murmur of shrubs and trees.

I am the guest of Thiam and his brother, Yamar. They work in Dakar, where we met. What do they do? Different things. Half the people in African towns don't have defined occupations, permanent jobs. They sell this and that, work as porters, guard something. They're everywhere, always at one's disposal, ready to serve, for hire. They perform their task, take their wages, and vanish without a trace. Or they can stay with you for years. That depends on you, on your money. They tell rich tales about what they have done in life. And what is it that they have done? Thousands of things—everything, really! They stay in the city because it is easier to live there, and one can earn something now and then. If they manage to make a few pennies, they purchase a few presents and travel home, back to the countryside, to their wife, children, cousins.

I met Thiam and Yamar just as they were preparing to leave for Abdallah Wallo. They proposed that I go with them, but I had to stay in Dakar for another week. If I wanted to come after that, however—they would be waiting for me. The only way for me to get there was by minibus. I must arrive at the bus terminal at dawn, they admonished, when it is easiest to get a seat.

So, a week later, I went to the terminal. Gare Routière is an enormous, flat square, still empty at this hour. A group of young boys materialized instantly at the gate, asking where I wanted to go. To Podor, I said, because the village I was traveling to was in the department of that name. They led me to more or less the center of the square and, without a word, left me there. Because I was alone in this desolate place, a group of vendors, shivering in the still-cool air (the nights are cold here), gathered around me, pushing their wares—chewing gum, biscuits, baby rattles, cigarettes, sold individually or by the pack. I didn't want anything, but they kept standing there; they had nothing else to do. A white man is such an anomaly, a foundling from another planet, that it is possible to stare at him with interest almost forever. After a while another passenger appeared at the gate, then one more after him, and the vendors moved off in their direction.

Finally, a small Toyota van pulled up. These vehicles are built to seat twelve, but here they accommodate more than thirty passengers. It is difficult to describe the number and nature of all the additions, the welded-on extensions, the little benches inside such a bus. When it is full, for one passenger to either get out or get in, all the others must do so as well; the intricate calibration of the internal arrangements is as tight and precise as the workings of a Swiss watch, and whoever occupies a place must take into account the fact that for the next several hours, for all intents and purposes, he will not be able to move so much as a toe. The worst are the hours of waiting, when one must sit in the hot, airless bus while the driver collects his full ensemble of passengers. In the case of our Toyota, this process lasted four hours. We were just about to set off when the driver—a powerful, well-built young man named Traoré—announced upon getting into the bus that someone had stolen a package that had been lying on his seat, with a girl's dress inside. Thefts like this are a common occurrence the world over, but Traoré fell into such a rage, a fury bordering on insanity, that we all cringed, fearing that he would tear us— innocent passengers!—limb from limb. It was yet another instance of something I had observed in Africa before: the reaction to a thief—although there is plenty of theft here—has an irrational dimension, akin to madness. Because there is something inhuman about stealing from a poor man, who often has but one bowl or one tattered shirt, that man's response to the theft can likewise be inhuman. If a crowd catches a thief in the market, on the square, on the street, it can kill him on the spot—which is why, paradoxically, the task of the police here is not so much the pursuit of thieves as their protection.

Initially, the road skirts the Atlantic coast, passing through an avenue of baobabs so formidable, gigantic, lofty, monumental, we might as well have been driving among the skyscrapers of Manhattan. Like elephants among other animals, so are baobabs among trees: they have no equals. They are from some other geological era, from another context, from another nature. They cannot be compared with anything else. They live for themselves, and have their own individual biological program.

After this kilometers-long forest of baobabs, the road turns east, toward Mali and Burkina Faso. In the town of Dagana, Traoré stops the bus. There are several eateries here. We will have our meal in one of them. The passengers divide up into groups of six to eight, and sit down in a circle on the floor. In the middle of each circle, a boy from the restaurant sets down a metal basin half filled with rice generously covered with a brownish, heavily spiced sauce. We begin to eat. And this is how we do it: one by one, in turn, each person extends his right hand into the bowl, takes a handful of rice, squeezes out the excess sauce, and lifts this compressed dumpling to his mouth. We eat slowly, seriously, mindful of the order, so that no one is wronged. There is great tact and restraint in this ritual. Everyone is hungry, and the amount of rice is limited, yet not one goes out of turn, hurries another, cheats. When the basin is empty, the boy brings a bucket of water from which everyone, again in sequential order, drinks a large cupful. Then we each wash our hands, pay, step outside, and get back on the bus.

A moment later we are on our way again. By afternoon we reach a town called Mboumba. I get out. I have ahead of me ten kilometers of country road, through dry, burnt-out savannah, hot, loose sand, and crushing heat.

So, morning in Abdallah Wallo. The children have already scattered throughout the village. Now the adults emerge from the huts. Men spread out small rugs in the sand and begin their morning prayers. They pray enclosed within themselves, hermetically oblivious to the bustle around them—children running, women going about their chores. At this early hour the sun already fills the horizon, illuminates the earth, pours into the village. One feels its presence immediately; all at once, it is already hot.

Now begins the ritual of morning visits and salutations. Everyone visits everyone else. These are backyard scenes—no one enters the houses. For the mud huts serve only as sleeping quarters. Thiam, after prayers, starts his rounds with his nearest neighbors. He walks up to them. A mutual exchange of questions and answers follows. How did you sleep? Well. And your wife? Also well. And the children? Well. And cousins? Well. And your guest? Well. And did you dream? I did. Etc., etc. This goes on for a very long time, and the longer we ask, the more detailed is this exchange of courtesies, the greater the respect that we each evince for the other. At this time of day, it is impossible simply to traverse the village; with each person encountered one must enter into this unending exchange of questions and greetings, and one must engage each one individually: addressing a group, collectively, would be rude.

I accompanied Thiam for the entire length of the ritual. It took a long time to complete the full circle. As we moved in our morning orbit, I noticed others circulating in theirs; the entire village was in motion, and from all directions one could hear those ritualized "How did you sleep?" and the reassuring, positive "Well. Well." As we walked the village, it became clear that in the tradition of its inhabitants, and even in their imagination, the concept of divided, differentiated, segmented space does not exist. There are no fences, boards, or wires, no hedges, nets, ditches, or demarcation lines anywhere. The space is single, communal, open—transparent even; there are no screens in it, no erected barriers, dams, and walls; it puts up no limits, offers no resistance.

Now a portion of the people go work in the fields. The fields are far away; you cannot even see them. The soil near the village has long been exhausted—barren, sterile sand and dust. You must walk for kilometers before you can plant something with the hope that, if the rains come, the earth will yield a crop. Man has as much land here as he can manage to cultivate, but the fact is that he will cultivate very little of it. The hoe is his only tool, he has no plow, no draft animals. I look at those setting out for the fields. Their only nourishment for the entire day is the bottle of water they carry. Before they reach their destination, the heat will already be frightful. What do they cultivate? Manioc, corn, dry rice. Wisdom and experience dictate to these farmers that they work little and slowly, take long breaks, conserve their strength, rest. For these are weak people, poorly nourished, without much energy. If someone were to start working intensively, toiling, going all out, he would grow weaker still and, in his exhaustion, easily succumb to malaria, tuberculosis, or any of the hundreds of other tropical diseases lying in wait, half of which are fatal. Life here is a constant struggle, an endlessly repeated effort to tilt in one's favor the fragile, flimsy, and shaky balance between survival and extinction.

The women, from the morning on, prepare the meal. I say "the meal" for one eats once a day, and terms such as breakfast, dinner, or supper are not applicable: one doesn't eat at any predetermined time, only when the meal is ready. This occurs most frequently in the late afternoon. And one always eats the same thing. In Abdallah Wallo, as in this entire region, it is rice with a sharp, spicy sauce. There are rich and poor in the village, but the difference in what they eat lies not in the variety of dishes, but merely in the amount of rice. The poor man will have only a scant portion, the rich man a heaping bowlful. But this distinction holds only in years of plenty. A drought of long duration pushes everyone down to the same level: the poor and the rich alike eat precious little, if they don't simply die of hunger.

Preparing the meal takes a woman the greater part of the day—the whole day, really. She must set out first thing in search of wood for the fire. There are no trees anywhere, the land was deforested long ago, and searching for slivers, splinters, and sticks on the savannah is an onerous and time-consuming task. When she finally collects and brings back a bundle of firewood, she must set out again, this time for water. In Abdallah Wallo the water is nearby, but elsewhere she would have to walk for kilometers to get it, and in times of drought she must wait for hours until the water truck delivers it. Having fuel and water, she can begin cooking the rice. But not always: she may first have to buy it in the market, for she rarely has enough money to purchase a supply of it. And then, on top of all this, noon arrives, and with it hours of such debilitating heat that everything stops, grows numb, dies down. The bustle around the fireplace and the pots likewise subsides. The whole village appears deserted, all life drains from it.

One day I summoned my strength and set off on a walk from hut to hut. It was noon. In all the dwellings, on the earthern floors, on mats, on bunks, lay silent, inert people. Their faces were bathed in sweat. The village was like a submarine at the bottom of the ocean: it was there, but it emitted no signals, soundless, motionless.

In the afternoon we went with Thiam to the river. Muddy, dark gray, it flows between steep, sandy banks. No greenery, plants, or shrubs in sight. One could, of course, build canals here, irrigate the desert. But who is to do this? With what money? What for? The river flows as if for itself alone, unnoticed, of little use. We ventured far out into the desert, and the dark caught us as we were returning. There is no light in the village. No one has a fire going, because that would be a waste of wood. No one has a lamp. No one has a flashlight. On a moonless night like tonight, you can see nothing. You can only hear voices, here and there, snatches of conversations and calls, stories being recounted that I do not understand, words ever less frequent, softer, for the village, taking advantage of the bit of coolness, grows silent for a few hours and falls asleep.

Rising in the Darkness

D awn and dusk—these are the most pleasant hours in Africa. The sun is either not yet scorching, or it is no longer so—it lets you be, lets you live.

It is twenty-five kilometers from Addis Ababa to the Sabeta waterfall. Driving a car in Ethiopia is a kind of unending process of compromise: everyone knows that the road is narrow, old, crammed with people and vehicles, but they also know that they must somehow find a spot for themselves on it, and not only find a spot, but actually move, advance forward, make their way toward their destination. Every few moments, each driver, cattle herder, or pedestrian is confronted by an obstacle, a conundrum, a problem that needs solving: how to pass without colliding with the car approaching from the opposite direction; how to hurry along one's cows, sheep, and camels without trampling the children and crawling beggars; how to cross without getting run over by a truck, being impaled on the horns of a bull, knocking over that woman carrying a twenty-kilogram weight on her head. And yet no one shouts at anyone else, no one falls into a fury, no one curses or threatens—patiently and silently, they all perform their slalom, execute their pirouettes, dodge and evade, maneuver and hedge, turn here, converge there, and, most important, move forward. If a bottleneck occurs, people will participate harmoniously and calmly in diffusing it; if a traffic jam forms, everyone will set about resolving it, millimeter by millimeter.

The shallow river rushes over a cracked, rocky bed, descending lower and lower, until it reaches an abrupt threshold and from there falls over the precipice. This is the Sabeta waterfall. A small Ethiopian boy, perhaps eight years old, makes money from visitors by stripping off all his clothes and riding the swift current on his naked bottom down to the edge of the falls. When he comes to a stop right above the thundering abyss, the assembled crowd emits two cries: the first of dread, and the second, immediately after, of relief. The boy stands up, turns his back, and shows the tourists his bum. There is nothing rude in this gesture, no intended insult. On the contrary, there is pride, and a desire to reassure us, the onlookers, that because he has such a properly tanned hide on his buttocks—look, please!—he can slide down the riverbed, which bristles with sharp rocks, without harming himself in the least. It is true: his skin looks as tough as the soles of hiking boots.

The next day, the prison in Addis Ababa. Before the entrance, under a tin roof, a line of people await visiting hours. The government is too poor to provide uniforms for the police, the guards, and so on, and these barely dressed barefoot young men milling about near the gate are in fact the prison guards. We must simply accept that they have power, that it is they who decide whether or not to admit us; we must believe this, and must wait until they have concluded their deliberations. The old prison, built by the Italians, was used by Mengistu's pro-Soviet regime for holding and torturing the opposition, and now the current authorities have shut behind these bars Mengistu's closest entourage—members of the Central Committee, ministers, generals of the army and the police.

On the gate, a enormous star with a hammer and sickle,

erected by Mengistu, and inside the prison, in the courtyard, a bust of Marx (it was a Soviet custom: portraits of Stalin hung at the entrances to the gulags, and statues of Lenin stood inside).

Mengistu's regime fell in the summer of 1991 after seventeen years in power. He himself escaped at the last minute by plane to Zimbabwe. The fate of his armed forces is extraordinary. With Moscow's help, Mengistu had built up the most powerful army in sub-Saharan Africa. It numbered 400,000 soldiers; it had rockets and chemical weapons. Its opponents were guerrillas from the northern mountains (Eritrea, Tigre) and from the south (Oromo). In the summer of 1991, these rebel forces had driven the government troops into Addis Ababa. The guerrillas: barefoot boys, often children, ragged, hungry, poorly armed. Europeans began fleeing the city, expecting a bloodbath once the guerrillas entered. But something quite different occurred, something that could have been the subject of a film entitled "The End of a Great Army." At the news that their commander had fled, this powerful force, armed to the teeth, collapsed in a matter of hours. Hungry, demoralized soldiers transformed all at once, before the stunned eyes of the city's residents, into beggars. Holding a Kalashnikov in one hand, they stretched out the other, asking for food. The guerrillas took the capital essentially without a fight. Mengistu's soldiers, having abandoned their tanks, rocket launchers, airplanes, armored vehicles, and artillery pieces, set off, each man for himself, on foot, on mules, by bus, for their villages and homes. If by chance you find yourself driving through Ethiopia, you will notice in many villages and small towns strong, healthy, young men sitting idly on the thresholds of houses, or on the stools of humble roadside bars. They are the soldiers of General Mengistu's great army, which was to conquer Africa yet fell apart in the course of a single day in the summer of 1991.

. . .

The prisoner with whom I am speaking is named Shimelis Mazengia and was one of the ideologues of Mengistu's regime, a member of the Political Bureau and a secretary of the Central Committee for ideological matters—in short, a kind of Ethiopian Mikhail Suslov. Mazengia is forty-five years old, intelligent. He weighs his words carefully as he speaks. He is dressed in light-colored sweats. All the prisoners here are in "civilian" clothing—the government lacks the funds for prison garb. The guards and the prisoners are dressed alike. I asked one of the guards whether the prisoners do not try to take advantage of the fact that they look like everyone out on the street, and escape. He looked at me with bewilderment. Escape? Here at least they have a bowl of soup, and if they were free they would be dying of hunger like the rest of the nation. They are enemies, he emphasized, but they are not madmen!

Anxiety, even fear, in Mazengia's dark eyes. They are in constant motion, running this way and that, as if he were feverishly searching for a way out of a trap. He says that Mengistu's flight was a shock to them all, that is, to the commander's closest entourage. Mengistu worked day and night; he was uninterested in material goods, only in absolute power. To rule—that was enough for him. He had a rigid mentality, incapable of any compromise. Mazengia describes the massacres of the red terror, which ravaged the country for several years, as "the struggle for power." He maintains that "both sides killed." How does he judge his participation in the highest ranks of the fallen regime, a regime that brought so much misfortune, destruction, and death? (More than thirty thousand people were shot on Mengistu's orders, and some estimates put that figure at more than three hundred thousand.) I remember driving in the morning through Addis Ababa in the late 1970s and seeing corpses strewn in the streets—the previous night's harvest. Mazengia answers philosophically: History is an intricate process. It errs, advances and retreats, searches here, there, and sometimes gets trapped in a dead end. Only the future can judge, can find the appropriate measure.

He and 406 others associated with the old regime (the Ethiopian *nomenklatura*) have been here for three years already, not knowing what next—more prison? a trial? execution? freedom? The government is asking itself the same question: what do we do with them?

We were sitting in a small office, probably a guardroom. No one was listening to our conversation, and no one was pressuring us to end it. As is often the case in Africa, there was chaos all around, people wandered in and out, on the table next to us a telephone that no one answered rang continually.

At the end of the conversation I said that I would like to see where the prisoners were kept. I was ushered into a courtyard surrounded by a two-story building with arcades. Along them stretched cells, doors opening onto the courtyard. A throng of prisoners milled about. I observed their faces. They were the bearded, bespectacled visages of university professors, their assistants, their students. Mengistu's regime had many followers from this milieu—mostly adherents of the Albanian version of socialism as practiced by Enver Hoxha. When Tirana broke with Beijing, in Addis Ababa Ethiopian pro-Hoxha activists shot at Ethiopian Maoists. For months, the streets of the city flowed with blood. After Mengistu's escape, his army dispersed and went home, and only the academics were left. They were seized without great difficulty and imprisoned in this crowded courtyard.

Someone brought from London a Somali quarterly that had been published there in the summer of 1993—*Hal-Abuur: Journal of Somali Literature and Culture*. I counted: of the seventeen authors represented—preeminent Somali intellectuals, scientists, and writers—fifteen reside abroad. Here is one of Africa's problems: its intelligentsia lives for the most part outside its borders, in the United States, in London, Paris, Rome. Remaining in their native countries are, at the bottom, masses of illiterate, downtrodden, utterly exploited peasants; at the top, the corrupt bureaucracy or arrogant, coarse soldiers (the lumpenmilitariat, as the Ugandan historian Ali Mazrui calls them). How is Africa to develop, to participate in the great transformation of the world, without an intelligentsia? Without its own educated middle class? Furthermore, if an African scholar or writer is persecuted in his own country, most frequently he will not seek shelter in another country on his continent, but in Boston, in Los Angeles, in Stockholm, or in Geneva.

I went to the university in Addis Ababa. It is this country's only institution of higher learning. I visited the university bookstore, which is this country's only bookstore. Empty shelves. No books, no periodicals—nothing. It is this way in most African countries. Once, I remember, there was a good bookshop in Kampala, another (three, even) in Dar es Salaam. Now—everywhere, nothing. Ethiopia is the size of France, Germany, and Poland put together. More than fifty million people live here; in several years there will be sixty million of them, in a dozen or so, more than eighty million. And so on.

Maybe then?

If only one?

In my free time, I walk to Africa Hall, a great ornamental structure on one of the hills upon which this city is built. The first African summit meeting took place here in May of 1963. I saw Nasser here, Nkrumah, Haile Selassie, Ben Bella, Modibo Keita. Very big names at the time. In the hall in which they met, some boys are now playing Ping-Pong; a woman is selling leather jackets.

Africa Hall—it reflects perhaps a corollary of Parkinson's Law untrammeled and triumphant. Whenever I arrive in Addis Ababa, I always notice the same thing: a new building is being erected near Africa Hall, each one more magnificent and luxurious than the one before. Political systems come and go in Ethiopia—first a feudal-aristocratic one, then a Marxist-Leninist one, currently a federal-democratic one. Africa too is changing, growing poorer and more wretched. But all this is of no consquence; the imperturbable and victorious law of the constant expansion of the seat of Africa's rulers—Africa Hall—operates freely and without constraints.

Inside—corridors, rooms, conference halls, offices piled with papers from floor to ceiling. The papers are spilling out of cabinets and files, falling from shelves. Desks are squeezed in tightly everywhere, and behind them sit the most beautiful girls from all over Africa.

Secretaries.

I am looking for one particular document. It is called "Lagos Plan of Action for the Economic Development of Africa 1980–2000." African leaders convened in Lagos in 1980 to consider solutions to the continent's crisis. How could Africa be saved? And they resolved on this particular plan of action—the bible, the panacea, the grand strategy for development.

I search and inquire, but to no avail. Most of the workers here have not even heard of any such plan. Others have heard of it, but they know nothing more specific. Others have heard of it, know a bit about it, but still do not have the text. They can give me copies of the resolution concerning how the production of peanuts in Senegal might be increased. How the tsetse fly should be combated in Tanzania. How the drought in the Sahel can be curtailed. But how to save Africa? This plan they do not have.

Several conversations in Africa Hall. One, with Babashola Chinsman. He is vice director of the United Nations Development Program. Young, energetic, from Sierra Leone. One of those Africans upon whom fate has smiled. A representative of a new global class: members of Third World nations occupying seats in international organizations. A villa in Addis Ababa (official), a villa in Freetown (private, which he rents to the German embassy), a private apartment in Manhattan (because he doesn't care for hotels). A limousine, a driver, servants. Tomorrow, a conference in Madrid; three days from now, one in New York; a week from now, another in Sydney. Always the same, the eternal, subject: how to relieve hunger in Africa.

The conversation is pleasant, interesting.

Chinsman: "It is not true that Africa is stagnant. Africa is developing; it is not merely a continent of famine.

"The problem is larger, worldwide. One hundred and fifty poorly developed countries are leaning on twenty-five developed ones, in which, moreover, there is recession and a stagnant population growth.

"It is extremely important to promote regional development in Africa. Unfortunately, the obstacle is a backward infrastructure: unsatisfactory means of distribution, bad roads, insufficient trucks and buses, a poor public transportation system.

"This inadequate transportation network results in ninety percent of the continent's villages and towns living in isolation— they have no access to the market, and thus no access to money.

"The paradox of our world: If one figures in the cost of transporting, servicing, warehousing, and preserving food, then the cost of a single meal (typically, a handful of corn) for a refugee in some camp, for example in Sudan, is higher than the price of a dinner in the most expensive restaurant in Paris.

"After thirty years of independence, we are finally beginning to understand that education is important for development. The farm of a literate peasant is ten to fifteen times more productive than the farm of an illiterate one. Education alone, without any additional investments, brings material benefits.

"The most important thing is to have a multidimensional approach to development: develop regions, develop local societies, develop interdependence rather than intercompetition!"

John Menru from Tanzania: "Africa needs a new generation

of politicans who know how to think in a new way. The current one must depart. Instead of thinking about development, they think about how to stay in power.

"The solution for Africa? Create a new political climate:

a. *adopt as binding the principle of dialogue;*
b. *ensure society's participation in public life;*
c. *observe fundamental human rights;*
d. *begin democratization.*

"Do all this, and new politicians will emerge all by themselves. New politicians, with a clear, well-defined vision. A precise vision—that is what we lack today.

"What is dangerous? Ethnic fanaticism. It can cause an ethnic principle to assume a religious dimension, to become a substitute religion. This is extremely dangerous!"

Sadig Rasheed—a Sudanese, one of the directors of the Economic Commission for Africa: "Africa must wake up.

"One must arrest the process of Africa's increasing marginalization. Whether this will succeed, I don't know.

"I worry about whether African societies will be able to assume a self-critical stance, and much depends on this."

That is precisely the subject of a conversation I have one day with A., an elderly Englishman and longtime local resident. His view: That the strength of Europe and of its culture, in contrast to other cultures, lies in its bent for criticism, above all, for self-criticism—in its art of analysis and inquiry, in its endless seeking, in its restlessness. The European mind recognizes that it has limitations, accepts its imperfections, is skeptical, doubtful, questioning. Other cultures do not have this critical spirit. More—they are inclined to pride, to thinking that all that belongs to them is perfect; they are, in short, uncritical in relation to themselves. They lay the blame for all that is evil on others, on other forces (conspiracies, agents, foreign domination of one sort or another). They consider all criticism to be a malevolent attack, a sign of discrimination, of racism, etc. Representatives of these cultures treat criticism as a personal insult, as a deliberate attempt to humiliate them, as a form of sadism even. If you tell them that the city is dirty, they treat this as if you said that they were dirty themselves, had dirty ears, or dirty nails. Instead of being self-critical, they are full of countless grudges, complexes, envies, peeves, manias. The effect of all this is that they are culturally, permanently, structurally incapable of progress, incapable of engendering within themselves the will to transform and evolve.

Do all African cultures (for there are many of them, just as there are many African religions) belong to this touchy, uncritical mess? Africans like Sadig Rasheed have begun to consider this; they want to find the answer to why, in the race of continents, Africa is being left behind.

Europe's image of Africa? Hunger; skeletal children; dry, cracked earth; urban slums; massacres; AIDS; throngs of refugees without a roof over their heads, without clothing, without medicines, water, or bread.

The world, therefore, rushes in with aid.

Today, as in the past, Africa is regarded as an object, as the reflection of some alien star, as the stomping ground of colonizers, merchants, missionaries, ethnographers, large charitable organizations (more than eighty are active in Ethiopia alone).

Meantime, most importantly, it exists for itself alone, within itself, a timeless, sealed, separate continent, a land of banana groves, shapeless little fields of manioc, jungles, the immense Sahara, rivers slowly drying up, thinning forests, sick, monstrous cities—a world charged, at the same time, with a restless and violent electricity.

. . .

Two thousand kilometers across Ethiopia. Empty, unpopulated roads. Mountains and more mountains. At this time of year (it is winter in Europe), the mountains are green. They are sky-high and magnificent in the sun. Profound silence everywhere. But stop for just a moment, sit down by the side of the road, and listen. Somewhere, far off, you will hear high monotonous voices. It is children singing on the nearby slopes—children collecting brushwood, tending herds, cutting grass for the cattle. You will not hear the voices of adults. It is as if this were a world only of children.

And this is a world of children. Half the population of Africa is under fifteen years of age. There are innumerable children in all its armies; children constitute the majority in refugee camps; children work in the fields, buy and sell in the markets. But the child's biggest role is in the home: he is responsible for supplying water. While everyone else is still asleep, little boys are rising in the darkness and running to springs, ponds, rivers—for water. Modern technology has proven to be their great ally: it gave them a gift—the cheap, light, plastic container. A dozen years ago, this container revolutionized life in Africa. Water is the sine qua non of survival in the tropics. Because there is generally no plumbing here and water is scarce, one must carry it over long distances, sometimes ten or more kilometers. For centuries, heavy clay or stone vessels were used for this purpose. Traditional African cultures did not know wheeled transport, so human beings carried everything themselves, most often on their heads. The division of domestic labor was such that carrying water was women's work. A child could never manage such a large and heavy receptacle, and in this bare-bones world each house usually had only one.

Then, the plastic container appeared. A miracle! A revolution! First of all, it is relatively inexpensive (although in certain houses it is the only thing of any value): it costs around two dollars. Most important, however, it is light. And it comes in various sizes, so even a small child can fetch several liters of water.

All the children carry water. You see entire flocks of youngsters, playing and teasing one another as they walk to a distant spring. What a relief this is for the exhausted African woman! What a transformation in her life! How much more time she now has for herself, for her household!

The plastic container possesses countless advantages. Among the most important is that it holds your place in line. Often, you have to stand for days in a line for water (in those places, that is, where it is delivered by truck). Standing in the tropical sun is torture. It used to be that you couldn't just set down the clay pot and go sit in the shade: it was too valuable to risk its being stolen. Now, however, you place your plastic container in the line and then go find yourself some shade, or go to the market, or visit friends. Driving through Africa, one sees these kilometer-long, colorful rows awaiting the arrival of water.

More about the children. It is enough to stop briefly in a village, a town, or simply in a field—a group of children will instantly materialize. All of them indescribably tattered. Little shirts, pants—all frayed and shredded beyond belief. Their entire treasure, their sole nourishment, is a small calabash with a bit of water in it. Each piece of bread or banana will disappear, inhaled, in a fraction of a second. Hunger for these children is something permanent, a way of life, second nature. And yet they do not ask for bread or fruit, or even for money.

They ask for a pencil.

A mechanical pencil. The price? Ten cents. Yes, but where can they possibly get ten cents?

They would all like to go to school, they would like to learn. And sometimes they do go to school (a village school is simply a spot in the shade of an enormous mango tree), but they cannot learn to write because they have nothing to write with—they do not own a pencil.

Somewhere near Gondar (you will come to this town of Ethiopian kings and emperors by traveling from the Gulf of Aden through Djibouti in the direction of Al-Ubayyid, Tersaf, N'Djamena, and Lake Chad), I met a man who was walking south. That is really the most important thing one can say about him: that he was walking north to south. Oh, yes, and that he was searching for his brother.

He was barefoot, dressed in short, patched-up pants, and on his back he had something that might have been called a shirt once. Besides that, he had three things: a wanderer's walking stick; a piece of cloth, which in the morning served him as a towel, shielded his head during the afternoon heat, and at night covered his body while he slept; and, slung over his shoulder, a wooden water dish. He had no money. If people along the way gave him something to eat, he would eat; if they did not, he walked hungry. But he had been hungry his whole life; there was nothing extraordinary about hunger.

He was walking south, because his brother had once set out from home in a southerly direction. When was this? Long ago. (I was speaking with him through the driver, who knew scant English, and had only one expression at his disposal for referring to the past: long ago.) And he has been walking a long time, from somewhere in the Eritrean mountains, from near Keren.

He knows about walking south: in the morning, you must head straight into the sun. When he meets someone, he asks whether they have seen, or know, Solomon (that's his brother's name). No one is surprised at such a question. All of Africa is in motion, on the road to somewhere, wandering. Some are running away from war, others from drought, still others from hunger. They are fleeing, straying, getting lost. This one, walking north to south, is an anonymous drop in the human deluge flooding the roads of the continent, a deluge driven either by fear of death or by the hope of finding a place under the sun.

Why does he want to find his brother? *Why?* He doesn't understand the question. The reason is obvious, self-evident, not requiring an explanation. He shrugs his shoulders. It is possible that he feels pity for the man he has just encountered and who, though well dressed, is poorer than he in some important, priceless way.

Does he know where he is? Does he know that the place we are sitting is no longer Eritrea, but already Ethiopia, another country? He smiles the smile of a man who knows many things, or who, in any event, knows one thing: that for him there are no boundaries here in Africa, and no states—there is only the burned earth, on which brother seeks brother.

Near this same road—but one must walk down, deep into a nearly impenetrable cleft between two steep mountain slopes—lies the monastery of Debre Libanos. Inside, the church is dark and cool. After hours of driving in blinding sun, the eyes must adjust to this place, which at first impression seems submerged in total darkness. After a time you begin to discern frescoes on the walls, and see Ethiopian pilgrims dressed in white lying facedown on the mat-covered floor. In one corner an old monk is chanting a psalm in a drowsy voice, which periodically dies away altogether, in the already dead language of Ge'ez. In this atmosphere replete with a concentrated and quiet mysticism, everything seems beyond time; beyond measure and weight, beyond life.

Who knows how long these pilgrims lay there, for I walked in and out of the church several times in the course of that day, and each time they were still resting motionless on the mats.

All day? A month? A year? Eternity?

The Cooling Hell

The pilots have not yet turned off the engines, and already people are rushing toward the airplane. Steps are pulled up. We walk down and fall straight into a panting, yelling crowd, which has now reached the plane and is shoving, grabbing at our shirts, pushing at us with all its might: "Passport? Passport?" insistent voices are barking. And immediately after, in the same threatening tone: "Return ticket?" And still others, sharply: "Vaccination? Vaccination?" These demands, this attack, are so violent and disorienting that, shoved, asphyxiated, pawed at, I start to commit error upon error. Asked about my passport, I obediently take it out of my bag. Instantly, someone rips it out of my hands and vanishes. Hectored about a return ticket, I show that I have it. A second later, it, too, is gone. The same thing with my record of vaccinations: someone pulled the form out of my hand and evaporated. I was left with no documents! What do I do now? To whom should I complain? To whom should I appeal? The crowd that had accosted me has suddenly dispersed and disappeared. I am left all alone. A few minutes later, two young men approach. They introduce themselves: "Zado and John. We will protect you. Without us, you will perish."

I didn't ask any questions. All I could think was: how terribly hot it is here! It was early afternoon, the air so humid and heavy, thick, burning, that I couldn't breathe. If only I could leave here, get to a place with a smidgen of coolness! "Where are my documents!" I started to shout, irritated, despairing. I was beginning to lose control; in heat like this you become nervous, enraged, aggressive. "Try to calm down," said John, when we got into his car, which was parked in front of the airport building. "Soon you will understand everything."

We drove through the streets of Monrovia. On both sides jutted forth the black, charred stumps of burned, demolished houses. Not much remains here of such destroyed buildings, because everything—bricks, tin, and surviving beams included— will be instantly dismantled and plundered. There are tens of thousands of people in the city who have fled the bush, have no roof over their heads, and are just waiting for a bomb or a grenade to strike a house. When it does, they descend upon it at once. With the materials they are able to carry away, they will erect a hut, a shack, or simply a roof to protect them from the sun and the rain. The city, which was probably built initially of simple, low buildings, is now cluttered with these haphazardly knocked together structures and looks even more stunted, having assumed the appearance of something makeshift, impermanent, recalling more than anything an encampment of nomads.

I asked John and Zado to take me to a hotel. I don't know if there were any choices in this matter, but without a word they drove me to a shabby, two-story building with the sign El Mason Hotel. The entrance was through a bar. John opened the door, but could go no farther. Inside, in the artificial colored twilight and hot stagnant air, stood prostitutes. To say that the prostitutes "stood" does not begin to convey the situation. There were maybe a hundred girls in the small room, sweaty, exhausted, and so tightly pressed together, squeezed, jammed in, that one could scarcely push one's hand in, let alone enter. It worked this way: if a client opened the door from the street, the pressure inside the bar propelled one of the girls, as though from a catapult, straight into the arms of the surprised customer. Then another girl took her place near the exit.

John retreated and looked for another way in. In a small currency-exchange booth next door sat a young Lebanese man with a sunny, kindly appearance—the owner. The girls belonged to him, as did this disintegrating building with its slimy, mold-covered walls, on which long black water stains arranged themselves into a mute procession of elongated, thin, and hooded apparitions, chimeras, and ghosts.

"I don't have any documents," I confessed to the Lebanese, who just smiled. "That's not important," he said. "Here, few people have them. Documents!" he laughed, and looked knowingly at John and Zado. To him, I was clearly a visitor from some other planet. On the one called Monrovia, the main preoccupation was how to survive from one day to the next. Who cared about papers? "Forty dollars a night," he said. "But food is not included. You can eat around the corner. At the Syrian's place."

I invited John and Zado for a meal. The old, distrustful proprietress, looking constantly at the door, had only one dish: shish kebabs with rice. She stared at the door because she never knew who might come in—customers, to eat something, or robbers, to take everything from her. "What else can I do?" she asked us, setting the plates down in front of us. She had already lost all her nerve and all her money. "I lost my life," she said, without despair, matter-of-factly even, just so that we would know. The restaurant was empty, a motionless fan hung from the ceiling, flies buzzed, one beggar after another stopped in the door and held out his hand. More beggars crowded on the other side of the dirty window, staring at our plates. Men in tatters, women on crutches, children whose legs or arms had been blown off by land mines. Here, at this table, over this plate, one didn't know how to behave, what to do with oneself.

For a long time, we were silent; finally, I inquired about my documents. Zado answered that I had disappointed the airport personnel, because I had all my papers. It would have been best if I had had nothing. Unregulated airlines fly in various con men and adventurers here—this, after all, is a country of gold, diamonds, and narcotics. Most of their ilk do not have visas or vaccination records; they pay to be let in. The airport staff live off this, because the government has no funds and does not pay them their salaries. These aren't even particularly corrupt people. They are simply hungry. I will have to buy back my documents. Zado and John know from whom and where. They can arrange it.

The Lebanese came and left me the key. It was near dusk, and he was going home. He advised that I too should go to the hotel. In the evening, he said, I will not be able to walk around the city by myself. I returned to the hotel, entered through a side door, and walked up to the second floor, where my room was located. By the ground-floor entrance and along the stairs I was accosted by ragged men, who assured me that they would guard me during the night. Saying this, they stretched out their hands. From the manner in which they looked at me, I understood that unless I gave them something, in the night while I slept they would come and slit my throat.

The only window in my room (number 107) gave out on a gloomy, fetid air shaft, from which a revolting odor arose. I turned on the light. The walls, the bed, the table, and the floor were black. Black with cockroaches. I have encountered throughout the world all imaginable types of insects, and have even developed indifference toward the fact, even come to accept, that we live among countless millions of flies, roaches, and ticks, among ever-replenished swarms of wasps, spiders, earwigs, and scarabs, amid billows of gadflies and mosquitoes, clouds of voracious locusts. But this time I was stunned; not so much by the number of cockroaches—although that, too, was shocking—but by their dimensions, by the size of each one of these creatures. These were roach giants, as big as small turtles, dark, gleaming, covered in bristles, and mustached. What made them grow so large? What did they feed on? Their monstrous proportions paralyzed me. For years now I had been swatting flies and mosquitoes, fleas and spiders, with impunity; now, however, I was facing something of an entirely different order. How should I deal with such colossi? What should I do with them? What stance should I adopt toward them? Kill them? With what? How? My hands shook at the very prospect. I felt that I wouldn't know how, that I wouldn't even have the courage to try. More—because of the cockroaches' extraordinary dimensions, I felt certain that if I leaned over them and listened, I would hear them emitting some sound. After all, many other creatures their size communicate in a variety of ways. They squeal, croak, purr, grunt—so why not a cockroach? A normal one is too small for us to be able to hear it, but these giants? Surely they will make noises! But the room remained absolutely quiet: they were all silent—closed, voiceless, mysterious.

I noticed, however, that when I leaned over them, straining my ears, they rapidly retreated and huddled together. Their reaction was identical whenever I repeated the gesture. Clearly, the cockroaches were revulsed by a human being, recoiled with disgust, regarded me as an exceptionally unpleasant, repugnant creature.

I could embellish upon this scene and describe how, infuriated by my presence, they advanced on me, attacked, crawled over me; how I became hysterical, started to tremble, fell into shock. But this would not be true. In reality, if I didn't come near them, they behaved indifferently, moved about sluggishly and sleepily. Sometimes they pattered from one place to another. Sometimes they crawled out of a crack, or else slid into one again. Other than that—nothing.

I knew that a difficult and sleepless night awaited me (also because the room was inhumanly airless and hot), so I reached into my bag for some notes about Liberia.

. . .

In 1821, a ship arrived at a place near where my hotel now stands (Monrovia lies on the Atlantic, on a peninsula), bringing from the United States an agent of the American Colonization Society, Robert Stockton. Stockton, holding a pistol to the head of the local tribal chief, King Peter, forced him to sell—for six muskets and one trunk of beads—the land upon which the aforementioned American organization planned to settle freed slaves (mainly from the cotton plantations of Virginia, Georgia, Maryland). Stockton's organization was of a liberal and charitable character. Its activists believed that the best reparation for the injuries of slavery would be the return of former slaves to the land of their ancestors—to Africa.

Every year from then on, ships came from the United States carrying groups of liberated slaves, who began to settle in the area of present-day Monrovia. They did not constitute a large population. By the time the Republic of Liberia was proclaimed in 1847, there were only six thousand of them. It is quite possible that their number never even reached twenty thousand: less than 1 percent of the country's population.

The fate and behavior of these settlers (they called themselves Americo-Liberians) is fascinating. Yesterday still they were black pariahs, slaves from America's southern plantations, with no legal rights. The majority of them did not know how to read or write, and had no trade or professional skills. Their fathers had been kidnapped years earlier from Africa, transported to America in chains, and sold in slave markets. And now they, the descendants of those unfortunates, until recently slaves themselves, found themselves once again in Africa, in the land of their ancestors, among kinsmen with whom they shared common roots and skin color. At the will of liberal white Americans, they were brought here and left to themselves, to their own fate. How would they conduct themselves? What would they do? In contrast to their benefactors' expectations, the newcomers did not kiss the ground or throw themselves into the arms of the local Africans.

From their experience in the American South, the Americo-

Liberians knew only one type of relationship: master-slave. Their first move upon arrival in this new land, therefore, was to re-create precisely that social structure, only now they, the slaves of yesterday, are the masters, and it is the indigenous communities whom they set out to conquer and rule.

Liberia is the voluntary continuation of a slave society by slaves who did not wish to abolish an unjust order, but wanted to preserve it, develop it, and exploit it for their own benefit. Clearly, an enslaved mind, tainted by the experience of slavery, a mind born into slavery, fettered in infancy, cannot conceive or conjure a world in which all would be free.

A large portion of Liberia is covered in jungle. Thick, tropical, humid, malarial, and inhabited by small, impoverished, and weakly organized tribes. (Powerful communities, with strong military and state structures, lived most often on the wide, open expanses of the savannah. The unhealthy conditions and difficulty of movement and communication in the African jungle prevented such societies from arising there.) Now, newcomers from across the ocean start to move onto these terrains, traditionally occupied by an indigenous population. Relations develop badly and are hostile from the very start. To begin with, the Americo-Liberians proclaim that only they can be citizens. They deny that status, that right, to the rest—to 99 percent of the population. Laws are passed defining this majority as merely "tribesmen," people without culture, savage, heathen.

The two groups usually live far from each other, and their contacts are infrequent and sporadic. The new masters keep to the coast and to the settlements they have built there, of which Monrovia is the largest. It would not be until one hundred years after the creation of Liberia that its president (it was then William Tubman) ventured for the first time into the country's interior. The newcomers from America, unable to set themselves apart from the locals by skin color or physical type, try to underline their difference and superiority in some other way. In the frightfully hot and humid climate, men walk about in morning coats and spencers, sport derbies and white gloves. Ladies usually stay at home, or if they do go out into the street (until the middle of the nineteenth century there were no asphalt roads or sidewalks in Monrovia), they do so in stiff crinolines, heavy wigs, and hats decorated with artificial flowers. The houses the members of these high, exclusive echelons live in are faithful reproductions of the manors and palaces built by white plantation owners in the American South. The religious world of the Americo-Liberians is similiarly closed and inaccessible to the native Africans. They are ardent Baptists and Methodists. They build their simple churches in the new land, and spend all their free time within, singing pious hymns and listening to topical sermons. With time, these temples will come to serve also as venues for social gatherings, as exclusive private clubs.

As early as the middle of the nineteenth century, long before apartheid was instituted in southern Africa by the Afrikaners, it had been invented and made flesh by the rulers of Liberia—descendants of black slaves. Nature and the impenetrability of the jungle alone created a natural barrier between the natives and the newcomers, an uninhabited no-man's-land that divided them and fostered segregation. But this was not enough. In the small, bigoted world of Monrovia, an ordinance is instituted forbidding close contacts with the local population, particularly intermarriage. Everything is done to ensure that the "savages know their place." To this end, the government in Monrovia allocates to each tribe (there are sixteen of them) a territory where they are allowed to live—not unlike the typical "homelands" created for Africans decades later by the white racists from Pretoria. All who speak out against this are severely punished. Punitive military and police expeditions are dispatched to places of rebellion and resistance. The chiefs of unsubmissive tribes are eliminated on the spot, the rebellious population murdered or imprisoned, its villages destroyed, its crops set afire. In accordance with the ancient, worldwide custom, these expeditions, incursions, and local wars have a single overriding goal: to capture slaves. The Americo-Liberians need laborers. And indeed, they start using slaves on their farms and in their businesses as early as the second half of the nineteenth century. They also sell them to other countries, especially to Fernando Po and Guinea. In the late 1920s, the world press discloses the existence of this trade, plied officially by the Liberian government. The League of Nations intervenes. The then president, Charles King, is forced to resign. But the practice will continue, only conducted in stealth.

From the very outset, the black settlers from America thought about how to preserve and strengthen their dominant position in the new country. At first, they did not allow its indigenous inhabitants, denied the rights of citizenship, to participate in government. They let them live, but only in designated tribal territories. Then they went further: they invented the single-party system of rule. In 1869, a year before the birth of Lenin, the True Whig Party is formed in Monrovia; it will enjoy a monopoly on power for the next 111 years, until 1980. The party's directorship, its political bureau—a National Executive—decides everything, and in detail: who will be president, who will participate in the government, what sort of politics this government will conduct, which foreign company will get what concession, who will be appointed chief of police, head of the postal service, and so on, down to the lowest rungs of the civil service. The leaders of the party are the presidents of the republic, or the other way around—the positions are treated interchangeably. You can achieve something only if you are a member of the party. Its opponents are either in prison or abroad.

In the spring of 1963 I met its then chief and Liberia's president, William Tubman, in Addis Ababa, during the first conference of Africa's heads of state. Tubman was then close to seventy. He never took a plane—he was afraid. A month before the conference, he set out by ship from Monrovia, sailing to Djibouti, and from there he traveled by train to Addis Ababa. He was a short, slight, jovial gentleman with a cigar in his mouth. To troublesome questions he responded with long, resounding laughter, which devolved into an explosion of loud hiccups, followed by an attack of wheezing, convulsive breathlessness. He trembled, his eyes bugged out and filled with tears. The discomfited and frightened interlocutor would fall silent and dared not insist further. Tubman brushed the ashes from his suit and, calm once more, hid again behind a thick cloud of cigar smoke.

He was the president of Liberia for twenty-eight years, and belonged to what is today a rare category of political boss who rules his country like a squire his manor: they know everyone, decide everything. (Rafael Leonidas Trujillo, a contemporary of Tubman's and the dictator of the Dominican Republic for thirty years, exercised power in a similar fashion. During his rule, the church organized mass baptisms of Dominican children, with Trujillo standing as godfather. With time, he became the godfather of all his subordinates. The CIA could find no volunteers to organize a coup against the dictator: no one wanted to raise a hand against his own godfather.)

Tubman received around sixty people daily. He made appointments to all official positions in the country himself, decided who should receive a concession, which missionaries were to be allowed in. He sent his own people everywhere, and his private police reported to him everything that was happening in this village, or in that one. Not much happened. The country was a small, forgotten African backwater; on Monrovia's sandy streets, in the shade of old tumble-down houses, fat women vendors dozed behind their stalls, and dogs sick with malaria roved. Now and then, a group passed before the gates to the government palace carrying a large banner reading "A gigantic manifestation of gratitude for the progress that has taken place in the country thanks to the Incomparable Administration of the President of Liberia—Dr. WVS Tubman." Musical ensembles from the countryside also stopped at these gates, praising in song the greatness of the president:

Tubman is the father of us all,
the father of the whole nation.
He builds us roads,
brings water.
Tubman gives us food to eat,
gives us food to eat,
ye, ye!

The guards, hidden from the sun in their sentry booths, applauded the enthusiastic singers.

What elicited the greatest respect, however, was the fact that the president was protected by benevolent spirits, which endowed him with extraordinary powers. If someone wanted to hand him a poisoned drink, the glass containing the liquid would shatter in midair. The bullet of an assassin could not strike him—it would melt before it reached its target. The president had herbs that allowed him to win every election. And a lens through which he could see everything that was happening, anywhere—there was no sense in opposition or conspiracy, since it would always be found out.

Tubman died in 1971. He was replaced by his friend, vice president William Tolbert. Whereas Tubman was amused by power, Tolbert was fascinated by money. He was a walking embodiment of corruption. He dealt in everything—gold, cars, passports. The entire elite, those descendants of black American slaves, followed his example. People who begged in the street for bread or water were shot on Tolbert's orders. His police killed hundreds.

In the predawn hours of April 12, 1980, a group of soldiers forced their way into the president's villa and hacked Tolbert to pieces in his bed. They disemboweled him and threw his internal organs out into the courtyard for dogs and vultures to devour. There were seventeen soldiers. Their leader was a twenty-eight-year-old sergeant, Samuel Doe. He was barely literate, from the small tribe of Krahn, which lived deep in the jungle. People just like him, driven from their villages by poverty, had been flowing into Monrovia for years, in search of work and money. In the course of thirty years, between 1956 and 1986, the population of Liberia's capital increased tenfold, from 42,000 to 425,000—and this in a city without industry or a system of public transportation, in which few houses had electricity, and fewer still running water.

The trek from the jungle to Monrovia requires many days of difficult marching across roadless tropical expanses. Only young, strong people can manage it. And it is they who arrived in the city. But nothing awaited them here: neither jobs, nor a roof over their heads. From the very first day, they became *bayaye*—that army of the young unemployed squatting idly on all the larger streets and squares of African cities. The existence of this multitude is one of the causes of turmoil on the continent: it is from their ranks that local chieftains, for a pittance, often with only the promise of food, recruit the armies they will use in their struggles for power, organizing coups, fomenting civil wars.

Doe, like Amin in Uganda, was one such *bayaye*. And like Amin, he won the lottery: he got into the army. One would have thought that he had thereby attained the peak of his career. As it turned out, however, he had greater ambitions.

Doe's coup was not simply the exchange of a corrupt political boss/bureaucrat for a semi-illiterate in uniform. It was simultaneously a bloody, cruel, and caricature-like revolt of the downtrodden, half-enslaved masses from the African jungle against their hated rulers—the descendants of slaves from American plantations. In a sense, it was a revolution within the slave world: current slaves rose up against former ones, who had imposed their rule upon them. The entire episode seemed to bear out a most pessimistic and tragic thesis: that in a certain sense, if only the mental or cultural one, there is no way out of slavery; or if there is, it is extremely difficult and takes a very long time.

. . .

Doe immediately declared himself president. He ordered thirteen ministers from Tolbert's administration killed at once. The executions were drawn out and staged before a large crowd of curious gaping onlookers.

The new president constantly announced that yet another attempt on his life had been uncovered and thwarted. A total of thirty-four, he said. He had the conspirators shot. The fact that he lived and continued to rule was proof that he was protected by spells and powerful forces—the work of sorcerers from his village. One could shoot at him—the bullets simply stopped in midair and fell to the ground.

There is not much to say about his administration. He governed for ten years. The country simply came to a standstill. There was no electricity, the shops were closed, the traffic on Liberia's few roads died out.

He didn't really know what it was that he was supposed to do as president. Because he had a childish, chubby face, he bought himself some gold-framed glasses, to look serious and affluent. He was lazy, and so spent entire days sitting in his residence playing checkers with subordinates. He also spent a great deal of time in the courtyard, where the wives of his presidential guards cooked over fires or did their washing. He talked with them, joked, sometimes took one to bed. Uncertain as to what he should do next, and how to save himself from vengeance after having killed so many, he saw as the only solution to surround himself with people from his own tribe, the Krahn. He summoned them in huge numbers to Monrovia. Power now devolved from the hands of the wealthy, settled, and worldly Americo-Liberians (who had managed meantime to flee the country) into those of a poor, illiterate tribe of forest dwellers unnerved by their new situation and who, pulled abruptly from their huts woven of vines and leaves, were seeing a city, a car, or shoes for the first time. They understood one thing, however: that their only means of survival would be to frighten or liquidate all actual or eventual enemies, meaning all non-Krahn. And so a handful of these erstwhile paupers, lost and benighted, wanting to hold fast to the riches and power that had fallen into their hands like a golden egg, set out to terrorize the nation. They beat, tortured, hanged, most often for no reason. "Why did they do this to you?" the neighbors ask a battered man. "Because they determined that I am not Krahn," the poor wretch answers.

It is hardly surprising that in such a situation the country awaits the slightest opportunity to rid itself of Doe and his people. A certain Charles Taylor comes to its aid, a former Doe associate who, as the president claimed, stole a milllion dollars from him before decamping for the United States, where he got into some business trouble, went to prison, escaped, and surfaced suddenly on the shores of the Ivory Coast. From here, with a group of sixty fighters, he begins a war against Doe in December of 1989. Doe could have easily destroyed Taylor, but he sent out against him an army of barefoot Krahn, who, the minute they left Monrovia, instead of fighting Taylor, fell to plundering and stealing whatever and wherever they could. News of this army of robbers spread quickly through the jungle, and the terrified populace, hoping for refuge and protection, started to flee to Taylor. Taylor's army grew at lightning speed, and in a mere six months arrived at the outskirts of Monrovia. A quarrel erupts in the Taylor camp: who will get to actually take the city and seize the spoils? Taylor's chief of staff, Prince Johnson, also a former associate of Doe, breaks with Taylor and forms his own army. Now three forces—Doe's, Taylor's, and Johnson's—are fighting in the city for its possession. Monrovia lies in ruins, entire neighborhoods go up in flames, corpses line the streets.

Finally, the countries of West Africa intervene. Nigeria sends a landing party by sea, which reaches the port in Monrovia in the summer. Doe hears of this and decides to pay the Nigerians a visit. On September 9, 1990, he gathers his entourage and sets out for the port in a Mercedes. The president drives through an exhausted, devastated, plundered, and deserted town. He reaches the port, but Johnson's people are already waiting for him there. They open fire. Doe's entire security detail is killed. He himself takes several bullets in the legs and is unable to escape. He is captured, his hands are tied behind his back, and he is dragged off to be tortured.

Johnson, hungry for publicity, orders the torture scene to be carefully recorded on film. We see Johnson sitting and drinking beer. A woman stands next to him, fanning him and wiping the sweat from his brow. On the floor sits a bound Doe, dripping with blood. His face is so battered you can barely see his eyes. Johnson's men crowd around, mesmerized by the sight of the dictator's agony. For six months now this regiment has been crossing the country robbing and killing, yet the sight of blood can still work them up into a state of ecstasy, a frenzy. Young boys push closer; each wants to see, to sate his eyes. Doe, his head swollen from blows, is sitting naked in a pool of blood, wet from the blood, sweat, and the water they pour over him to keep him from fainting. "Prince!" Doe mutters to Johnson (he addresses him by his first name, because these men who are fighting one another and devastating the country are all friends—Doe, Taylor, and Johnson are friends). "Just have them loosen the ropes on my hands. I will tell you everything, just loosen the ropes!" Clearly, his hands have been tied so tightly that this hurts him more than his bullet-riddled legs. But Johnson just yells at Doe in a local creole dialect. It is impossible to understand most of what he says, except for one thing: he demands that Doe tell him his bank account number. Whenever a dictator is seized in Africa, the entire ensuing inquisition, the beatings, the tortures, will inevitably revolve around one thing: the number of his private bank account. In local opinion, the politician is synonymous with the leader of a criminal gang, who does business trading arms and narcotics and stashes away money in foreign accounts, knowing that his career will not be long, that eventually he will have to flee and will need the wherewithal to live.

"Cut off his ears!" Johnson shouts, furious that Doe will not talk (although Doe says that he is willing to!). Soldiers throw the president down on the floor, hold him down with their boots, and one of them cuts off his ear with a bayonet. An inhuman roar of pain resounds.

"The second ear!" Johnson yells. There is pandemonium; everyone is excited, quarreling, each would like to cut off the president's ear. The same screams again.

They raise the president. Doe sits propped by a soldier's boots, swaying, his earless head flowing with blood. Johnson simply doesn't know what to do next. Order that his nose be cut off? His hand? Leg? He has clearly run out of good ideas. The whole thing is beginning to bore him. "Take him away!" he commands the soldiers, who carry him off for further tortures (also filmed). Doe lived for several hours more, and died from loss of blood. When I was in Monrovia, the video showing him being tortured was the hottest ticket in town. However, there were few video cassette players in the city, and, furthermore, there were frequent power outages. To see Doe's torment (the entire film lasted two hours), people had to invite themselves to the homes of their more well-to-do neighbors or go to those bars where the tape was running nonstop.

Those who write about Europe have a comfortable life. For example, the writer can stop for a while in Florence (or place his hero there). And that's it—history does the rest for him. Endless subject matter is provided to him by the works of architects who erected Florentine churches; of sculptors, who created the extraordinary statues; of wealthy citizens, who could afford the ornamental Renaissance houses. All this he can describe without moving from one place, or by taking a short walk through the city. "I stood in the Piazza del Duomo," writes an author who found himself in Florence. He can follow this up with many pages of description of the richness of objects, of the miracles of art, the creations of human genius and taste that surround him on all sides, which he sees everywhere, in which he is immersed. "And now I am walking through Il Corso and Borgo degli Albizi toward the Michelangelo Museum, since I must see the bas relief of the Madonna della Scala," our author writes. How pleasant for him! It is enough that he walk and look. What is all around him practically writes itself. He can create an entire chapter out of this short walk. There is such a diversity of everything here, such profusion, such inexhaustibility! Take Balzac. Take Proust. Pages upon pages listing, recording, cataloguing objects and articles invented and executed by thousands of cabinetmakers, carvers, fullers of cloth, and stonecutters, by countless skilled, sensitive, and solicitous hands, which built streets and cities in Europe, erected houses and appointed their interiors.

Monrovia puts the newcomer in an entirely different situation. Identical cheap and unkempt houses stretch on for kilometers, streets changing into streets and neighborhoods into neighborhoods so imperceptibly that only fatigue, which you will feel quickly in this climate, will inform you that you have passed from one part of the city into another. The interiors of the houses (with the exception of a few villas belonging to the eminent and the rich) are also uniformly poor and monotonous. A table, chairs or stools, a metal conjugal bed, mats out of raffia or plastic for the children, nails on the wall for hanging clothes, some pictures, most often torn out of glossy magazines. A large pot for cooking rice, a smaller one for preparing the sauce, cups for drinking water and tea. A plastic washbowl, which in the event of flight (lately a frequent occurrence here, as battles kept on erupting) serves as a handy suitcase women can carry on their heads.

Is that all?

Yes, more or less.

It is easiest and cheapest to build a house out of corrugated sheet metal. A calico curtain takes the place of a door and the window openings are small; in the rainy season, which is long and onerous, they are covered with pieces of plywood or thick cardboard. A house like this is hot as a furnace by day, its walls blazing and flaming, its roof sizzling and practically melting in the sun. No one dares enter from dawn to dusk. The earliest daybreak, as the first light streaks the sky, will catapult the still sleepy residents into the yard and the street, where they will remain until evening. They will step outside wet from sweat, scratching blisters from mosquito and spider bites, and peering inside the pot to see if there might be a bit of rice left over from yesterday.

They look at the street, at the houses of their neighbors, without interest, without expectations.

Maybe one should do something. . . .

But what? Do what?

In the morning I set off along Carrey Street, where my hotel is. This is the downtown, the center, the commercial district. It is impossible to get very far. Everywhere against the walls sit groups of *bayaye*—idle hungry boys, with no hope of anything, with no chance for a life. They accost me, asking either where am I from, or can they be my guides, or would I arrange a scholarship to America for them. They don't even want a dollar to buy some bread. No. Right from the start, they aim as high as they possibly can—at America.

I haven't gone a hundred meters and I'm already surrounded by small boys with swollen faces and bleary eyes, sometimes missing an arm or a leg. They beg. These are the former soldiers from Charles Taylor's Small Boys Units, his most frightful divisions. Taylor recruits small children and gives them weapons. He also gives them drugs, and when they are under the influence, he makes them attack. The stupefied youngsters behave like kamikaze fighters, throwing themselves into the heat of battle, advancing straight into flying bullets, getting blown up by mines. When they become addicted to the point of uselessness, Taylor throws them out. Some of them reach Monrovia and end their short lives in ditches or on garbage heaps, consumed by malaria or cholera, or by jackals.

It is unclear why Doe drove down to the port (thereby provoking his own murder). It could be that he forgot that he was the president. He had assumed the office ten years before, essentially by accident. With a group of sixteen companions, like him noncommissioned career officers, he went to President Tolbert's residence to demand overdue wages. They encountered no one from the security forces, and Tolbert was sleeping. Taking advantage of the situation, they stabbed him with their bayonets. And Doe, the oldest among them, assumed his place. Normally, no one in Monrovia shows respect to noncommissioned officers, and now suddenly everyone started to greet him, applaud, push forward to shake his hand. He took a liking to this. And he quickly learned several things: That when the crowd is clapping, one must stretch one's arms upward in a gesture of salutation and victory. That to various evening functions one must wear not a field uniform but a dark double-breasted suit. That if and when an opponent materializes, one must fall upon him and kill him.

But he didn't learn everything. For example, he didn't know what to do when his former friends, Taylor and Johnson, occupied his whole country, occupied the capital, and started laying siege to his residence. Taylor and Johnson had their gangs and were competing with each other for power (which was still in Doe's hands). Of course, these aspirations had nothing to do with any social programs, any democratic principles or issues of national sovereignty. The only question was, who controls the till. Doe had controlled the till for ten years. They deemed that long enough. Why, they even said so outright! "We only want," they repeated in dozens of interviews, "to remove Samuel Doe. The very next day there will be peace."

Doe did not know how to respond to this; he simply became

confused. Instead of acting, either militarily or peacefully, he did nothing. Shut in his residence, he seemed not to comprehend fully what was happening all around, although by then there had been fierce fighting in the city for three months. And suddenly someone informed him that Nigerian troops had sailed into the harbor. As the president of the republic, he had the right to inquire officially about foreign troops entering his country's territory. He could order the commander of these troops to present himself at his residence with an explanation. But Doe did nothing of the kind. The noncommissioned officer-scout, the sergeant-burrower, reared up in him. He would see for himself what was cooking! He got into his car and drove to the port. But didn't he know that that part of the city was under the control of Johnson, who wanted to cut him into pieces? And that it was unseemly for a country's president to report in effect to the commander of a foreign division?

Maybe he really did not know. Or maybe he did, but his imagination failed him, he didn't properly consider things, acted thoughtlessly. History is so often the product of thoughtlessness: it is the offspring of human stupidity, the fruit of benightedness, idiocy, and folly. In such instances, it is enacted by people who do not know what they are doing—more, who do not want to know, who reject the possibility with disgust and anger. We see them hastening toward their own destruction, forging their own fetters, tying the noose, diligently and repeatedly checking whether the fetters and the noose are strong, whether they will hold and be effective.

Doe's final hours allow us to see history at the point of total disintegration—the dignified and haughty goddess transformed into its bloody and pitiful caricature. Johnson's henchmen shoot the nation's president in the legs so that he cannot escape, grab him, break and bind his arms. They then go on to torture him for more than a dozen hours. This takes place in a small city, with a legal government. Where are the ministers during this time? What are the other bureaucrats doing? Where is the police? The president is being tortured right next door to a building just occupied by Nigerian forces who have arrived in Monrovia to protect the lawful regime. So what about these soldiers—what, nothing? Don't they care about this? And that's not all! A few kilometers from the harbor are stationed several hundred soldiers from the elite presidential guard, whose sole mission and purpose in life is to protect the head of state. Meantime, the head of state set off in the morning on a short visit to the port, hours have passed, and there is no sign of him. Aren't they even curious about what might have happened to him? About where he could be?

Let us return to the scene in which Johnson is interrogating the president. He wants to find out where Doe keeps his bank account. Doe is moaning, his wounds are painful; less than an hour ago he was struck by a dozen or more bullets. He is babbling something, who knows what. Is he giving the number of the account? Does he even have an account? Johnson, furious, orders his ears cut off. Why? Is this wise? Doesn't Johnson understand that at the very moment this is done, blood will flood Doe's ear passages and communicating with him will be even more difficult?

One can see how these people are unable to cope with anything, how the situation is getting the better of them, how they botch everything in turn. And then, enraged, they try to recover. But can one make things right by shouting? By sadism? By killing others?

The war continued after Doe's death. Taylor fought with Johnson, the two of them fought with the remnants of the Liberian army, and all of them with the interventionist forces dispatched by other African countries, under the name of ECOMOG, to restore order in Liberia. After drawn-out battles, ECOMOG seized control of Monrovia and the city's closest suburbs, leaving the rest of the country to Taylor and other chieftains like him. You could move about the capital, but after driving twenty to thirty kilometers, you would inevitably arrive at a guardpost manned by soldiers from Ghana, Guinea, or Sierra Leone. They stopped everyone—you could go no farther.

Farther on, hell began, and even these well-armed foreign soldiers did not have the courage to peer into it. It was country under the control of Liberian chieftains. It has become customary to call these chieftains, numerous also in other African countries, the masters, or lords, of war—warlords.

The warlord—he is a former officer, an ex-minister or party functionary, or some other strong individual desiring power and money, ruthless and without scruples, who, taking advantage of the disintegration of the state (to which he contributed and continues to contribute), wants to carve out for himself his own informal ministate, over which he can hold dictatorial sway. Most often, a warlord uses to this end the clan or tribe to which he belongs. Warlords are the sowers of tribal and racial hatred in Africa. They will never admit to this. They will always proclaim that they are leading a national movement or party. Most often it will be called the Something or Other Liberation Movement, or the Movement to Protect Democracy or Independence—never anything less grand or idealistic.

Having chosen the name, the warlord sets about enlisting an army. This is not difficult. In each country, in each city, thousands of hungry and unemployed boys dream of joining a warlord's brigade. The commander will give them arms, and, equally important, a sense of belonging. Most frequently, their caudillo will not pay them. He will say, You have weapons, feed yourselves. That permission is enough: they know what to do next.

Obtaining weapons is also simple. They are cheap and plentiful. Besides, warlords have money. They either grabbed it from state institutions (as ministers or generals), or they reaped profits by seizing valuable sections of the country, those with mines, factories, forests to be cut down, maritime harbors, airports. For instance, Taylor in Liberia or Savimbi in Angola occupy territories with diamond mines. The war over diamonds was waged in the province of Kasai in the Congo, and has lasted years in Sierra Leone. But it is not only mines that yield money. Roads and rivers also generate a good income: one can set up guardposts and collect tolls from everyone who passes.

International relief for the poor, starving population is an inexhaustible source of profit to the warlords. From each transport they take as many sacks of wheat and as many liters of oil as they need. For the law in force here is this: whoever has weapons eats first. The hungry may take only that which remains. The dilemma faced by international organizations? If the robbers aren't given their cut, they will not let the shipments of aid get through, and the starving will die. Therefore you give the chieftains what they want, in the hope that at least the leftovers will reach those suffering from hunger.

The warlords are at once the cause and the product of the crisis in which many of the continent's countries found themselves in the postcolonial era. When we hear that an African country is beginning to totter, we can be certain that warlords will soon appear on the scene. They are everywhere and control everything—in Angola, in Sudan, in Somalia, in Chad. What does a warlord do? Theoretically, he fights with other warlords. Most frequently, however, he is busy robbing his own country's unarmed population. The warlord is the opposite of Robin Hood. He takes from the poor to enrich himself and feed his gangs. We are in a world in which misery condemns some to death and transforms others into monsters. The former are the victims, the latter are the executioners. There is no one else.

The warlord doesn't have to look far to find his victims. They are right there: the inhabitants of nearby villages and towns. Bands of half-naked condottieri shod in ragged Adidas sneakers prowl ceaselessly over the lands of their warlord in search of food and other plunder. For these brutal, hungry, and often drugged wretches, everything is booty. A handful of rice, an old shirt, a piece of a blanket, a clay pot—all are objects of desire, bring a gleam to the eye. But people have grown experienced. It is enough for them to receive word that a warlord's army is approaching, and instantly everyone in the area starts packing and fleeing. It is these people, walking in kilometer-long columns, that the residents of Europe and America see on their television screens.

Let us look at them. Most often, they are women and children. The warlords' forays are aimed at the weakest, at those who cannot defend themselves. They do not know how to defend themselves; they do not have anything to defend themselves with. Let us turn our attention to what these women are carrying on their heads: a bundle or a bowl containing their most indispensible possessions—a little sack of rice or millet, a spoon, a knife, a piece of soap. They have nothing more. That bundle, that bowl, is their entire treasure, their life's earnings, the riches with which they enter the twenty-first century.

The number of warlords is growing. They are the new power, the new rulers. They take for themselves the best morsels, the richest parts of the country, with the result that the state, even if it does survive, will be weak, poor, and ineffective. That is why, in order to defend themselves, states enter into alliances and confederations: to fight for their lives, their very existence. It is the reason there are few international wars in Africa: countries are united in adversity, share the same anxiety about their fate. On the other hand, there are many civil wars, i.e., wars during which warlords divide up a country among themselves and plunder its population, raw materials, and land.

Sometimes the warlords decide that everything worthy of plunder has been extracted, and that the hitherto rich sources of revenue have dried up. Then they begin the so-called peace process. They convene a meeting of the opposing sides (the "warring factions conference"), they sign an agreement, and set a date for elections. In response, the World Bank extends to them all manner of loans and credits. Now the warlords are even richer than they were before, because you can get significantly more from the World Bank than from your own starving kinsmen.

John and Zado arrive at the hotel. They will drive me around town today. But first we must get something to drink, because already the heat is exhausting and oppressive. Even at this early hour the bar is full of people; they are afraid to walk the streets, they feel safer inside. Africans, Europeans, Indians. I met one of them earlier: James P., a retired colonial bureaucrat. What is he doing here? He doesn't answer, just smiles and executes a vague gesture with his hand. Idle prostitutes sit at the sticky, rickety tables. Black-skinned, sleepy, very pretty. The Lebanese owner leans toward me across the counter and whispers in my ear: "These are all thieves. They want to make some money and go to America. They are all diamond dealers. They buy the stones for a pittance from the warlords and fly them out to the Middle East on Russian airplanes." "Russian airplanes?" I ask, surprised. "Yes," he answers. "Go to the airport. There are Russian planes there, which transport these diamonds to the Middle East. To Lebanon, Yemen, Dubai. Especially Dubai."

In the course of our conversation the bar suddenly emptied. It became roomy, spacious. "What happened?" I asked the Lebanese. "They noticed that you had a camera. They'd rather leave than risk being caught on film."

We too walked out. Wet, hot air instantly enveloped us. One doesn't know what to do with oneself here. Inside, it's hot; outside, it's hot. It is impossible to walk, impossible to sit, lie down, or drive. Such temperatures drain all energy, sensation, curiosity. What does one think about? How to get through the day. OK, morning is already past. Good, noon is over. Dusk is finally approaching. But there isn't much relief at dusk; things are hardly better. Dusk too is stifling, sticky, slimy. And evening? The evening steams with a hot, smothering mist. And night? Night envelops us like a wet, burning sheet.

Fortunately, one can take care of many things in the hotel's close vicinity. First—exchange money. Only one banknote is in circulation, one bill: five Liberian dollars. It is worth approximately five cents U.S. Stacks of these five-dollar bills lie on tables set up in the streets—for exchange. To buy almost anything, you must carry a large bag of money. But our transaction is simple: we exchange money at one table, and buy fuel at the next. Gasoline is sold in one-liter bottles; gas stations are closed, there is only a black market. I look at how much people are buying: one liter, two liters; they have no money. John is rich, so he buys ten liters.

We set off. I am curious about what John and Zado will want to show me. First, I must see the impressive things. Everything impressive is American. Several kilometers beyond Monrovia a great metal forest begins. Masts upon masts. Tall, massive, and sprouting ever higher branches, spurs, webs of antennas, poles, wires. These structures go on for kilometers, and we have the impression of being in a science fiction world, hermetic, incomprehensible, not of this earth. It is a Voice of America relay station for Europe, Africa, and the Middle East, built in the presatellite era, during World War II, and now inactive, abandoned, consumed by rust.

Next, we drive to the other side of the city, where we see before us an enormous, flat stretch of land, an endless plain bisected by a concrete landing strip. This is the Robertsfield airport, the largest in Africa and one of the largest in the world. Now deserted, ruined, closed (the only airport open is the small one in town, at which I landed). The airport building: bombed out. The landing strip: riddled with craters from shells and bombs.

Finally, the largest object, the state within the state: the Firestone rubber plantation. Getting to it is difficult. We are constantly encountering military guardposts. There is a roadblock in front of each, and one must stop. Stop and wait. After a while, a soldier emerges from the booth. From a booth, from behind sandbags—this varies. He begins to interrogate—who? what? The slowness of gestures, the sparse words (syllables, really), the flat, enigmatic expression, the deliberation and solemnity evident in his face, are meant to imbue his person and function with seriousness and authority. "Can we drive farther?" Before he answers, he will wipe the sweat from his brow, adjust his weapons, inspect the car from various angles, and so on. Finally, John decides to turn around; we will not be able to reach our destination before evening, and from dusk on all the roads are closed—we risk being stranded somewhere.

We are back in the city again. They take me to a square to see the remnants of the statue of President Tubman, overgrown with vegetation. It was ordered blown up by Doe, to show that the rule of the ex-slaves from America had come to an end and that power was now in the hands of the oppressed Liberian people. Here, if anything is destroyed, broken, ruined, it will simply be left that way. Along the road we notice rusted scraps of metal imbedded in a tree trunk: years ago a car collided with the tree, and what's left of it is there to this day. If a tree trunk falls across the road, it will not be removed; people will go around it, onto the adjoining field, and eventually beat out a new road. An unfinished house will stay unfinished, a ruined one will stay ruined. Similarly with this statue. They have no intention of ever rebuilding it, but they will also not cart away the debris. The act of destruction itself ends the matter: if some material trace remains, it has no meaning anymore, no weight, and therefore is not worth paying attention to.

A bit further, closer to the harbor and the sea, we stopped in an empty area, before an atrociously foul mountain of garbage. I saw rats scurrying everywhere. Vultures circled above. John jumped out of the car and vanished amid the tumbledown shacks scattered nearby. After a moment he reemerged with an old man. We followed him. I could not keep from shuddering, because the rats were walking between our feet, fearlessly. I squeezed my nose between my thumb and fingers, I was suffocating. Finally, the old man stopped and pointed at a slope of rotting garbage. He said something. "He said," Zado translated for me, "that they threw Doe's corpse here. Somewhere here, somewhere in this place."

To breathe cleaner air, we drove on to the St. Paul River. The river constituted the border between Monrovia and the territory of the warlords. It was spanned by a bridge. On the Monrovia side, shacks and the huts of a refugee camp stretched almost as far as the eye could see. There was also a large market—a colorful kingdom of impassioned, zealous women vendors. Those from the other side of the river, from the warlords' inferno, a realm governed by terror, hunger, and death, could cross over to our side to shop, but before stepping onto the bridge they had to leave their weapons behind. I observed them as they crossed and, once on this side, how they stopped, distrustful and uncertain, surprised that a normal world exists. How they stretched out their hands, as if this normalcy were something material, something that could be touched.

I also saw a naked man, walking about with a Kalashnikov over his shoulder. People stepped out of his way, avoided him. He was probably a madman. A madman with a Kalashnikov.

The Lazy River

I am met in Yaoundé by a young Dominican missionary named Stanisław Gurgul. He will take me into the forests of Cameroon. "But first," he says, "we will go to Bertoua." Bertoua? I have no idea where this is. Until now, I had no idea it even existed! Our world consists of thousands—no, millions—of places with their own distinct names (names, moreover, that are written or pronounced differently in different languages, creating the impression of even greater multiplicity), and their numbers are so overwhelming that traveling around the globe we cannot commit to memory even a small percentage of them. Or—which also often happens—our minds are awash with the names of towns, regions, and countries that we are no longer able to connect meaningfully with any image, view, or landscape, with any event or human face. Everything becomes confused, twisted, blurred. We place the Sodori oases in Libya instead of in Sudan, the town of Tefé in Laos instead of in Brazil, the small fishing port of Galle in Portugal instead of where it actually lies—in Sri Lanka. The oneness of the world, so unachievable in the realm of empirical reality, lives in our minds, in the superimposed layers of tangled and confused memories.

It is 350 kilometers from Yaoundé to Bertoua, along a road that runs east, toward the Central African Republic and Chad, over gentle, green hills, through plantations of coffee, cacao, bananas, and pineapples. Along the way, as is usual in Africa, we encounter police guardposts. Stanisław stops the car, leans his head out the window, and says: *"Évêché Bertoua!"* (the bishopric of Bertoua!). This has an instantaneous and magical effect. Anything to do with religion—with the supernatural, with the world of ceremony and spirits, with that which one cannot see or touch but which exists, and exists more profoundly than anything in the material world—is treated with great seriousness here, and immediately elicits reverence, respect, and a little bit of fear. Everyone knows how toying with something higher and mysterious, powerful and incomprehensible, ends: it ends badly, always. But there is more to it. It is about the way in which the origins and nature of existence are perceived. Africans, at least those I've encountered over the years, are deeply religious. *"Croyez-vous en Dieu, monsieur?"* I would always wait for this question, because I knew that it would be posed, having been asked it so many times already. And I knew that the one questioning me would at the same time be observing me carefully, registering every twitch of my face. I realized the seriousness of this moment, the meaning with which it was imbued. And I sensed that the way in which I answered would determine our relationship. And so when I said, *"Oui, je suis croyant"* (yes, I believe), I would see in his face the relief this brought him, see the tension and fear attending this scene dissipate, see how close it brought us, how it allowed us to overcome the barriers of skin color, status, age. Africans valued and liked to make contact on this higher, spiritual plane, to which often they could not give verbal definition, but whose existence and importance each one sensed instinctively and spontaneously.

Generally, it isn't a matter of belief in any one particular god, the kind one can name, and whose appearance or characteristics one can describe. It is more an abiding faith in the existence of a Highest Being, one that creates and rules and also imbues man with a spiritual essence that elevates him above the world of irrational beasts and inanimate objects. This humble and ardent belief in the Highest Being trickles down to its messengers and earthly representatives, who as a consequence are held in special esteem and granted reverential acceptance. This privilege extends to Africa's entire multitudinous layer of clergymen from the most varied sects, faiths, churches, and groups, of which the Catholic missionaries constitute only a small percentage. For there are countless Islamic mullahs and marabouts here, ministers of hundreds of Christian sects and splinter groups, not to mention the priests of African gods and cults. Despite a certain degree of competition, the level of tolerance among them is astonishingly high, and respect for them among the general population universal.

That is why, when Father Stanisław stops the car and tells the policemen, *"Évêché Bertoua!"* they don't check our documents, do not inspect the car, do not demand a bribe. They only smile and make a consenting gesture with their hand: we can drive on.

After a night in the chancery building in Bertoua, we drove to a village called Ngura, 120 kilometers away. Measuring distances in kilometers, however, is misleading and essentially meaningless here. If you happen upon a stretch of good asphalt, you can traverse that distance in an hour, but if you are in the middle of a roadless, unfrequented expanse, you will need a day's driving, and in the rainy season even two or three. That is why in Africa you usually do not say "How many kilometers is it?" but rather "How much time will it take?" At the same time, you instinctively look at the sky: if the sun is shining, you will need only three, four hours, but if clouds are advancing and a downpour looks imminent, you really cannot predict when you will reach your destination.

Ngura is the parish of the missionary Stanisław Stanisławek, whose car we are now following. Without him, we would never be able to find our way here. In Africa, if you leave the few main roads, you are lost. There are no guideposts, signs, markings. There are no detailed maps. Furthermore, the same roads run differently depending on the time of year, the weather, the level of water, the reach of the constant fires.

Your only hope is someone local, someone who knows the area intimately and can decipher the landscape, which for you is merely a baffling collection of signs and symbols, as unintelligible and bewildering as Chinese characters to a non-Chinese. "What does this tree tell you?" "Nothing!" "Nothing? Why, it says that you must now turn left, or otherwise you will be lost. And this rock?" "This rock? Also nothing!" "Nothing? Don't you see that it is telling you to make a sharp right, at once, because straight ahead lies wilderness, a wasteland, death?"

In this way the native, that unprepossessing, barefoot expert on the writing of the landscape, the fluent reader of its inscrutable hieroglyphics, becomes your guide and your savior. Each one carries in his head a small geography, a private picture of the world that surrounds him, a most priceless knowledge and art, because in the worst tempest, in the deepest darkness, it enables him to find his way home and thus be saved, survive.

Father Stanisławek has lived here for years, and so guides us without effort through this remote region's intricate labyrinth. We arrive at his rectory. It is a poor, shabby barracks, once a country school but now closed for lack of a teacher. One classroom is now the priest's apartment: a bed and a table, a little stove, an oil lamp. The other classroom is the chapel. Next door stand the ruins of a little church, which collapsed. The missionary's task, his main occupation, is the construction of a new church. An unimaginable struggle, years of labor. There is no money, no workers, no materials, no effective means of transport. Everything depends on the priest's old car. What if it breaks down, falls apart, stops? Then everything will come to a standstill: the construction of the church, the teaching of the gospel, the saving of souls.

. . .

Later, we drove along the hilltops (below us stretched a plain covered in a thick green carpet of forest, enormous, endless, like the sea) to a settlement of gold diggers, who were searching for treasure in the bed of the winding and lazy Ngabadi River. It was afternoon already, and because there is no dusk here, and darkness can descend with sudden abruptness, we went first to where the diggers were working.

The river flows along the bottom of a deep gorge. Its bed is shallow, sandy, and gravelly. Its every centimeter has been plowed, and you can see everywhere deep craters, pits, holes, ravines. Over this battlefield swarm crowds of half-naked, black-skinned people, streaming with sweat and water, all of them feverish, in a trance. For there is a peculiar climate here, one of excitement, desire, greed, risk, an atmosphere not unlike that of a darkly lit casino. It's as though an invisible roulette wheel were spinning somewhere near, capriciously whirling. But the dominant noises here are the hollow tapping of hoes digging through the gravel, the rustle of sand shaken through handheld sieves, and the monotonous utterances, neither calls nor songs, made by the men working at the bottom of the gorge. It doesn't look as if these diggers are finding anything much, putting much aside. They shake the troughs, pour water into them, strain them, inspect the sand in the palm of their hand, hold it up to the light, throw everything back into the river.

And yet sometimes they do find something. If you gaze up to the top of the gorge, to the slopes of the hills that it intersects, you will see, in the shade of mango trees, under the thin umbrellas of acacias and tattered palms, the tents of Arabs. They are gold merchants from the Sahara, from neighboring Niger, from N'Djamena and from Nubia. Dressed in white djellabahs and snowy, gorgeously wound turbans, they sit idly in tent entrances drinking tea and smoking ornate water pipes. From time to time, one of the exhausted, sinewy black diggers climbs up to them from the bottom of the crowded gorge. He squats in front of an Arab, takes out and unrolls a piece of paper. In its crease lie several grains of gold sand. The Arab looks at them indifferently, deliberates, calculates, then names a figure. The grime-covered black Cameroonian, master of this land and of this river—it is, after all, his country and his gold—cannot contest the price, or argue for a higher one. Another Arab would give him the same measly sum. And the next one, too. There is only one price. This is a monopoly.

Darkness descends, the gorge empties and grows quiet, and one can no longer see its interior, now a black, undifferentiated chasm. We walk to the settlement, called Colomine. It is a hastily thrown together little town, so makeshift and scruffy that its inhabitants will have no qualms abandoning it once the gold in the river runs out. Shack leaning against shack, hovel against hovel, the streets of slums all emptying into the main one, which has bars and shops and where evening and nightlife take place. There is no electricity. Oil lamps, torches, fires, and candles are burning everywhere. What their glow picks out from the darkness is flickering and wobbly. Here, some silhouettes slip by; over there, someone's face suddenly appears, an eye glitters, a hand emerges. That piece of tin, that's a roof. That flash you just saw, that's a knife. And that piece of plank—who knows what it's from and what purpose it serves. Nothing connects, arranges itself, can be composed into a whole. We know only that this darkness all around us is in motion, that it has shapes and emits sounds; that with the assistance of light we can bring bits of it up to the surface and momentarily observe them, but that as soon as the light goes out, everything will escape us and vanish. I saw hundreds of faces in Colomine, heard dozens of conversations, passed countless people walking, bustling about, sitting. But because of the way the images shimmered in the flickering flames of the lamps, because of their fragmentation and the speed with which they followed one another, I am unable to connect a single face with a distinct individual or a single voice with some particular person that I met there.

In the morning we drove south, to the great forest. First, however, was the Kadeï River, which runs through the jungle (it is a tributary of the Sangha River, which flows into the Congo River north of Yumbi and Bolobo). In keeping with the operative local principle that a thing broken will never be repaired, our ferry looked like something fit only for the scrap heap. But the three little boys scampering around it knew exactly how to compel the monster into motion. The ferry: a huge, rectangular, flat metal box. Above it, a metal wire stretching across the river. Turning a squeaky crank, alternately tightening and releasing the wire, the boys move the ferry (with us and the car on board)—slowly, ever so slowly—from one bank to the other. Of course, this operation can succeed only when the current is sluggish and somnolent. Were it to twitch, to come alive, suddenly we would end up, carried off by the Kadeï, the Sangha, and the Congo, somewhere in the Atlantic.

After that—driving, plunging into the forest—sinking, slipping, into the labyrinths, tunnels, and underworlds of some alien, green, dusky, impenetrable realm. One cannot compare the tropical forest with any European forest or with any equatorial jungle. Europe's forests are beautiful and rich, but they are of average scale and their trees are of moderate height: we can imagine ourselves climbing to the top of even the highest ash or oak. And the jungle is a vortex, a giant knot of tangled branches, roots, shrubs, and vines, a heated and compressed nature endlessly proliferating, a green cosmos.

This forest is different. It is monumental, its trees—thirty, fifty, and more meters high—are gigantic, perfectly straight, loosely positioned, maintaining clearly delineated distances between one another and growing out of the ground with virtually no undercover. Driving into the forest, in between these sky-high sequoias, mahogany trees, and others I do not recognize, I have the sensation of stepping across the threshold of a great cathedral, squeezing into the interior of an Egyptian pyramid, or standing suddenly amid the skyscrapers of Fifth Avenue.

The journey here is often a torment. There are stretches of road so pitted and rough that for all intents and purposes one cannot drive, and the car is flung about like a boat on a stormy sea. The only vehicles that can deal with these surfaces are the gigantic machines with engines like the underbellies of steam locomotives, which the French, Italians, Greeks, and Dutch use to export timber from here to Europe. For the forest is being cut down day and night, its surface shrinking, its trees disappearing. You constantly come across large, empty clearings, with huge fresh stumps sticking out of the earth. The screech of saws, their whistling, penetrating echo, carries for kilometers.

Somewhere in this forest, in which we all appear so small, live others smaller still—its permanent inhabitants. It is rare to see them. We pass their straw huts along the way. But there is no one around. The owners are somewhere deep in the forest. They are hunting birds, gathering berries, chasing lizards, searching for honey. In front of each house, hanging on a stick or stretched out on a line, are owl's feathers, the claws of an anteater, the corpse of a scorpion, or the tooth of a snake. The message is in the manner in which these trifles are arranged: they probably tell of the owners' whereabouts.

At nightfall we spotted a simple country church and beside it a humble house, the rectory. We had arrived at our destination. Somewhere, in one of the rooms, an oil lamp was burning, and a small, wavering glow fell through the open door onto the porch. We entered. It was dark and quiet inside. After a moment, a tall, thin man in a light habit came out to greet us: Father Jan, from southern Poland. He had an emaciated, sweaty face with large, blazing eyes. He had malaria, was clearly running a fever, his body probably wracked by chills and cramps. Suffering, weak and listless, he spoke in a quiet voice. He wanted to play the host somehow, to offer us something, but from his embarrassed gestures and aimless puttering about it was plain he didn't have the means, and didn't know how. An old woman arrived from the village and began to warm up some rice for us. We drank water, then a boy brought a bottle of banana beer. "Why do you stay here, Father?" I asked. "Why don't you leave?" He gave the impression of a man in whom some small part had already died. There was already something missing. "I cannot," he answered. "Someone has to guard the church." And he gestured with his hand toward the black shape visible through the window.

I went to lie down in the adjoining room. I couldn't sleep. Suddenly, the words of an old altar boy's response started to play in my head: *Pater noster, qui es in caeli . . . Fiat voluntas tua . . . sed libera nos a malo . . .*

In the morning, the boy whom I had seen the previous evening beat with a hammer on a dented metal wheel rim hanging on a wire. This served as the bell. Stanisław and Jan were celebrating morning mass in the church, a mass in which the boy and I were the sole participants.

Madame Diuf Is Coming Home

At first, nothing portends what is to come. At dawn, the train station in Dakar is empty. There is only one train on the tracks, which will leave for Bamako before noon. Trains rarely arrive or depart from here. In all of Senegal, there is only one international rail connection, to Bamako, the capital of Mali, and only one short internal one, to St. Louis, with a train running once every twenty-four hours. Most frequently, therefore, there is no one at the station. It is difficult even to find the cashier, who, reportedly, is also the stationmaster.

Only when the sun is already high in the sky do the first passengers appear. They take their places in the compartments unhurriedly. The cars here are smaller than in Europe, the tracks narrower, the compartments more cramped. At first, however, there is no shortage of seats. I met a young couple on the platform, Scots from Glasgow, who were traveling through western Africa from Casablanca to Niamey. "Why from Casablanca to Niamey?" They have difficulty answering. That's just what they decided. They are together, and that, it seems, is enough for them. What did they see in Casablanca? Nothing, really. And in Dakar? Nothing much either. They are not interested in sightseeing. They want only to travel. Travel and travel. What is important for them is an exotic route, and experiencing this route together.

They look very much alike: pale complexions, which in Africa look almost transparent, light brown hair, many freckles. Their English is very Scottish, meaning that I understand little of it. For a while, it's just the three of us in the compartment, but right before departure we are joined by a heavy, energetic woman in an ample, puffy, brightly colored bou-bou (the local ankle-length dress). "Madame Diuf!" she introduces herself, and settles herself comfortably on the bench.

We set off. At first, the train rolls along the edge of old, colonial Dakar. A beautiful coastal city, pastel-colored, picturesque, laid out on a promontory amid beaches and terraces, slightly resembling Naples, the residential areas of Marseilles, the posh suburbs of Barcelona. Palm trees, gardens, cypresses, bougainvillea. Stepped streets, hedges, lawns, fountains. French boutiques, Italian hotels, Greek restaurants. The train, gathering more and more speed, passes this showcase city, enclave city, dream city, then suddenly, in the space of a second, it grows dark in the compartment, there are loud thudding, crashing sounds outside, and we hear blood-curdling screams. I lunge at the window, which Edgar, the young Scot, is trying unsuccessfully to slam shut in order to keep out the clouds of dust, garbage, and debris forcing their way in.

What has happened? I can see that the lush, flowering gardens have disappeared, swallowed beneath the ground, and a desert has commenced, but a populated desert, full of shacks and lean-tos, sand upon which sprawls a neighborhood of squalor, a chaotic and swarming district of slums, one of the typical, depressing bidonvilles that surround most African cities. And in this cramped bidonville, the shanties crowd one another, press together, even climb up on one another; the only open space for a market is the train tracks and embankment. It's busy here from dawn. Women display their merchandise on the ground, in bowls, on trays, on tables—their bananas, tomatoes, soap, and candles. They stand next to one another, elbow to elbow, as is the African custom. And then—here comes the train. It arrives at full speed, unchecked, thundering and whistling. And then everyone, shouting, terrified, panicked, grabbing whatever they can manage to, starts to run as fast as their legs can carry them. They cannot move out of the way earlier, because no one knows for certain when the train will arrive, and, moreover, one cannot see it from a distance: it comes barreling out from behind a bend. Thus there is only one thing to do: save yourself at the last minute, in those seconds when the enraged iron giant is already coming at you headlong, rushing like a lethal rocket.

Through the window I see the fleeing crowds, the frightened faces, hands instinctively raised in a protective gesture. I see people falling, rolling down the embankment, covering their heads. And all this in clouds of sand, flying plastic bags, shreds of paper, rags, bits of cardboard.

It is some time before we finish rushing through the market, leaving in our wake a trampled battlefield and billowing dust. And people, who no doubt will now try to restore some semblance of order. We come to a spacious, peaceful, unpopulated savannah, on which grow acacias and blackthorn bushes. Madame Diuf says this moment when the train knocks down and, as it were, blows up the market is ideal for thieves, who are lying in wait for just this moment. Taking advantage of the confusion, concealed behind the curtain of dust raised by the train wheels, they pounce upon the scattered merchandise and steal as much as they can.

"Ils sont malins, les voleurs!" she exclaims, almost admiringly.

I tell the young Scots, who are on this continent for the first time, that in the last two to three decades the character of African cities has changed. What they saw just a moment ago—the beautiful Mediterranean-like Dakar giving way to the frightful desert Dakar—is an apt illustration of this change. In the past, the cities were administrative, commercial, and industrial centers, practical constructs, performing productive, creative functions. Typically of moderate size, they were inhabited only by those who had employment there. What remains of these cities today is merely a shred, a fraction, a fragment of the former cities, which even in small and thinly populated countries have expanded monstrously, become great metropolises. True, urban centers the world over are growing at an accelerated pace, because people pin on them their hopes for an easier and better life. But in Africa's case additional factors came into play, which further intensified this hyper-urbanization. The first was the calamity of the drought that descended on the continent in the 1970s, and then again in the 1980s. Fields were drying up, cattle were perishing. Millions of people were starving to death. Millions of others sought salvation in cities. The cities offered a better chance of survival, because international relief supplies were distributed here. Transport in Africa is too difficult and costly for such supplies to reach the countryside; therefore, the inhabitants of the countryside must journey to the city in order to take advantage of them. But once a clan abandons its fields and loses its herds it will not have the means to regain them. These people, now permanently condemned to depend on international relief, will live only as long as it is not interrupted.

The city also tempted with the mirage of peace, the dream of safety. This was especially so in countries tormented by civil wars and the terror of warlords. The weak, the defenseless, fled to the cities, hoping to increase their chances of survival. I remember the little towns of eastern Kenya—Mandera, Garissa—during the Somalian war. When evening approached, Somalis arrived from pastures with their herds and converged around these hamlets, which each night were encircled by a glowing ring of lights: it was the newcomers burning their lamps, tallow candles, torches. They felt calmer closer to town, more secure somehow. At dawn, the band of lights died out. The Somalis dispersed, walking with their herds to distant pastures.

That is how drought and war depopulated villages and drove their inhabitants into cities. The process took years. It involved millions, tens of millions, of people. In Angola and in Sudan, in Somalia and in Chad. Everywhere, really. Go to the city! It was an expression of hope, and also a gesture of despair. After all, no one was waiting for them there, no one had invited them. They came spurred on by fear, with the last ounces of strength, just to find a hiding place, to be saved somehow.

I think of the camp we passed leaving Dakar, of the fate of its residents. The impermanence of their existence, the questions about its purpose, its meaning, which they probably do not pose to anyone, not even to themselves. If the truck does not bring food, they will die of hunger. If the tanker does not bring water, they will die of thirst. They have no reason to go into the city proper; they have nothing to come back to in their village. They cultivate nothing, raise nothing, manufacture nothing. They do not attend schools. They have no addresses, no money, no documents. All of them have lost homes; many have lost their families. They have no one to complain to, no one they expect anything from.

The increasingly important question in the world is not how to feed all the people—there is plenty of food, and preventing hunger is often only a matter of adequate organization and transport—but what to do with them. What should be done with these countless millions? With their unutilized energy? With the hidden powers they surely possess? What is their place in the family of mankind? That of fully vested members? Wronged brothers? Irritating intruders?

The train was slowing down; we were nearing a station. I saw a throng of people dashing toward the train cars, desperately, as if a crowd of would-be suicides who in a minute would fling themselves beneath the wheels. They were women and children, selling bananas, oranges, grilled corn, dates. They pressed around the windows of the cars, but because their goods were laid out on trays which they held atop their heads, one could not see the sellers' faces, only competing heaps of bananas, which were being pushed aside by stacks of dates and pyramids of watermelons and jostled by tumbling oranges.

Madame Diuf immediately commandeered the entire span of the window with her magnificent self. She picked through the heaps of fruits and vegetables swaying above the platform. She haggled and quarreled. Occasionally, she would turn from the window and show us a bunch of green bananas, or a ripe papaya. She would weigh her loot in her soft, plump hand, and exclaim triumphantly: *"À Bamako? Cinq fois plus cher! À Dakar? Dix fois plus cher! Voilà!"* And she would stash the purchased fruit on the floor and on the shelves. There weren't many other buyers. The fruit bazaar undulated before our eyes practically untouched. I wondered how these besieging people made a living. The next train would not pass this way for several days. No settlement was visible nearby. Who do they sell to? Who buys from them?

The train jerked and set off, and Madame Diuf sat down, satisfied. But she sat down in such a way that there was now noticeably more of her. She not only sat down but sprawled out imperiously, as if she had decided to liberate her massive body from its hitherto invisible corsets, to let it breathe, set it free. The compartment filled up with the ever expanding, panting, and sweaty Madame, whose shoulders and hips, arms and legs lorded over us, pushing Edgar and Clare (the Scot and his girlfriend) into one corner and me into the other, until I had barely any room left at all.

I wanted to step out of the compartment to stretch my legs, but this turned out to be impossible. It was the hour of prayer, and the corridors were filled with men kneeling on rugs, bowing rhythmically. The corridor was the only place where they could pray. Even so, the train ride posed a liturgical problem: Islam commands its faithful to pray facing Mecca, whereas our train constantly swerved, turned and changed direction, positioning itself at such angles as to put the faithful in danger of prostrating themselves with their backs to the holy places.

The train twisted and turned, but the landscape was always the same. The Sahel: an arid, sandy, beige, at times brown plain, heated by the sun. Here and there, above the sand and the rocks, patches of dry, rough, straw-yellow grass. Bushes of pink barberries and slender, bluish tamarisks. Scattered over the shrubs, grasses, and earth, the thin, pale shadows of the knotty, thorny acacias, growing all around. Quiet. Emptiness. The quivering, white air of a hot day.

In the large Tambacounda station, the locomotive broke down. Some valves burst, and a stream of oil trickled down the embankment. The local boys hastily filled their bottles and cans with it. Nothing is wasted here. If grain spills, it will be carefully gathered; if a pitcher of water cracks, every drop possible will be saved and drunk.

It looked as if we were going to be standing here quite some time. A crowd of curious onlookers from the town quickly assembled. I encouraged the two Scots to step outside, have a look around, talk a little. They categorically refused. They did not want to meet or speak to anyone. They did not want to get to know anyone, visit with anyone. If someone started to approach them, they turned and walked away. Ideally they would prefer simply to run. Their attitude was the result of limited but bad experience. They had seen that whenever they engaged in conversation with anyone, that that person always wanted something from them later. Different things: help securing a scholarship, employment, money. He or she invariably had sick parents, younger siblings in their care, and had not eaten for several days now. These complaints and lamentations were constantly repeated. They didn't know how to react. They felt helpless. Finally, discouraged and disappointed, they made a joint decision: no contact, encounters, conversations. And they were now sticking by this.

I told the Scots that these requests on the part of the people they had met follow from the belief of many Africans that the white man has everything, or that, in any event, he has a great deal, much more than the black man. And if a white man suddenly crosses an African's path, it's as if a chicken has laid him a golden egg. He must take advantage of this opportunity—he must remain focused, must not miss his chance. All the more so because so many of these people really have nothing, need everything, and want so much.

But this behavior is also a manifestation of a great cultural difference, a dissimilarity of expectations. African culture generally is a culture of exchange. You give me something, and it is my responsibility to reciprocate. It is not only my responsibility; my dignity, my honor, my humanity require it. Human relations assume their highest form during the process of exchange. The union of two young people, who through their progeny prolong man's presence on earth and ensure the continuation of the species—why, even that union comes into being through an act of interclan exchange: the woman is traded for various material goods indispensible to her clan. In this culture, everything assumes the form of a gift, a present demanding requital. The unreciprocated gift lies heavily on the head of the one who has received it, torments his conscience, and can even bring down misfortune, illness, death. Thus the receipt of a present is a signal, a goad to immediate reciprocal action, to a quick restoring of equilibrium: I received? I repay!

Many misunderstandings arise because one side does not understand that things of a very different order can be exchanged; for example, we can exchange something of symbolic value for something of material value, and vice versa. If an African approaches the Scots, he showers various gifts on them: he bestows upon them his presence and attention, imparts information (warning them about thieves, for example), ensures their safety, etc. It goes without saying that this generous man now awaits reciprocity, recompense, the satisfaction of his expectations. It is to his astonishment that he observes the Scots make sour faces; more, that they turn on their heels and walk away!

In the evening we continued on our way. It grew a bit cooler, one could breathe. We were traveling east, deeper and deeper into the Sahel, into Africa's interior. The train tracks led through Goudiry,

Diboli, and a larger town already across the border in Mali: Kayes. At each station Madame Diuf shopped. The compartment was already bursting with oranges, watermelons, papayas, grapes; now she bought carved stools, brass candleholders, Chinese towels, French soaps. Each transaction was punctuated with her triumphant cries: *"Voilà, m'sieurs, dames! Combien cela coûte à Bamako? Cinq fois plus cher! Et à Dakar? Dix fois! Bon Dieu! Quel achat!"* She now took up the entire length of one banquette. I lost my seat entirely, but even the Scots had only a small sliver left on the other side of the compartment, now packed to the rafters with fruit, laundry detergents, blouses, bunches of dried herbs, sacks of seeds, millet, and rice.

I had the impression—I was a little drowsy and felt that I was coming down with a fever—that Madame was becoming ever more immense, that there was more and more of her. Her full bou-bou caught the wind coming in through the window, swelled, ballooned like a sail, undulated and fluttered. She was returning home to Bamako, proud of her cheap purchases. Satisfied, victorious, she filled the whole compartment with her person.

Looking at Madame Diuf, at her ubiquitousness, her dynamic and commanding presence, her monopolizing and unapologetic omnipotence, I realized how much Africa had changed. I remembered how I had ridden this railroad years ago. I was then alone in my compartment; no one dared to disturb the peace and encroach upon the comfort of a European. And now the proprietress of a stall in Bamako, the mistress of this land, without so much as blinking an eye, pushes three Europeans out of the compartment, demonstrating unequivocally that there is no room for them here.

We reached Bamako at four in the morning. The station was full of people, a dense crowd stood on the platform. A band of feverish boys burst into our compartment: Madame's crew, come to carry her purchases. I walked out of the compartment. Suddenly, I heard a man shouting. Pushing my way in that direction, I came upon a Frenchman in a torn shirt sitting on the platform, moaning and cursing. He had been robbed of everything the second he stepped off the train. All he had left was the handle of his suitcase, and now, brandishing this scrap of leather, he was shaking his fist at the world.

Salt and Gold

In Bamako I live in a guest house called the Centre d'Acceuil, run by Spanish nuns. The rooms are cheap—a bed, mosquito netting. The bad thing about the Centre d'Acceuil is that although there are ten rooms for rent, there is only one shower. Moreover, it is constantly occupied these days by a young Norwegian, who came here not realizing just how hot it gets in Bamako. The African interior is always white-hot. It is a plateau relentlessly bombarded by the rays of the sun, which appears to be suspended directly above the earth here: make one careless gesture, it seems, try leaving the shade, and you will go up in flames. For newcomers from Europe, there is also a psychological factor at work: they know they are in the depths of hell, far from the sea, from lands with a gentler climate, and this feeling of distance, of exile, of imprisonment, makes life here even harder for them to bear. The Norwegian, after several suffocating, sweltering days, decided to leave everything and return home. But he had to wait for the plane. And the only way he could survive until then, he concluded, was by never coming out from under the shower.

There is no question: the temperatures here during the dry season are overwhelming. The street where I live is dead still from early morning. People slump motionlessly against walls, in passageways, beneath entrance gates. They sprawl in the shade of eucalyptus and mimosa trees, beneath a great, spreading mango and a tall, flaming amaranthine bougainvillea. They sit on a long bench in front of the bar run by a Mauritanian, and on empty crates in front of the corner grocery shop. Despite having observed them all at length on several occasions, I have been unable to determine what exactly it is that they are doing. Perhaps that's because they are not doing anything. They don't even talk. They resemble people sitting for hours in a doctor's waiting room. Although this is perhaps not the best comparison, because in the end the doctor will arrive. Here no one arrives. No one arrives, no one leaves. The air trembles, undulates, stirs restlessly, like over a kettle of boiling water.

One day a fellow countryman from Valencia, Jorge Esteban, arrived to stay with the sisters. He had a travel agency back home and was driving around West Africa collecting materials for a tourist brochure. Jorge was a cheerful, merry, energetic man, naturally convivial. He felt at home everywhere, at ease with everyone. He spent only one day with us. He paid no heed to the scorching sun; the heat only seemed to energize him. He unpacked a bag full of cameras, lenses, filters, rolls of film, and began walking around the street, chatting with people, joking, making various sorts of promises. That done, he placed his Canon on a tripod, took out a loud referee's whistle, and blew it. I was looking out the window and couldn't believe my eyes. Instantly, the street filled with people. In a matter of seconds they formed a large circle and began to dance. I don't know where the children came from. They had empty cans, which they beat rhythmically. Everyone was keeping the rhythm, clapping their hands and stomping their feet. People woke up, the blood flowed again through their veins, they became animated. Their pleasure in this dance, their happiness in finding themselves alive again, was palpable. Something started to happen in this street, around them, within them. The walls of the houses moved, the shadows stirred. More and more people joined the ring of dancers, which grew, swelled, and accelerated. The crowd of onlookers was also dancing, the whole street, everyone. Colorful bou-bous, white djellabahs, blue turbans, all were swaying. There is no asphalt or pavement here, so billows of dust soon began to rise above the dancers, dark, thick, hot, choking, and these clouds, just like ones from a raging fire, drew more people still from the surrounding areas. Before long the entire neighborhood was shimmying, shaking, partying—right in the middle of the worst, most debilitating and unbearable noontime heat.

Partying? No, this was something different, something bigger, something loftier and more important. You had only to look at the faces of the dancers. They were attentive, listening intently to the loud rhythm the children beat on their tin cans, concentrating, so that the sliding of their feet, the swaying of their hips, the turns of their arms, and the bobbing of their heads corresponded to it. And they looked determined, decisive, alive to the significance of this moment in which they were able to express themselves, participate, prove their presence. Idle and superfluous all day long, all at once they had become visible, needed, and important. They existed. They created.

All the while, Jorge was photographing. He needed pictures in which the street of an African town makes merry and dances, beckons and invites. Finally, he grew weary, stopped shooting, and with a gesture of his hand thanked the dancers. They stopped, adjusted their clothing, wiped off sweat. They talked, exchanged comments, laughed. Then they started to disperse, seek out the shade, vanish inside houses. Once again the street reverted to a still, scorching emptiness.

I was in Bamako because I wanted to see the war with the Tuareg. The Tuareg are eternal wanderers. But can one really call them that? A wanderer is someone who roams the world searching for a place to call his own, a home, a country. The Tuareg has his home and his country, in which he has lived for a thousand years: the interior of the Sahara. His home is just different from ours. It has no walls or roof, no doors or windows. There are no fences or walls, nothing that limits or confines. The Tuareg despises whatever hems him in, strives to demolish every partition, destroy every barrier. His country is immeasurable—thousands upon thousands of kilometers of burning sand and rocks, an immense, treacherous, barren expanse, which everyone fears and tries to bypass. Its border is where the Sahara and the Sahel end and the green fields, villages, and houses of the sedentary societies hostile to the Tuareg begin.

Wars have been waged between them for centuries. For often the drought in the Sahara is so severe that all the wells vanish, and then the Tuareg must wander with their camels beyond the desert, to the green regions, toward the Niger River and Lake Chad, to water and feed their herds and also to find a little something to eat.

The sedentary Bantu peasants treat these visits as invasions, raids, acts of aggression, hecatombs. The hatred between them and the Tuareg is fierce, because the latter not only burn villages and steal livestock but also enslave the villagers. The Tuareg, who are light-skinned Berbers, consider the black Africans a low and abject race of wretched subhumans. These, in turn, hold the Tuareg to be bandits, parasites, and terrorists, and wish that the sands of the Sahara would swallow them up once and for all. The Bantu have fought off two colonialisms in this part of Africa: the external French one and the intra-African colonialism practiced by the Tuareg, which has existed here for centuries.

The two societies, the settled, agricultural Bantu people and the restless, fleet Tuareg, have always had divergent philosophies. The source of strength, of life, for the Bantu is the land—the domain of the ancestors. The Bantu bury their dead in their fields, often in close proximity to their houses, and even beneath the floors of the huts in which they live. In this way, the one who has died continues symbolically to participate in the existence of the living, watches over them, advises, intervenes, blesses, or metes out punishments. The tribal, familial land is not only a source of livelihood, but also a sacred thing, the place from which man sprung and to which he will return.

The Tuareg—a nomad, a man of open spaces and limitless horizons, the cavalryman and Cossack of the Sahara—has a different relation toward the ancestors. The one who died is erased from the memory of the living. The Tuareg bury their dead in the desert, in arbitarily chosen locations, making sure of one thing only: never to pass that way again.

Between the people of the Sahara and the sedentary tribes of the Sahel and the green savannah there had existed for centuries in this part of Africa a form of commerce known as silent trading. The inhabitants of the Sahel traded salt and received gold in return. This salt, a highly coveted and priceless commodity, especially in the tropics, was carried from the interior of the Sahara on the heads of the black slaves of the Tuareg and the Arabs, probably to the River Niger, where the transaction took place. "When the Negroes reach the river, they proceed as follows," tells a fifteenth-century Venetian merchant, Alvise Ca' da Mosto. "Each of them forms a little hillock out of the salt he brought, and marks it. Leaving the salty piles arranged in one straight line, they retreat a half day's travel time in the direction from whence they came. Then, people from another Negro tribe arrive. They come on large boats, probably from nearby islands, disembark, and place next to each mound of salt a certain amount of gold. Then they, too, withdraw, leaving behind the gold and the salt. When they are gone, those who brought the salt return, and if they deem the amount of gold to be sufficient, they take it, leaving the salt; if not, they take neither the gold nor the salt, and go away once again. Then the other ones come back and take those piles of salt that have no gold next to them; next to the others they place more gold, if they consider it appropriate, or leave the salt. In this manner they conduct their commerce, never seeing one another and never speaking. This practice has gone on for a very long time already, and although the whole business sounds improbable, I assure you that it is true."

I read this story on the bus on which I'm traveling from Bamako to Mopti. "Go to Mopti!" friends advised me. The idea is that from there I might be able to get to Timbuktu, which is already on the threshold of the Sahara, hence of Tuareg territory.

The Tuareg are perishing, their way of life is ending. In the past, a portion of them lived by robbing caravans, which these days are both infrequent and well armed. Most important, severe and constant droughts are pushing them out of the Sahara. They must go where there is water, but all those regions are already occupied. The Tuareg live in Mali, Algeria, Libya, Niger, Chad, and Nigeria, as well as a few other Saharan countries. But they do not consider themselves to be the citizens of any state, do not want to subordinate themselves to anyone else's government, to any authority.

There are around a half million of them left, perhaps one million. No one has ever counted this mobile, mysterious, reclusive community. They live apart, secreted not only physically but also mentally in their impenetrable Sahara. The outside world holds no interest for them. It does not occur to them to explore the oceans, as the Vikings did, or to tour Europe or America. When a European traveler they had captured told them that he was headed for the Niger, they refused to believe him: "Why the Niger? Are there no rivers in this country?" Despite the fact that the French occupied the Sahara for more than half a century, the Tuareg had no desire to learn French, were interested neither in Descartes nor in Rousseau, in Balzac or Proust.

My neighbor on the bus, a merchant from Mopti called Diawara, does not like the Tuareg. He is afraid of them and pleased that in Mopti the troops have dealt with them successfully.

"Dealt with them" means that some of the Tuareg were killed, and others chased so deep into the Sahara that they would soon die from lack of water. When we arrive (the bus trip lasts a whole day), Diawara will ask his cousin, one Mohamed Kone, to show me the traces of the Tuareg's presence. Mopti is a great port on the Niger, and the Niger is one of the three largest rivers in Africa, after the Nile and the Congo. For two thousand years Europeans argued about which way the Niger flows, and into which lake, river, or sea it empties. The reason for these controversies was the strange course of the river, which originates not far from the western shores of Africa, in Guinea, flows deep into the continent, toward the heart of the Sahara, until suddenly, as if encountering in the great desert some insurmountable barrier, it turns in the opposite direction, south, and on the territory of present-day Nigeria, near Cameroon, empties into the Gulf of Guinea.

As seen from the high bank upon which Mopti is situated the Niger is a wide, dark brown, slowly flowing river. It is an extraordinary sight: all around, blazing hot desert, and then suddenly, in a stony channel, this immense expanse of water. Moreover, the Niger, in contrast to other Saharan rivers, never dries up, and this image of an eternally flowing stream amid limitless sands inspires such awe and devotion in people, that they regard the waters of the river as miraculous and holy.

Mohamed Kone turned out to be a young boy with no clearly defined occupation, a typical *bayaye,* living off whatever he could. He had a friend called Thiema Djenepo who owned a boat (he later gave me his business card—Thiema Djenepo, Piroguer, BP 76, Mopti, Mali) and took us, rowing with difficulty against the current, to a little island on which stood the scattered remnants of recently demolished mud houses: vestiges of a Tuareg attack on a village of Mali fishermen. *"Regardez, mon frère,"* Mohamed said to me in a familiar way. *"Ce sont les activités criminelles des Tuaregs!"* I asked him where would be the best place to meet them, in response to which Mohamed just laughed and looked at me with pity: to him, this was akin to my inquiring about how best to commit suicide.

The most difficult thing was getting from Mopti to Timbuktu. The road through the desert was closed by the army, for battles were still being fought somewhere in the interior. One could get closer to them, but this would take weeks. The only real option was a small Air Mali plane, which flew sporadically, sometimes once a week, sometimes once a month. In this part of the world, time has no measure, no reference points, shape, or tempo. It spreads, melts, and it is difficult to seize it, to give it form. I secured a seat by bribing the manager of the Mopti airport. One flies over the Sahara—moonlike, surreal, full of mysterious lines and signs. The desert is clearly telling us something, communicating something, but how can we understand it? What do these two straight lines mean, which appear suddenly in the sand and just as quickly vanish? And those circles, an entire chain of them, symmetrically positioned? And these zigzags, broken triangles, and rhomboids, followed by arched lines and twisting ones? Are they the traces of lost caravans? Of human settlements? Of campgrounds? But how could one possibly live on this sizzling pan? Along what road would one have traveled to arrive here? And which way would one flee?

We landed in Timbuktu straight into the muzzles of the anti-aircraft guns guarding the runway. The town consists of clay houses built on sand. The clay and the sand are the same color, so the town looks like an organic part of the desert—a fragment of the Sahara shaped into rectangular blocks and elevated. The heat curdles the blood, paralyzes the body, stuns. I did not encounter a living soul in the narrow streets and back alleys. But I found a house with a plaque informing that here, from September 1853 until May 1854, lived Heinrich Barth. Barth was one of the greatest travelers in the world. For five years he journeyed alone through the Sahara, keeping a diary in which he described the desert. Several times, sick and pursued by bandits, he bade his life farewell. Dying of thirst, he would cut his veins and drink his own blood to survive. Eventually he returned to Europe, where no one appreciated the unique feat he had accomplished. Bitter, worn out by the hardships of his voyage, he died in 1865 at the age of forty-four, not understanding that the human imagination is incapable of traveling to the frontier he had crossed in the Sahara.

Behold, the Lord Rideth
upon a Swift Cloud

When I entered, the interior was already filled by a throng of the faithful. All were kneeling, motionless on simple, backless benches. Their heads were bowed and their eyes were closed. There was total silence.

"They are confessing their sins and humbling themselves before God, so as to lessen His anger," whispered the parishioner who had earlier arranged permission for me to enter and who now accompanied me.

We were in the city of Port Harcourt, situated in the hot and humid Niger delta. The temple belonged to a congregation called the Church of the Faith of the Apostles, one of the several hundred Christian sects active in southern Nigeria. The Sunday mass was about to begin.

It is not easy for an outsider to gain admittance to such a rite. I had tried my luck to no avail in other towns and with other congregations (I am using terms interchangeably here—sect, congregation, gathering, church—because they are used this way in Africa). The sects engage in a politics characterized by a certain contradiction: on the one hand, each tries to have as many adherents as possible, but on the other makes acceptance a long and painstaking procedure, with extremely careful screening and selection. This is the consequence not only of doctrinal demands;

there are also important economic reasons. The majority of these sects have their headquarters in the United States, in the Antilles and the Caribbean, or in Great Britain. It is from there that donations of money as well as medical and educational assistance flow to the African affiliates. That is why, in indigent Africa, there is no end to those who want to join a sect. But the sects are intent on their followers having suitable social and material standing. The poor and the down-and-out are not admitted. There are many thousands of these congregations in Africa, and millions of members.

I looked around the interior of the temple. It was a spacious, sprawling hall, resembling a great hangar. The walls had wide grilles, so that fresh air could enter and the breeze offer some relief, all the more important given the corrugated tin roof, warmed by the sun. I didn't notice an altar anywhere. There were also no sculptures or paintings. An orchestra several dozen strong, however, with large brass and percussion sections, stood on an elevated platform near the presbytery, and right behind it, on the uppermost level, a mixed choir dressed in black. The center of the proscenium was occupied by a massive mahogany pulpit.

The priest who now stepped up to it was a graying, heavy Nigerian, perhaps over fifty. He leaned his hands on the edge of the pulpit and looked at the faithful. They had raised themselves by now from their kneeling position and were sitting, watching him attentively.

The proceedings began with the choir singing the fragment of the prophecies of Isaiah in which God announces that he will punish the Egyptians with a great drought:

Behold, the Lord rideth upon a swift cloud and shall come into Egypt: and the idols of Egypt shall be moved . . .

And the waters shall fail from the sea, and the river shall be wasted and dried up.

And they shall turn the rivers far away; and the brooks of defence shall be emptied and dried up: the reeds and flags shall wither.

The paper reeds by the brooks, by the mouth of the brooks, and every thing sown by the brooks, shall wither, be driven away, and be no more.

The fishers also shall mourn, and all they that cast angle into the brooks shall lament, and they that spread nets upon the waters shall languish.

If the goal was to instill anxiety and dread in the faithful, to evoke the atmosphere of Apocalypse, the text was aptly chosen. For these were local people, from the land upon which the mighty Niger splits into dozens of smaller rivers, into numerous twisting branches and canals, creating Africa's largest delta. This watery net has given them sustenance for generations, and the biblical vision of drying and disappearing rivers was bound to awaken in those gathered the direst forebodings and fears.

The priest now opened the large Bible bound in red leather, paused for a long while, then started to read:

Moreover the word of the Lord came unto me, saying, Jeremiah, what seest thou? And I said, I see a rod of an almond tree.

He looked at the assembled and continued reading:

And the word of the Lord came unto me the second time, saying, What seest thou? And I said, I see a seething pot . . .

Thou therefore gird up thy loins, and arise, and speak unto them all that I command thee: be not dismayed at their faces . . .

He laid the Bible aside and, pointing at the congregation, shouted: "And I am not dismayed at your faces! I did not come here to be afraid of you, but to tell you the truth and to cleanse you!"

From the very first moments of his sermon, from the first words and sentences, he was in high gear, brimming with accusations, anger, irony, and fury. He continued: "Above all else, the

Christian must be clean. Internally clean. And are you all clean? Are *you* clean?" He motioned somewhere toward the back of the hall, but because he didn't actually single out any one person, a whole group of people standing there cringed guiltily, as if they had been caught in the act.

"And perhaps you consider yourself to be clean?" He moved his finger, pointing at another place in the hall, and now the people standing there cowered and hid their faces in embarrassment.

"No, you are not clean! You have a long way to go before you are clean! None of you are clean!" He said this categorically and almost triumphantly. Just then the orchestra blared, the trumpets, trombones, cornets, and horns roared. They were accompanied by the dull thud of drums and the chaotic moaning of the choir.

"And you probably think that you are Christians!" he exclaimed after a moment, mockingly. "I can swear that is what you think. That you are certain of this. Each one of you walks around, proudly sticking out his chest and announcing: 'I am a Christian! Look at me, look and admire—now here is a Christian! A true one, so true, there isn't a truer one in the world!' That is how you think. I know you well. A Christian! Ha! ha! ha! ha!"— he burst into loud, nervous, scathing laughter, so suggestive that the atmosphere in the hall began to communicate itself to me, and I felt shivers running up and down my spine.

The people stood there bewildered, crestfallen, condemned. Who were they, if they couldn't be considered Christians? What were they supposed to be, where were they supposed to go? Each of the priest's utterances brought them lower, reduced them to dust. Standing in the middle of this rapt, emotional, terrified crowd, it would have been unseemly of me to observe them too openly and obviously. It sufficed that I was white; that alone drew attention. But out of the corner of my eye I could see that the women standing next to me had beads of sweat on their brows, and that their hands, which were folded on their breasts, were trembling. Perhaps what they were most fearful of was the priest pointing at any one of them individually, destroying their reputations, denying them the right to call themselves Christians. The priest had enormous, hypnotic power over them, and the authority to mete out the most heartless, severe judgments.

"Do you know what it means to be a Christian?" he asked. The audience, which until now had been standing still, dejected and humbled, stirred, expecting to hear an answer, some advice, a helpful recipe or definition. "Do you know what it means?" he repeated, and one could sense the tension rising among the faithful. But before they were able to hear the reply, the orchestra resounded once again. The tubas, bassoons, and saxophones thundered. Drums beat and rumbled. The priest sat down in an armchair, leaned his head on his hands, and rested. The orchestra fell silent. The priest rose again.

"To be a Christian," he said, "means to hear within yourself the voice of the Lord. To hear the Lord asking, 'Jeremiah, what seest thou?' "

After the word "Lord," the congregation started to sing:

Oh, Lord,
You are my Lord,
Oh, yes,
Oh, yes, yes, yes,
Oh, yes,
You are my Lord.

They began rhythmically rocking and undulating, and billows of brick dust rose from the floor. Then everyone sang the psalm "Praise the Lord on loud cymbals . . ."

The tension diminished somewhat, the mood mellowed, and people loosened up a bit, breathed easier. But only for a brief moment, because soon the priest spoke again:

"But you cannot hear the voice of the Lord. Your ears are plugged up. Your eyes do not see. Because there is sin in them. And sin renders you deaf and blind."

Absolute silence descended. The only ones now moving in the hall full of people sitting motionless—but moving carefully, almost on tiptoe—were a number of young, strong, well-built men. They wore identical dark suits, white shirts, and black ties. I had counted twenty of them earlier, at the gate leading into the churchyard: they were checking who was arriving. Then, right before the mass, they spread out through the hall and took up positions near the pews, in such a way that each of them could observe a different sector of the temple. Observe, intervene, lead. Their gestures, their whole behavior, were characterized by absolute concentration and decisiveness. No African muddling or lolling about here. On the contrary—efficiency, attentiveness, alacrity. They were in control of the situation, and one sensed that that was their mission.

The silence after the priest informed them that the road to the Christian ideal is blocked by sin, which they carry within themselves and commit continually by the mere fact of their own existence, sprung from a profound source. The members of the congregation belonged to the Ibo tribe, and the traditional religion of the Ibo, like that of the majority of African communities, does not know the concept of sin. The African belief system has a radically different understanding of guilt from that espoused by Christian theology. In Africa, the notion of metaphysical, abstract evil—evil in and of itself—does not exist. A deed first becomes evil when it is discovered, and, second, when the community or the individual declares it to be evil. Moreover, the criterion here is not axiomatic, but practical, concrete: that which does harm to others is evil. Evil intentions do not exist, because evil is not evil until it materializes, assumes an active form. There are only evil actions.

If I wish illness upon my enemy, I am doing nothing wrong, committing no sin. Only when my enemy actually falls ill can I be accused of an evil deed: of sowing the seeds of illness in him (illnesses here are not believed to have biological causes, but to result from spells cast by one's adversaries).

But perhaps most important, undiscovered evil is not evil, and therefore does not give rise to a feeling of guilt. I can cheat with a clean conscience until someone realizes that he is being cheated and points a finger at me. The Christian tradition, on the other hand, internalizes guilt: our soul aches, our conscience torments us, we are plagued by worries. That is the state in which we experience the full weight of sin, its stinging presence, its harrowing intrusiveness. It is different in societies in which the individual does not exist in and of himself, but only as part of a collective. The collective relieves us of private responsibility, therefore there is no individual guilt, and by the same token no sensation of having sinned. Awareness of sin takes place in time: I did something wrong, I feel that I committed a sin, I am tortured by this, and I look for a way to cleanse myself, to atone, to confess—to erase the sin. This is a process, and it requires the passage of time to unfold. To the African mind, this time simply does not exist; there is no space for sin and its consequences. Either I have not done anything wrong, since I was not found out, or else, if the evil is brought to light, it is at the very same moment, instantly, punished—and thus purged. Guilt and punishment go hand in hand here, form an inseparable unit, with no open space between them, no chink. In the African tradition, the conflicts and drama of Raskolnikov are an impossibility.

"Sin makes you deaf and blind," the priest repeated for emphasis. His voice started to tremble slightly. "But do you know what awaits those who do not hear and do not see? Who think they can live at a distance from the Lord?"

He reached again for the Bible, and lifting one arm up high, as if it were the antenna along which the word of the Lord would flow down from the heavens, called out:

Then said the Lord unto me, . . . cast them out of my sight, and let them go forth.

> *And it shall come to pass, if they say unto thee, Whither shall*
> *we go forth? then thou shalt tell them, . . . Such as are for death, to*
> *death; and such as are for the sword, to the sword; and such as are*
> *for the famine, to the famine; and such as are for the captivity, to the*
> *captivity.*
> *And I will appoint over them four kinds, saith the Lord: the*
> *sword to slay, and the dogs to tear, and the fowls of the heaven, and*
> *the beasts of the earth, to devour and destroy.*

The drums boomed hollowly. But the choir and the orchestra were silent. Then, all was quiet. The congregation stood still, their faces lifted high. Out of the corner of my eye I noticed sweat pouring down. And I saw tense strained features, taut necks, hands stretched upward in a dramatic gesture that was partly a plea for salvation, partly an instinctive form of self-defense, as if in anticipation of a huge boulder that any moment now would come crashing down.

It occurred to me that the participants at this mass must be experiencing an inner conflict, maybe even a drama, although I wasn't sure to what degree they would be conscious of it. They were for the most part young people from an industrial African town—the new Nigerian middle class. They belonged to a social group modeling itself on European and American elites, whose culture is essentially Christian. They wanted to familiarize themselves with this culture and this faith, get a feel for their nature, identify with them. So they joined one of the Christian congregations, which accepted them while at the same time imposing upon them doctrinal and ethical requirements alien to their native traditions. One of these was instruction in sin, a type of transgression and burden about which they knew nothing. As followers of the new faith, they now had to acknowledge the presence of sin, had to swallow that bitter, repugnant pill. And also to search immediately for ways to uproot it from their being—to become true, pure Christians. Relentlessly, the priest was hammering home the great and painful price they would have to pay. Hence the nature of his sermon: threats, humiliation. And they, for their part, fervidly accepted their status as sinners weighed down by the greatest of trespasses, were duly frightened by the specter of imminent infernal punishment, ready at a moment's notice to don sackcloth and ashes.

Their eager submission to all the priest's charges, grumblings, and accusations proved they considered this a price worth paying for the right to be in the church. The Ibo fear loneliness, regarding it as a curse and a condemnation. Here, they could participate in rites that gave them a sense of community, of belonging. And perhaps something greater still: many African societies have given rise to secret associations, a type of ethnic Freemasonry—secretive, closed, yet important and influential. Sects in Africa often try to model themselves on these traditional institutions, creating an atmosphere of secrecy and exclusivity, instituting their own system of signs and slogans, a distinct liturgy.

To avoid the rudeness of scrutinizing the hall during the service, I did not so much observe as intuit much of what was going on. I had within the scope of my vision only those standing closest to me. I was unable to see the others, but their presence was palpable: the atmosphere of this congregation was so concentrated, so full of vibrant, ecstatic emotion, so pervasive and poignant, that it couldn't but penetrate and affect everyone. There was so much spontaneity, abandonment, and feeling in these people, so much ardent desire and quivering will and freely expressed sentiment, that one could deduce and comprehend everything that was going on behind one's back, even far away.

As I was walking toward the exit at the end of the mass, I had to step carefully, because the crowd, their faces concealed from prying eyes, was again kneeling motionless. It was completely silent. The choir was not singing, the orchestra was not playing. The priest stood on the pulpit, tired and depleted, his eyes closed, saying nothing.

The Hole in Onitsha

Onitsha! I have always wanted to see Onitsha. There are certain magical names with seductive, colorful associations—Timbuktu, Lalibela, Casablanca. Likewise Onitsha. It is a small town in eastern Nigeria, and it has the largest market in Africa, perhaps in the world.

In Africa there is a very clear distinction between the open market and what we might call a commercial center or a market hall. The market hall is a fixed structure, one with an architectonic shape, a relatively planned layout, a more or less consistent group of merchants, and a stable clientele. It has permanent reference points—signboards of well-known firms, plaques with the names of big merchants, colorful advertisements, decorative displays. The open market is an entirely different universe. It is vitality, spontaneity, improvisation. It is a folk festival, an outdoor concert. It is first and foremost the domain and kingdom of women, part of their very being. Their life, whether in the countryside or in town, revolves around the fact that they will soon be going to market, to buy or to sell something—or both. Usually, the market is far away, the expedition takes at least a day, and the road there and back (because they walk in a group) gives them an opportunity for conversation, for an exchange of observations and gossip.

And the market itself? It is a place for commerce, but also a meeting place, an escape from the monotony of everyday life, a social event. Going to the market, women first painstakingly arrange each other's hairdos and put on their best attire. Shopping is accompanied by a fashion show—discreet, unwitting, improvised. If you look at what many of these women are selling or buying, it is difficult to resist the impression that the merchandise is merely a pretext for establishing or maintaining contacts with others. Here is a woman selling three tomatoes. Or several ears of corn. Or a little pot of rice. What profit does she make from this? What can she buy with it? And yet she sits in the market all day. Let us observe her carefully. She sits and talks nonstop with her neighbors, arguing about something, watching the passing crowds, voicing her opinions, making comments. Hungry, she and her friends all swap the products and dishes they had brought to sell, and eat them on the spot. I once observed a fish market in Mopti. Some two hundred women were sitting in a small, sandy square, in the scorching heat. Each had several small fish for sale. I didn't see anyone who seemed in the least interested in purchasing them, anyone who so much as looked at them, or asked the price. And yet these women were content, chatting, engaged in loud debate, preoccupied with themselves, oblivious to their surroundings. If a customer had appeared, I thought, he would have met with displeasure, for he would have spoiled their fun.

A great marketplace is a huge crowd, a crush. People are pressing on one another, pushing, shoving. As far as the eye can see, an ocean of black heads, as if identically sculpted in basalt, and bright, colorful clothes.

And then trucks drive into all this. They are distributing merchandise. So that no one is run over or killed, there are established rules of conduct governing the trucks' motion. First, the truck drives a meter into the crowd. It advances slowly, centimeter by centimeter, a little at a time. The women standing or sitting in its path gather their goods into baskets, bowls, and aprons, and, pushing those standing or sitting behind them, wordlessly and obediently move out of the fender's way, only to return to their places a second later, like waves cut by the prow of a ship.

The African market is a great repository of everything and anything. A veritable mine of the cheap and the shoddy. A mountain of rubbish, gimcrack, and kitsch. There is nothing of any value to a Westerner here, nothing to catch your attention, arouse your admiration, tempt you to possess it. At one end are stacks of identical red and yellow buckets and bowls; at the other, billowing piles of thousands of identical undershirts and sneakers; someplace else still, pyramids of multicolored calicos and glittering rows of nylon dresses and men's jackets. Only in such a place can one fully appreciate the extent to which the world is swamped with material tenth-rateness, how it is drowning in an ocean of camp, knockoffs, the tasteless and the worthless.

Finally, an opportunity presented itself to go to Onitsha. Now, sitting in the car, I tried to imagine how everything there must look, my mind monstrously multiplying images of markets I had seen, blowing them up many times over until they had attained the proportions of the largest marketplace in the world. My driver was called Omenka and belonged to the shrewd and crafty people raised among the riches of the local oil fields, people who know what money is and exactly how to extract it from their passengers. On the day we first met, I gave him nothing as we parted. He walked away without so much as a good-bye. I dislike cold, formal relations between people and I felt bad. So the next time I gave him 50 naira (the local currency). He said good-bye, and even smiled. Encouraged, I gave him 100 naira the following time. He said good-bye, smiled, and shook my hand. At the subsequent parting, I gave him 150 naira. He said good-bye, smiled, wished me well, and warmly shook my hand, grasping it in both of his. The next time I raised the rate again and paid him 200 naira. He said good-bye, smiled, shook and squeezed my hand, asked me to pay his respects to my family, and with concern in his voice inquired after my health. Without stretching this story out any longer, suffice it to say that I ended up showering him with so many naira that we were simply unable to part. Omenka's voice was always trembling with emotion, and with tears in his eyes he would swear his everlasting devotion and fidelity.

I had what I wanted, and more: tenderness, warmth, good-will.

And so Omenka and I were now driving to Onitsha, north from the Bight of Benin, passing the little towns of Aba, Owerri, and Ihiala. The countryside in these parts is invariably green, malarial, humid, populated. Some people work extracting oil, some cultivate little fields of manioc and cassava, others collect and sell coconuts, still others manufacture moonshine out of bananas and millet. But everybody trades. In Africa, the division into farmers and shepherds, soldiers and office workers, tailors and mechanics exists and is very real, but something else is more important, something they all have in common and which unites them: they all trade.

One of the differences between African and European soci-eties is the latter's division of labor: specialization, strictly defined expertise, professionalism. These principles are only marginally in effect in Africa. Here, especially these days, one must try one's hand at dozens of occupations and do many things, most fre-quently not for long and—alas!—not too thoroughly. In any event, it is difficult to find anyone who has not had a brush with Africa's prime life force and passion: the exchange of goods.

And the market in Onitsha is where all the roads and paths of mercantile Africa converge.

I was also fascinated by Onitsha because it is the only market I know of that has spawned its own literature, the Onitsha Market Literature. Dozens of Nigerian writers live and work in Onitsha and are published by as many local publishing houses, which have their own printing presses and bookshops in the marketplace. It is a diverse literature—romances, poems, and plays (the latter staged by the numerous little theatrical companies in the market), folk comedies, farces, and vaudevilles. There are many didactic tales, countless self-help pamphlets, such as "How to Fall in Love?" or "How to Fall Out of Love?" Many little novellas like "Mabel, or Sweet Honey That Has Poured Away," or "Love Games, and Then Disenchantment." Everything is meant to move you, to make you weep, and also to offer instruction and disinterested advice. Literature must be useful, believe the authors from Onitsha, and in the market they find a huge audience thirsty for wisdom and vicarious experience. Whoever cannot afford the brochure masterpiece (or simply doesn't know how to read) can listen to its message for a penny—the admission fee to authors' readings, which take place often here in the shade of stalls piled high with oranges, yams, or onions.

Several kilometers before Onitsha the road turns in a gentle arc toward town. As we approached, we could see cars already backed up on the arc—a monumental traffic jam—and it was clear we would have to wait, since this was the only road into town from this direction. It is called Oguta Road, and it ends—far, very far, from here—in that famous market. For now, however, we were standing behind several trucks in an immensely long line. A half hour passed, then an hour. The local drivers were obviously familiar with this situation, for they spread out with insouciance in the roadside ditch. But I was in a hurry: I was supposed to return that same day to Port Harcourt, three hundred kilometers away. The road was narrow, two lanes, and our car stood squeezed amid other vehicles with no chance of maneuvering. So I set out on foot alone to investigate the cause of the obstruction. It was hot, at noon of course, so I dragged myself along slowly, one step at a time. Finally, I reached my goal. By now I was already in town; low brick houses covered in rusty corrugated iron stood on both sides of the street, and there were street-level shops. In the shade of wide verandas tailors sat at their sewing machines, women were washing and hanging up laundry. In one spot the street was crowded; there was a noisy, nervous commotion, engines were roaring, you could hear shouting and calling. Once I had pushed myself through the throng I saw an enormous gaping hole in the middle of the street: huge, wide, several meters deep. It had steep, sheer sides, and its bottom was an opaque, muddy pond. The street was so narrow here that you couldn't go around the hole, and everyone who wanted to drive into town had to descend first into this abyss, plunge into its swampy waters, and then hope that someone, somehow, would pull them out.

And that's exactly what was happening now. At the bottom of the hole, half immersed in water, stood a huge truck loaded with sacks of peanuts. A bunch of half-naked boys were unloading it, clambering up to street level with the sacks. Another group was fastening ropes to the truck, to help haul it out of the pit. Still others were sloshing about in the water, trying to lay planks and beams under wheels. Those who had no more strength would climb up to rest awhile. Rows of women were positioned around the brim, selling hot food—rice with a spicy sauce, cassava pancakes, baked yams, peanut soup. Others were hawking homemade lemonade, rum, banana beer. Some boys were selling cigarettes and chewing gum. In the end, when everything was ready and the peanuts had been unloaded, the teams set about extricating the truck. Some of the boys, cheered on with shouts, pulled on the ropes; others pushed with their shoulders against the vehicle's sides. The truck resisted, went in reverse, practically stood on end. But finally, as a result of all these joint efforts, it reared up and onto the asphalt. The onlookers applauded and slapped one another on the back; the neighborhood children danced and clapped their hands.

Barely a moment had passed, and the next car in line was already swimming at the bottom of the abysmal pit. I noticed that an entirely different group of people set about pulling it out. They had their own ropes, chains, planks, and shovels. Those who had been working on the previous vehicle had already dispersed somewhere. The work was immensely difficult and laborious— this was a particularly heavy machine, an enormous Bedford.

They had to haul it out by degrees, little by little. At the conclusion of each phase, work would cease and a long discussion would ensue about which methods of towing might now prove to be the most effective. The Bedford kept slipping, its engine roared as if it were demented, its platform tilted dangerously to one side.

With each vehicle the hole grew deeper and deeper. Its bottom was an increasingly slimy, sticky goo, in which tires spun in place, splashing and spraying everyone with lumps of mud and streams of gravel. I estimated that we had a two to three-day wait before our turn in the pit finally came. I wondered, how much would the rescuers charge to pull us out? But there was a more pressing question: how do we get out of this trap? I was no longer thinking about the market in Onitsha, about its colorful commotion, its fairground literature. I wanted to get out of here—I had to go back. But first I went to explore briefly the area around this catastrophically potholed, jammed Oguta Road. To see what it looks like. To gather some intelligence. Listen to what's being said.

I was immediately struck by how the area around the hole had become the epicenter of local life, how it drew people, engaged them, spurred them to initiative and action. In the normally sleepy, lifeless backwater on the outskirts of town, where the unemployed slumber in the streets and packs of homeless malarial dogs roam, there arose, suddenly and spontaneously, thanks solely to that unfortunate hole, a dynamic, humming, bustling neighborhood. The hole created work for the unemployed, who formed teams of rescuers and made money hauling cars out of the pit. It brought new customers for the women operating the portable sidewalk eateries. Because of the attendant traffic jam, shoppers appeared perforce in the previously empty local shops—the passengers and drivers of cars waiting to get through. Hawkers of cigarettes and cold drinks found buyers for their wares.

More: I noticed fresh, clumsy, hand-painted signs on the surrounding houses: "Hotel," aimed at those who were forced to spend the night waiting for their turn in the hole. Local car-repair shops revived as drivers, taking advantage of the enforced stop, used the time to repair damages, pump up tires, recharge batteries. Tailors and shoemakers had more work, barbers appeared; I noticed witch doctors making their rounds, offering herbs, snake skins, and rooster feathers, ready to cure anyone in an instant. In Africa, all these professions are performed by people in motion, wandering about, searching out clients, and if an opportunity like the hole in Onitsha arises, they quickly converge there in large numbers. Social life, too, was reinvigorated: the area around the hole became a place for meetings, conversation, and discussion, and, for the children, a playground.

The curse of drivers traveling to Onitsha became the salvation of the residents of Oguta Road, and of this entire neighborhood. It was further proof that every evil thing has its defenders, because everywhere there are those whom evil sustains, for whom it is an opportunity, life itself.

For a long time, people did not allow this hole to be repaired. I know this because when years later I was telling someone in Lagos with great emotion about my adventure in Onitsha, he replied with an absolutely indifferent tone of voice: "Onitsha? It's always like that in Onitsha."

Eritrean Scenes

A smara, five o'clock in the morning. Dark and cool. Suddenly two sounds soar simultaneously over the city: the powerful, low chiming of the bell from the cathedral on Via Independencia and the drawn-out, lilting calls of the muezzin from the mosque nearby. For several minutes these two sounds fill the air, combine and reinforce each other, creating a harmonious and triumphal ecumenical duet that shatters the quiet of the sleepy streets and awakens their inhabitants. The voice of the bell, rising and falling, is like a sonorous accompaniment, a lofty and bracing allegro punctuating the fervent Koranic suras with which the muezzin summons the faithful to the first prayer of the day, called *salad as-subh*.

Deafened by this morning music, I walk cold and hungry through the empty streets to the bus station: I am planning to go to Massawa today. Even on the large maps of Africa, the distance between Asmara and Massawa is barely the width of a nail, and in reality it is not great, only 110 kilometers, but it takes a bus five hours to traverse it, descending from an altitude of 2,500 meters down to sea level—the Red Sea, along which Massawa lies.

Asmara and Massawa are the principal cities of Eritrea, the youngest African state, with a population of only three million. It had never in the past been an independent state, being first a colony of Turkey, then of Egypt, and in the twentieth century of

Italy, England, and Ethiopia successively. In 1962, the latter, having already forcibly occupied Eritrea for ten years, declared it an Ethiopian province, to which the Eritreans responded with an anti-Ethiopian war of liberation, the longest-running war (thirty years) in the history of the continent. When Haile Selassie ruled in Addis Ababa, the Americans helped him fight the Eritreans, and when Mengistu overthrew the emperor and seized power for himself, the Russians did. You can see the relics of this history in the great park in Asmara, where the war museum is situated. Its charming and hospitable young director, Aforki Arefaine, is a poet and guitarist, and a former guerrilla. He first shows me American mortars and guns, and then a collection of Soviet tommy guns, mines, rocket launchers, and MIGs. "This is nothing!" he says. "If only you could see Debre Zeyit!"

It wasn't easy, because securing permission is complicated, but I finally did see Debre Zeyit. It is several dozen kilometers outside Addis Ababa. You drive along country roads, passing a series of military checkpoints. At the last one, the soldiers open the gate to a large enclosure at the top of a flat hill. The view from this place is unlike any in the world. Before us, as far as the eye can see, all the way to the distant, misty horizon, lies a flat and treeless plain—and it is completely covered with military equipment. To one side, stretching for kilometers, are fields of artillery pieces of various calibers: unending avenues of medium and large tanks; enclosures stacked with a veritable forest of antiaircraft guns and mortars; hundreds upon hundreds of armored trucks, small tanks, motorized radio stations, amphibious vehicles. And on the other side stand enormous hangars and warehouses, the hangars full of the body parts of still unassembled MIGs, the warehouses brimming with crates of ammunition and mines.

What's most shocking and astonishing is the monstrous quantity of everything, the improbable accumulation, the piles of hundreds of thousands of machine guns, mountainous-terrain howitzers, military helicopters. All of this wended its way for years by sea from the Soviet Union to Ethiopia, Brezhnev's gift to

Mengistu. Not even a tenth of these armaments could actually be operated by people in Ethiopia. Why, with this many tanks, you could conquer all of Africa, and with fire from all these guns and rocket launchers reduce the continent to ashes! Roaming through the still streets of this city of motionless steel, where dark, rusty barrels stared at me from everywhere and around whose every corner caterpillar tanks bared their massive metal teeth, I thought about the man who, dreaming of conquering Africa, of staging on this continent a showpiece blitzkrieg, constructed this military necropolis. Who could this have been? Moscow's ambassador to Addis Ababa? Marshal Ustinov? Brezhnev himself?

"And did you see Tira Avolo?" Aforki asked me once. Yes, I saw Tira Avolo. It is one of the wonders of the world. Asmara is a beautiful city, with an Italian, Mediterranean architecture and a delectable climate—an eternal warm and sunny spring. Tira Avolo is Asmara's luxurious residential neighborhood. Magnificent villas submerged in flowering gardens, royal palms, tall hedges, swimming pools, lush lawns and decorative borders, an inexhaustible parade of plants, colors, and scents—a veritable paradise on earth. When the Italians left Asmara in the course of the war, Tira Avolo was taken over by Ethiopian and Soviet generals. No Sochi, Sukhumi, or Gagra can rival Tira Avolo in climate and comfort. So half the High Command of the Red Army, having been forbidden access to the Côte d'Azur or Capri, spent their holidays in Asmara, simultaneously helping Mengistu's forces fight the Eritrean guerrillas.

The Ethiopian army regularly used napalm. To protect themselves, the Eritreans dug shelters, camouflaged corridors, and secret hiding places. With time, they had constructed a second, underground country—literally underground, a clandestine, covert Eritrea, impenetrable to strangers, which they could traverse from one point to another undetected by the enemy. The Eritrean war, they themselves proudly emphasize, was no bush war, no destructive and wasteful spasm of plunder whipped up by warlords. In their underground state they had schools and hospitals, courts and orphanages, workshops and gunsmiths. In a country of illiterates, each warrior had to know how to read and write.

The Eritreans' pride and achievement is now their problem and their drama. The war ended in 1991, two years later Eritrea became an independent nation, and now this small country, one of the poorest in the world, has a hundred-thousand-strong army of young, relatively well-educated people it doesn't know what to do with. Eritrea has no industry, agriculture is devastated, the towns are in ruin, the roads wrecked. One hundred thousand soldiers awake each morning with nothing to do; most important, they have nothing to eat. And it's not just the soldiers. The fate of their civilian friends and brothers is similar. All you have to do is walk through the streets of Asmara during dinnertime. The officials of the fledgling nation's few institutions are hurrying to little neighborhood restaurants and bars for a bite to eat. But the crowds of young people have nowhere to go—they don't work and are penniless. They walk around, peer into shop windows, stand on street corners, recline on benches—idle and hungry.

The bells of the cathedral fall silent, the muezzin's voice ceases calling, a fiery, blinding sun emerges from behind the mountains of Yemen, and our bus—an ancient Fiat whose body has been so corroded by rust and so often knocked and hammered that it is impossible to determine its color—sets off, rushing downhill past steep little fields from 2,500 meters above the sea. I can scarcely bring myself to describe this journey. The chauffeur seats me, the only European, next to him. He is a young, intelligent, and careful driver. He understands this road, knows its deadly traps. There are several hundred turns along the one-hundred-kilometer route—in fact, the entire road is just turns and bends, and, moreover, the narrow track, which is covered with loose gravel, runs the entire time above formidable precipices, without any protective railings or safeguards.

At many a turn, if you don't suffer from fear of heights, you can look down and see lying far, far below you, at the bottom of the chasm, the shattered remains of buses, trucks, armored vehicles, and the skeletons of all sorts of beasts—probably camels, perhaps mules or donkeys. Some are already very old, but others—and it is those that are most disturbing—are quite fresh. The driver and his passengers are in sync, clearly a well-practiced and smoothly functioning team: when we enter a turn, the driver calls out a protracted "Yyyaaahhh!" and at this signal the passengers lean in the opposite direction, giving the bus the counterweight it needs to keep from plunging headlong into the abyss.

Every now and then we come upon a brightly colored Coptic altar at a bend, decorated with ribbons, artificial puffy flowers, and naively painted icons, with several skinny, desiccated monks milling about. When the bus slows down on the turn, they hold clay bowls up to the windows, into which the passengers can throw offerings of some pennies. The monks will pray for their safe journey—safe at least until the next bend.

Every kilometer reveals different vistas, a different landscape emerges from behind each mountain; ever new panormas compose themselves before our eyes, the earth showing off the abundance of its charms, wanting to overwhelm us with its beauty. Because, indeed, this road is at once terrifying and beautiful. Down below, a village submerged in flowering shrubs; there, a monastery, its pale walls shining against the black of the mountains like a white flame. Over there, a gigantic, one-hundred-ton boulder, split in half as neatly as if by a thunderbolt—and thrust into the middle of a green pasture. Somewhere else, fields of loose stones, sparsely, carelessly scattered about—but in a certain spot these stones are more concentrated, lie nearer one another, nearer and neater: the sign of a Muslim cemetery. Here, as in a classical landscape painting, a rapid stream glitters with silver; over

there, massed cliffs create heaven-grazing gates, convoluted labyrinths, immense columns.

As we descend lower and lower, constantly spinning around
on the frenzied carousel of turns, ever balancing on the border
between life and death, we feel it getting warmer, and then very
warm, even hot, until finally, as though we'd been tossed with a
giant shovel, we are thrust into a blazing furnace—Massawa.

First, though, several kilometers before the city, the mountains end and the road runs straight and level. At this point, the
driver is transformed: his slim silhouette goes limp, his facial muscles relax, and his expression becomes gentler. He smiles. He
reaches for a stack of cassettes lying next to him and snaps one
into the tape player. From the scratched, gravelly recording comes
the hoarse voice of a local singer. The melody is Eastern; there are
many high, yearning, sentimental tones in it. "He is saying that
she has eyes like two moons," the driver explains to me. "And that
he loves those moonlike eyes."

We enter the ruined city. On either side of the road, mountains of artillery shells. The walls of burned houses, and broken,
splintered tree trunks. A woman is walking down an empty street,
two boys are playing in the cab of a demolished truck. We arrive
at a sandy rectangular square in the center of town. All around,
shabby single-story houses painted green, pink, and yellow, the
façades cracked, the paint peeling and falling. In one corner, in a
spot of shade, three old men are napping. They are sitting on the
ground, their turbans pulled down over their eyes.

Eritrea is two altitudes, two climates, two religions. In the
highlands, where Asmara lies and where it is cooler, lives the
Tigrinya ethnic group. The majority of the country's inhabitants
belong to it. The Tigrinya are Coptic Christians. The other part
of Eritrea is the hot, semidesert lowlands—the shores of the Red
Sea, between Sudan and Djibouti. Various pastoral people live
there, professing Islam (Christianity seems to tolerate the tropics
less well, while Islam takes to them). Massawa, the port and the

city, belong to that latter world. These areas of the Red Sea around Massawa and Assab, and on the Gulf of Aden at Djibouti, Aden, and Berbera, are the hottest spots on the planet. As I stepped off the bus, I was struck by such heat that I could barely catch my breath. I felt that the flaming air all around would soon choke me, and I realized I had to find shelter quickly because in a moment I would collapse. I began to scrutinize the lifeless town, searching for some hint, some trace of life. Seeing no signs anywhere, in despair I simply started walking straight ahead. I knew I wouldn't get far, but kept going, with great difficulty, lifting one leg, then the other, as if I were pulling them out of a bottomless, sucking quagmire. At long last I spotted a bar, its entrance shielded by a percale curtain. I parted the panels of fabric, walked in, and slumped on the nearest bench. My ears were buzzing; the heat seemed to be growing more intense, more abominable.

In the darkness, at the back of the empty bar, I noticed a dirt-encrusted, battered counter and two heads lying on it. From a distance, it appeared the heads had been severed, and left here by someone. Yes. That's what must have happened, because the heads were not moving. They were showing no signs of life whatsoever. But I was in no condition to ponder who might have brought these heads here and why he would have left them. My attention was diverted by the sight of a crate of water bottles next to the counter. With what strength I had left I dragged myself over to them and began drinking, bottle after bottle. Only then did one of the heads open an eye, which proceeded to observe what I was doing. But the two barmaids still did not so much as twitch, motionless from the heat, like lizards.

Having water and a shady place, I now calmly waited for the fierce afternoon hours to pass. Later, I ventured out to search for some sort of a hotel. One could see that the wealthy districts of Massawa must once have been an enchanting mixture of tropical, Italianate-Arabic architecture. But now, several years after the war, most of the houses still lay in ruins, and the sidewalks were littered with bricks, garbage, and glass. In one of the city's main intersections stood an enormous burned-out Russian T-72 tank. They clearly had no means of removing it. There wasn't a crane in Eritrea capable of lifting it, no platform on which it could be transported, no forge that could melt it down. Indeed, you can bring a great tank like this into a country like Eritrea, you can fire away with it, but when it breaks down, or someone torches it, there is really nothing to be done with the wreckage.

In the Shade of a Tree, in Africa

I t is already the end of the journey. All that remains now is a brief rest in the shade of a tree, on the way back home. The tree grows in a village called Adofo, which lies near the Blue Nile in the Ethiopian province of Wollega. It is an enormous mango tree, with thick, eternally green foliage. Whoever travels across Africa's plateaux, through the immensity of the Sahel and the savannah, repeatedly sees a startling sight: on the great stretch of sandy, sun-burned ground, on plains covered with parched yellow grasses and sparsely growing, dry, thorny shrubs, there appears every now and then a single, solitary, magnificently branching tree. Its canopy is lush and vibrant, of so intense and saturated a color that it is visible from far away, a pronounced, vivid stain on the horizon. Its leaves, with no apparent trace of wind, move and shimmer. What is this tree doing here, in this dead, moonlike landscape? Why in this precise spot? Why only one? Where does it draw its juices from? Sometimes you will have to travel many kilometers before encountering another one like it.

Perhaps a great many trees used to grow here once, an entire forest that was cut down and burned, and only this one mango tree was left. Everyone from the surrounding area nurtures it, knowing how important it is that it live. A village lies near each one of these solitary trees. Indeed, spotting such a tree from far away, you can head with confidence in its direction, assured that you will find people there, some water, and maybe even something to eat. The tree was saved because without it these people could not live: in this kind of sun, man needs shade to survive, and the tree is that shade's depository and source.

If there is a teacher in the village, the area under the tree serves as the schoolroom. Village children gather here in the mornings. There are no separate classes or age limits. Whoever wants to, comes. The teacher pins to the trunk a piece of paper with the alphabet printed upon it. He points to each letter with a stick, and the children look and repeat after him. They must learn it by heart—they have nothing to write on or with.

When noontime arrives and the sky turns white from the heat, whoever can do so takes shelter in the tree's shade: children, adults, and if there are farm animals in the village, they come too—cows, sheep, goats. It is better to sit out the scorching hours under the tree than in one's own clay house. The houses are cramped and airless, while beneath the tree it is roomy and there is more hope of a breeze.

The afternoons under the tree are very important: it's when the older people gather for a conference. The mango tree is the only place to meet and talk, the village has no larger venue. People assemble eagerly and willingly, because Africans are collectivist by nature, and possess a great need to participate in everything that constitutes communal life. All decisions, such as who should get how much land to farm, are made collectively, and conflicts and disputes are jointly resolved. According to tradition, each resolution must be adopted unanimously. If someone has a differing opinion, the majority must persuade him to change his position. This can drag on endlessly, because the discussions are famously garrulous. If someone in the village is quarreling with someone else, then the court convened beneath the tree will not try to ascertain the truth, or where justice lies, but will set itself the sole task of ending the conflict and conciliating the warring sides, while granting to each that he is in the right.

When the day ends and darkness falls, the meeting is adjourned and everyone goes home. It is impossible to argue in the dark; discussion requires being able to see one's interlocutor's face, to determine whether his words and his eyes are saying the same thing.

Now women and the elderly gather beneath the tree, and children, who are curious about everything. If there is wood, a fire is built. If there is water and mint, a thick, aromatic tea is brewed. Now begins the most pleasant, their favorite, time of day: the retelling of the day's events, stories that mix fact and fiction, the joyous and the frightening. What dark, savage thing was making such a racket in the bushes that morning? What was that strange bird that flew by overhead and suddenly vanished? The children drove a mole into its burrow. They dug up the burrow— the mole wasn't there. What happened to it? As the stories unfold, people start to remember—that once, long ago, the old people used to tell of a strange bird that did indeed fly by and vanish. Someone else recalls that his grandfather used to tell of something dark that had long been making a noise in the bushes. How long ago? As far back as one can remember. Because here the outer reaches of memory are the limits of history. Earlier, there was nothing. Earlier does not exist. History is what is remembered.

Africa, except for the Muslim north, did not know writing, and history here is an oral tradition, legends passed from mouth to mouth, a communal myth created invariably at the base of the mango tree in the evening's profound darkness, in which only the trembling voices of old men resound, because the women and children are silent, raptly listening. That is why the evening hour is so important: it is the time when the community contemplates what it is and whence it came, becomes conscious of its distinctness and otherness, defines its identity. It is the hour for conversing with the ancestors, who have departed yet are nevertheless present, who lead us on through life, and protect us from evil.

In the evening, the quiet beneath the tree is only seemingly so. In reality, the stillness is brimming with the most varied voices, sounds, and whispers. They come from everywhere—from the high branches, from the surrounding bush, from beneath the ground, from the sky. It is best to be close to others at such moments, to feel one another's presence, for this brings comfort and courage. The African always feels endangered. Nature on this continent strikes such monstrous and aggressive poses, dons such vengeful and fearsome masks, sets such traps and ambushes, that man lives with a constant sense of anxiety about tomorrow, in unabating uncertainty and dread. Everything here appears in an inflated, unbridled, hysterically exaggerated form. If there is a storm, then the thunderbolts convulse the entire planet, the lightning tears the sky to shreds; if there is a downpour, then a veritable wall of water pours from the heavens, threatening at any moment now to drown us and pound us into the ground; if there is a drought, then it is one that does not leave a drop of water behind, and we die of thirst. There is nothing here to temper the relations between man and nature—no compromises, no in-between stages, no gradations. Only ceaseless struggle, battle, a fight to the finish. From birth until death, the African is on the front line, sparring with his continent's exceptionally hostile nature, and the mere fact that he is alive and knows how to endure is his greatest triumph.

So it is evening, and we are sitting under the great tree. A girl hands me a glass of tea. I can hear people, whose faces, strong and lustrous, as if carved out of ebony, are barely discernible against the motionless darkness. I understand little of what they are saying, but their voices are serious and engaged. Speaking, they feel responsible for the history of their people. They must preserve it and enhance it. No one can say, "Read our history in books." For no one has written such books; they do not exist. History does not exist beyond that which they are able to recount here and now. The kind of history known in Europe as scholarly and objective can never arise here, because the African past has no documents or records, and each generation, listening to the version being transmitted to it, changed it and continues to change it, transforms it, modifies and embellishes it. But as a result, history, free of the weight of archives, of the constraints of dates and data, achieves here its purest, crystalline form—that of myth.

In these myths, instead of dates and mechanical measures of time—days, months, years—other designations appear, like "long ago," "very long ago," "so long ago that no one remembers." Within these time frames everything can still be placed and arranged in a temporal hierarchy, only that within it time will not evolve in a linear fashion, but will mimic the circular, uniform revolutions of our planet. In this view of time, the notion of development does not exist; it is replaced by the notion of the abiding. Africa is eternal abiding.

It is getting late and everyone is going home. The night is here, and the night belongs to the spirits. Where, for instance, do the witches gather? Everyone knows that they hold their meetings and councils in high branches, immersed and concealed in foliage. It is better not to disturb them, to move away from beneath the tree—they cannot stand to be spied and eavesdropped upon, and they are quite capable of vengeance, of persecution, spreading disease, inflicting pain, sowing death.

Therefore the place under the mango tree will remain unoccupied until dawn. At dawn, the sun and the shade of the tree will appear simultaneously. The sun will awaken people, who will immediately strive to hide from it, seeking the shelter of the tree. It is strange but true that human life depends on something as fleeting and fragile as shade. That is why the tree, which bestows it, is something greater than just a tree—it is life itself. If lightning strikes its crown and the mango goes up in flames, people here will have nowhere to find shelter from the sun, or to assemble. Without the means to assemble, they will be unable to make any decision, reach any resolution. But above all they will be unable to recount their history, which exists only in the process of being retold during evening gatherings beneath the tree. Because of this they will quickly lose their knowledge about their yesterday, will lose their memory of it. They will become people without history, meaning—they will be nobody. They will lose that which united them, will disperse, each one going off in a separate direction, alone. But solitude is impossible in Africa; a solitary man will not survive a single day, is automatically condemned to death. That is why if a thunderbolt shatters the tree, the people who lived in its shade will also perish. And so it is said: Man cannot survive longer than his shadow.

Besides shade, the second most valuable thing is water.

"Water is everything," says Ogotommelli, a wise man of the Dogon people, who live in Mali. "The earth comes from the water. Light comes from water. And blood."

"The desert will teach you one thing," a nomadic Saharan merchant told me in Niamey. "That there is something that one can desire and love more than a woman. And that is water."

Shade and water—two fluid, inconstant things, which appear, and then vanish who knows where.

Two kinds of life, two situations: anyone who finds himself for the first time in an American supermarket, one of those gigantic, unending malls, will be struck by the richness and variety of the goods assembled there, by the presence of every conceivable object that man has ever invented and produced, and subsequently transported, stowed, and piled up, all of which results in the customer not having to think about anything—the thinking was done for him earlier, and now he has everything ready and at hand.

The world of the average African is different indeed. It is a lean world, of the very simplest, most elementary sort, reduced to several objects: a single shirt, a single bowl, a handful of grain, a sip of water. Its richness and diversity are expressed not in a material, concrete, palpable, and visible form, but in the symbolic values and meanings that the African imparts to the most mundane things, imperceptible to the uninitiated on account of their utter ordinariness. Thus a rooster's feather can become a lantern lighting the way in darkness, and a drop of oil a shield that will protect you from bullets. The slightest object takes on symbolic, metaphysical weight, because man decided that it would be thus and through his choice elevated it, transported it into another dimension, into a higher realm of being—into transcendence.

Once, in the Congo, I was admitted to a secret: I was allowed to see a boys' initiation school. Upon finishing the school, boys became men, had the right to speak up in clan assemblies, could start a family. The European visiting this place, so critically important in the life of an African, will be stunned, will rub his eyes in puzzlement. How is this possible! Why, there is nothing here! No benches, no blackboard! A few thorny bushes, some bunches of dry grass, and instead of a floor, gray, ashy sand. This is supposed to be a school? And yet the young people here were proud and excited. They had attained a great honor. Everything here was based on a social contract, on an act of profound faith, which was treated very seriously: tradition said that this place was the school that initiated boys into adult life, and therefore it had a privileged status, was a distinguished, even sacred site. A nothing becomes a deeply significant something because we decide that it should be so. Our imagination anoints and exalts it.

A good example of this deifying metamorphosis might be the record of Leshina. She was a Zambian woman, around forty, a street merchant in the little town of Serenge. She did not distinguish herself in any particular way. These were the 1960s, and in various corners of the world one still came upon hand-cranked phonographs. Leshina had such a phonograph, and one completely worn and scratched-up record. It was a recording of Churchill's 1940 speech, in which he summoned Englishmen to wartime renunciations and sacrifice. The woman set the phonograph up in her yard and cranked the handle. From the green-painted metal tube rose a low, hoarse rumbling, grunting, and gurgling, in which one could pick out some traces of an emotional, dramatic voice, though the sounds were by now incomprehensible and devoid of meaning. Leshina explained to the onlookers—and the gaping crowds kept growing in number—that this was God's voice anointing her his emissary and commanding absolute obeisance. More and more gathered around her. Her followers, for the most part poor people without a penny to their names, with superhuman effort raised a temple to her in the bush and began conducting prayers there. At the start of each mass, Churchill's booming bass worked them up into an ecstatic trance. But African leaders are ashamed of such religious cults, and President Kenneth Kaunda sent out the army against Leshina. Several hundred innocent people were murdered, and tanks reduced the clay temple to dust.

The European in Africa sees only part of it, usually only the continent's exterior coating, the frequently not very interesting, and perhaps least important, part of it. His vision glides over the surface, penetrating no deeper and refusing to imagine that behind every thing a mystery may be hidden, and within as well. But European culture has ill prepared us for these excursions into the depths, into the springs of other worlds and other cultures—or of our own, for that matter. For historically, it was a fact of the drama of cultures that the first contacts between them were most frequently carried out by the worst sorts of people: robbers, soldiers of fortune, adventurers, criminals, slave traders, etc. There were, occasionally, others—good-hearted missionaries, enthusiastic travelers and explorers—but the tone, the standard, the atmosphere were for centuries set and sustained by a motley and rapacious international riffraff. Naturally, respect for other cultures, the desire to learn about them, to find a common language, were the furthest things from the minds of such folk, for the most part benighted, dull-witted mercenaries, lacking refinement and sensitivity, often illiterate, interested only in conquest, plunder, and carnage. As a result of such encounters, the world's cultures—

instead of becoming versed in one another's ways, drawing closer, permeating one another—became mutually hostile or, at best, indifferent. Their representatives, aside from the rogues, kept their distance, avoided and even feared one another—intercultural exchange was monopolized by a class of ignoramuses. As one consequence, interpersonal contacts were informed from the outset by the most primitive criterion: skin color. Thus racism became an ideology according to which people defined their place in the world. Whites-Blacks: a division that bred discomfort on both sides. In 1894, when the Englishman Frederick Lugard was advancing at the head of a small division deep into western Africa, with the aim of conquering the kingdom of Borgu, he demanded to meet the king. But a messenger arrived to announce that the ruler could not receive him. As he spoke with Lugard, the envoy kept spitting into a bamboo container hanging around his neck. Spitting, it turned out, was deemed protection and purification from the consequences of contact with a white man.

Racism, hatred and contempt for others, and the desire to exterminate them, have their roots in African colonial relations. Everything was invented and honed there centuries before totalitarian systems grafted those grim and disgraceful impulses onto twentieth-century Europe.

The cultural monopoly of crude know-nothings had a further consequence: European languages did not develop vocabularies adequate to describe non-European worlds. Entire areas of African life remain unfathomed, untouched even, because of a certain European linguistic poverty. How do we describe the dark, green, dank interior of the jungle? Those hundreds of trees and shrubs—what are they called? I know names like "palm," "baobab," "euphorbia," but they happen not to grow in the jungle. And those enormous, ten-meter-high trees in Ubangi and Ituri—what are they called? What about the countless species of insects, which are everywhere continually attacking and biting us?

Sometimes one can find a Latin name, but how might that help the average reader? And these are mostly the problems of botany and zoology. What of the immense realm of the psychology, faith, and mentality of Africans? The richness of every European language is a richness in ability to describe its own culture, represent its own world. When it ventures to do the same for another culture, however, it betrays its limitations, underdevelopment, semantic weakness.

Africa is a thousand situations, varied, distinct, even contradictory. Someone will say, "There is war there," and he will be right. Someone else, "It is peaceful there," and he too will be correct. Because everything depends on where and when.

During precolonial times, and hence not so long ago, more than ten thousand little states, kingdoms, ethnic unions, and federations existed in Africa. Roland Oliver, a historian at the University of London, draws attention to a general paradox in his book, *The African Experience* (1991): it has become common parlance to say that European colonialists partitioned Africa. Partitioned? Oliver marvels. Colonialism was a brutal unification, brought about by fire and sword! Ten thousand entities were reduced to fifty.

But much of the underlying variety, this mosaic—this shimmering collage of pebbles, bones, shells, bits of wood, pieces of tin, and leaves—has remained. The more closely we stare at it, the better we see how the bits and pieces of this tableau change place, shape, and hue, giving rise to a spectacle staggering in its mutability, richness, pulse of color.

Several years ago I was spending Christmas Eve with friends in the Mikumi National Park, deep in Tanzania. The evening was warm, clear, windless. In a clearing in the bush, under the open sky, stood several tables piled high with fried fish, rice, tomatoes, local *pombe* beer. Candles, lanterns, and oil lamps were burning. The atmosphere was jovial, easy. There were jokes, laughter, and much storytelling, as is always the case in Africa on such occasions. In attendance were Tanzanian government ministers, ambassadors, generals, clan chiefs. Midnight passed. Suddenly, I sensed in the impenetrable darkness, which began immediately beyond the illumination of the tables, a rocking and thundering. The din intensified rapidly, and then, just at our backs, from the depths of the night, an elephant emerged. It is one thing to find yourself eye to eye with an elephant in a zoo or a circus—quite another in the African bush, where the elephant is the formidable lord of his world. The lone elephant, apart from the herd, is often an animal running amok, a frenzied predator that attacks villages, tramples mud houses, kills people and cattle.

This one was truly immense, his glance gimletlike, strangely piercing. And he was silent. We could not tell what was going on in his gigantic head, what he would do a second from now. He stood for a while, and then began to stroll among the tables. Everyone was dead silent, frozen with fear, paralyzed. You cannot move—for what if that should trigger his fury? And he is fast: you cannot run away from an elephant. Sitting motionless, on the other hand, you expose yourself to a full frontal attack, and might die crushed under the giant's legs.

So the elephant sauntered about, looked at the set tables, at the flickering lights, at the motionless people. One could see by his movements, by the way he swayed his head, that he was hesitating, that he hadn't yet reached a decision. This went on and on, seemingly forever, an icy eternity. At a certain moment I intercepted his gaze. He was watching us attentively, heavily, and in his eyes was a profound, unwavering sadness.

Finally, having made his rounds of the tables and the clearing several times, the elephant left us, simply walked away and was swallowed up by the darkness. When the ground ceased rumbling, and the dark grew still again, one of the Tanzanians sitting next to me asked: "Did you see?"

"Yes," I answered, not quite daring to move yet. "It was an elephant."

"No," he replied. "The spirit of Africa always appears in the guise of an elephant. Because no other animal can vanquish an elephant. Not a lion, not a buffalo, not a snake."

Everyone walked in silence to their huts, and the boys snuffed out the lights on the tables. It was still night, but Africa's most dazzling moment was approaching—the break of day.